THE
DIFFICULT
WAR

THE DIFFICULT WAR

Perspectives on Insurgency and Special Operations Forces

Edited by
Dr. Emily Spencer

Foreword by
Major-General J.P.Y.D. Gosselin

CANADIAN DEFENCE ACADEMY PRESS
KINGSTON

THE DUNDURN GROUP
TORONTO

Catalogue No. D2-248/2009E

Published by The Dundurn Group and Canadian Defence Academy Press in cooperation with the Department of National Defence, and Public Works and Government Services Canada.

Editor: Michael Carroll
Copy Editor: Nigel Heseltine
Designer: Jennifer Scott
Printer: Webcom

Library and Archives Canada Cataloguing in Publication

The difficult war : perspectives on insurgency and special operations forces / edited by Emily Spencer.

Includes index.
ISBN 978-1-55488-441-4

1. Insurgency. 2. Counterinsurgency. 3. Special forces (Military science). 4. Asymmetric warfare. I. Spencer, Emily

U241.D54 2009   355.02'18   C2009-902068-8

1   2   3   4   5   13   12   11   10   09

    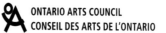

We acknowledge the support of the **Canada Council for the Arts** and the **Ontario Arts Council** for our publishing program. We also acknowledge the financial support of the **Government of Canada** through the **Book Publishing Industry Development Program** and **The Association for the Export of Canadian Books**, and the **Government of Ontario** through the **Ontario Book Publishers Tax Credit** program and the **Ontario Media Development Corporation**.

Printed and bound in Canada
www.dundurn.com

Canadian Defence Academy Press
PO Box 17000 Station Forces
Kingston, Ontario, Canada
K7K 7B4

Dundurn Press	Gazelle Book Services Limited	Dundurn Press
3 Church Street, Suite 500	White Cross Mills	2250 Military Road
Toronto, Ontario, Canada	High Town, Lancaster, England	Tonawanda, NY U.S.A.
M5E 1M2	LA1 4XS	14150

CONTENTS

Foreword by Major-General J.P.Y.D. Gosselin   7

Acknowledgements by Emily Spencer   9

Introduction by Emily Spencer and Bernd Horn   11

1   Mao Zedong and the People's War   23
    Tony Balasevicius

2   The End of Asymmetry: 43
    Force Disparity and the Aims of War
    Peter H. Denton

3   Intelligence and Its Application to Irregular Warfare   53
    Tony Balasevicius and Bernd Horn

4   "The People Puzzle":   79
    The Importance of Cultural Intelligence to Counterinsurgency
    Emily Spencer

5   Defining Terrorism   111
    Bernd Horn

6   Operational Alchemy in Northern Ireland: 123
    The Mutually Enabling Relationship Between SOF and Intelligence
    Andrew Brown

7   Fighting the Mujahideen: 147
    Lessons from the Soviet Counterinsurgency Experience
    in Afghanistan
    Tony Balasevicius and Greg Smith

8   Unconventional Warfare Operations in Afghanistan —   163
    September to December 2001
    V.I.

9   From the Cold War to Insurgency: 193
    Preparing Leaders for the Contemporary Operating Environment
    Bernd Horn

10 SOF for Sale: 231
    The Canadian Forces and the Challenge of Privatized Security
    Christopher Spearin

11 Building Coalition Special Operations Forces for the "Long War" 245
    J. Paul de B. Taillon

Contributors   269
Index   273

FOREWORD

I AM DELIGHTED TO introduce *The Difficult War: Perspectives on Insurgency and Special Operations Forces.* This book represents the latest of over 35 publications produced by the Canadian Defence Academy (CDA) Press. It is indicative of what we have tried to achieve — relevant operational material that will be of use to Canadian Forces (CF) personnel serving in today's complex security environment.

Founded in January 2005, the CDA Press continues to be a testament to its founding principles. Its original vision was to provide a place where key themes and operational topics of importance for military personnel could be gathered together. CDA serves those who interact with the profession of arms, as well as the Canadian public at large.

Significantly, so that we may build on our proud and rich military experience and legacy, these publications have been Canadian-centric in content and perspective. This focus has allowed us to populate our CF professional development centres and schools, as well as those of our allies, and civilian universities and libraries with books that provide a distinctly Canadian operational perspective and experience. We have always had a unique Canadian way of war, so it is logical that we produce material that allows us to learn from our own Canadian operational and combat experiences.

In that vein, there is no topic that could be more relevant at the current time than counterinsurgency. As such, *The Difficult War* is a timely volume that presents a collection of essays that deal with the topics of insurgency and counterinsurgency and many of the collateral issues, topics, and considerations that are wrapped up in what could arguably be considered one of the most complex forms of warfare. This book examines both theoretical and practical topics, and in sum provides an excellent collection of ideas that stimulate thought and debate on this relevant and complex subject.

As always, we at the Canadian Defence Academy hope that our efforts at providing well-researched, relevant, and authoritative books on key operational topics both enlighten and empower those who serve in, and for those who interact with, the profession of arms in Canada. We welcome any and all comments on our continuing pursuit to develop an authoritative body of Canadian operational literature.

MAJOR-GENERAL J.P.Y.D. GOSSELIN
COMMANDER, CANADIAN DEFENCE ACADEMY

ACKNOWLEDGEMENTS

by Emily Spencer

I WOULD BE NEGLIGENT if I did not formally recognize those individuals whose hard work and efforts made this volume possible. To begin, I would like to thank the authors for their dedication, interest, and desire to contribute to the greater cause. In our current hectic environment where work and life in general seemingly increase in tempo every year, endeavours such as writing a chapter for a collected volume or journal are efforts that are left for off-duty hours and involve sacrificing nights, weekends, and holidays. As such, I fully appreciate your participation.

Equally important, I wish to thank Lieutenant-Colonel Jeff Stouffer, the director of the Canadian Forces Leadership Institute (CFLI), and Greg Moore, the CFLI CDA Press project manager, for their support with the book specifically, and with the CDA Press concept in general. Their enduring support is a critical part of the continuing success of CDA Press.

Last, but certainly not least, I would like to thank the chair of CDA Press, Colonel Bernd Horn, Ph.D., without whose continuous guidance and encouragement this volume would not have been possible. His dedication to CDA Press, which he created in 2005, as well as the authors and editors who contribute to the press's publications, is inspiring. Moreover, he continues to ensure the production of high-quality, relevant publications, all within an environment in which the pursuit and dissemination of knowledge is not only enriching but enjoyable.

INTRODUCTION

by Emily Spencer and Bernd Horn

S OME MAY ARGUE THAT Canada is not at war. For instance, a former
minister of national defence (MND), Gordon O'Connor, told the
House of Commons, "I don't consider this [Afghanistan] war. We're
engaged in helping people move products around; we're helping them
build houses, we're helping to advise the police; and, when we're attacked,
we attack back."[1] The reality on the ground undeniably tells a different
story: Leopard main battle tanks, field artillery, light armoured vehicle
IIIs (LAV IIIs), and a variety of other armoured vehicles with heavy arma-
ments underscore the level of threat and combat present in Afghanistan.

The scope of the conflict, of the war, can also been seen in the combatants. There are few places where the true impact of the fighting is
more evident than in the eyes of the soldiers. They are hardened. The
fatigue and deep-seated pain can be seen in their faces. Their eyes —
"windows to the soul," in the words of William Shakespeare — betray a
sadness that belies their youth.

Intermingled with this image is the continual testimony of the
indisputable benchmark of war: the casualties — dead, wounded, and
maimed. At the time of writing this book, Canada has suffered 116
dead and hundreds of wounded (physically, emotionally, and mentally).

One of the war's veterans, Lieutenant-Colonel Omer Lavoie, perhaps expressed it best. "I challenge anyone to tell me that we're not at war." After only a month and a half in command in theatre in the late summer of 2006, Lavoie had suffered 15 killed in action within his unit. Moreover, he had awarded roughly 100 wound stripes.[2] Similarly, Bob Sweet, the mayor of the garrison town of Petawawa, which on the 2006 Labour Day weekend alone grieved with the families of the five soldiers killed and with those of the over 40 soldiers wounded, stated: "We are at war. I don't know whether the rest of Canada understands that, but certainly we do here in Petawawa."

Nonetheless, in many ways, it is not hard to comprehend why many fail to grasp the essence of the struggle in Afghanistan. It is a truly difficult war. It is difficult because it is not war as conceived by most of the general public. It does not fit the traditional image of uniformed combatants fighting to hold ground. There are no large battles between military machines. In fact, rarely do the soldiers, much less the public, actually see the enemy. It is often a war of words, punctuated by sudden attacks that end as quickly as they begin. It is a war in which attacks just as often kill civilians as they do combatants. The attacks are commonly senseless, brutal acts of violence aimed to terrorize and wear down the government, coalition, and public will. They are in essence attacks that fall in line with the tactics of insurgency: provocation, intimidation, protraction, and exhaustion. To disinterested publics, a counterinsurgency, such as the one now being waged by Canada and its allies in Afghanistan, is seen as a pointless waste of national blood and treasure.

It is also the difficult war to prosecute. One American special operations forces (SOF) officer mused, "Counterinsurgency isn't just thinking man's warfare — it is the graduate level of war."[3] It is a war among the people, which is simultaneously in support of the people.

From the ruling government perspective, counterinsurgency is "those political, economic, military, paramilitary, psychological, and civic actions taken by a government to defeat an insurgency."[4] It is a campaign that combines offensive, defensive, and stability operations that are prosecuted along multiple lines of operation."

An insurgency, in turn, is a "struggle between a non-ruling group and the ruling authorities in which the non-ruling group consciously uses political resources (e.g., organizational expertise, propaganda, and demonstrations) and violence to destroy, reformulate, or sustain the basis of legitimacy of one or more aspects of politics."[5] In simplest terms, insurgency is "an organized movement aimed at the overthrow of a constituted government through the use of subversion and armed conflict."[6]

Again, insurgency is anything but simple. Rather, it is the most difficult of conflicts to counter and rests on the notion of security. Additionally, as cultural anthropologists Montgomery McFate and Andrea V. Jackson note, "Security is the most basic precondition for civilian support of the government.... The motivation that provides the only real long-lasting effect is the elemental consideration of survival."[7] Yet this end state is difficult to achieve, especially when the enemy has the initiative, can ignore the conventions of war, targets indiscriminately, blatantly lies, and conducts operations while using the population around it as cover. Moreover, the enemy needs merely to discredit the government and coalition forces. All it needs to show is that the ruling authority is unable to protect itself or provide security for the population.

In essence, the insurgency is a battle for the people. Both the insurgent and the government need to win the "hearts and minds" of the people. Indeed, winning the respect and support of the host nation's population is fundamental to success in any counterinsurgency campaign. The local population can provide intelligence on enemy activity, location, and movements. With their co-operation, information operations (IO) initiatives, governmental programs, and military operations can be advanced. If this support is not forthcoming, the public is at best neutral, perhaps withholding vital information required for force protection. At worst, the public can assist the enemy, furnishing information, food, lodgings, caching of weapons, and potential recruits.

Strategist Major-General Robert Scales observed, "the enemy clearly understands the war he's involved in, that is to win and hold cultural high ground — that is his objective." Scales concluded, "we're playing catch up."[8] And that is another reason it is the difficult war.

Winning hearts and minds requires an understanding of the host nation society. In locations such as Afghanistan, which is largely rural, xenophobic, and tribal, the cultural divide between "us" and "them" is huge. Spanning that gap is not a function of contracting more linguists — it is about truly comprehending the society. As Scales observed, empathy is important. One must understand and work within an alien culture, create alliances with foreign armies, and communicate and shape perceptions of others so that they fully understand the intent of the government and coalition forces.

In the end, counterinsurgency is a difficult war because the greatest challenge on the modern battlefield is human, not technological. It comes down to influencing opinion; winning over the people. Importantly, this challenge must be met with both the host nation population and the domestic population back home. This requirement demands upholding the values of one's own society. "A military force in a democracy can only retain its legitimacy, its self-confidence, and its public support," insisted renowned Harvard professor Michael Ignatieff, "if it plays by the rules, if it refuses to fight dirty." He continued, "but all of the wars and challenges that you face are coming at you from people who definitely and most emphatically fight dirty."[9]

As these examples demonstrate, this "foreign" human component is the reason counterinsurgency is the difficult war. The enemies that we as a Western world now face are ruthless by our standards. "They are dedicated to TTPs [tactics, techniques, and procedures] unacceptable to western nations," Major-General Scales explained: "they are organized and networked; passionate and fanatical; committed; relentless; savage."[10] For many Canadian, or Western soldiers for that matter, the idea that a suicide bomber will walk into a crowd of soldiers and kill combatants and non-combatants is unfathomable.[11] But, as Ignatieff warned, "You're going to have people coming at you who don't play by the rules, and you're going to have people coming at you who have an infinitely greater willingness to risk anything, i.e., their lives, than you may and that's one of the challenges you have to face."[12]

Moreover, too often you just do not know who your enemy is. Lieutenant Toby Glover lamented, "One minute they [insurgents] will be walking down the street and have a woman and children surrounding them and the next the woman and children will disappear and he [the insurgent] will be firing at you. They were masters of using the art of cover. Very rarely did you see them."[13] Lieutenant-Colonel Lavoie commented, "It's not a linear battlefield and it's much harder to measure progress. The enemy has all the assets of an insurgent. One minute he has a hoe in his hand, the next minute it's an AK-47."[14] Lance-Corporal George Sampson recalled, "They attack you when you are least expecting it. We made two mistakes and they punished us for that."[15] Not surprisingly in such an environment interaction with the population becomes difficult. "We still think everyone approaching us wants to kill us," conceded Captain Ryan Carey, "We have no choice but to plan for a fight right 'till we leave."[16]

Consequently, there is no one single, simple solution. The kinetic, military component of counterinsurgency is just one piece of the campaign and, frankly, not the most important. Economic, political, and social reforms are normally the key drivers that will resolve conflict. Nonetheless, too often the emphasis is placed on the military solution. But, security and development are mutually supporting and must be conducted in tandem. Indeed, Sergei Akhrome'ev, the Soviet deputy minister of defence, in November 1986 commented:

> There is no single piece of land in this country which has not been occupied by a Soviet soldier. Nevertheless, the majority of the territory remains in the hands of the rebels ... There is no single military problem that has arisen and that has not been solved, and yet there is still no result. The whole problem is in the fact that military results are not followed up by political.[17]

This reality is another reason counterinsurgency is the difficult war. The provision of the required economic, social, and political reform must be done within the framework of the legitimate host government. However, lack of infrastructure, processes, and experience, as well as corruption, cultural realities, and historical memory can make progress seem impossible. Renowned author and strategist Robert Kaplan stated, "[we will face] warriors — erratic primitives of shifting alliance, habituated to violence, with no stake in civil order."[18] Brigadier-General David Fraser, a former International Security Assistance Force (ISAF) multinational brigade commander in the volatile southern province of Kandahar opined, "it's the most complicated environment you can have."[19]

When one considers the complexities noted thus far, it becomes easy to understand the difficulty of prosecuting a counterinsurgency. The multifarious levels of complexity take time — a commodity that is usually in short supply in Western, technologically advanced, info-centric societies. But the reality is, to change a "medieval culture," to convince the Afghan population that its new government and coalition are there for the long haul, to allow governance and rule of law to mature, and to ensure the economy becomes stable and strong — in short to give the population reasons for supporting the existing regime — takes time. "You cannot win without the trust of the local people," Lieutenant-Colonel Ian Hope asserted and continued, "that is only done over time by sustaining a presence."[20]

Additionally, sustaining domestic support for a prolonged insurgency far from one's own shores also contributes to the difficult war. While Western publics and politicians easily tire of the struggle, the Afghans believe warfare is a contest of endurance over time.[21] "You cannot stop us," taunted one Taliban leader named Ashoor, "We've been using these tactics for hundreds of years and they have always worked." He elaborated, "After an attack fighters can easily stash their weapons among villagers sympathetic to their cause. They can then melt in with the local population and move on to another village, where there are more caches of weapons available to them for mounting another attack."[22] He reiterated the old Afghan saying, "the foreigners have the watches, but we have the time." In a similar vein, Brigadier-General Fraser concluded, "It's a marathon and this [counterinsurgency] is hard, hard stuff."[23]

This volume contains a collection of essays that are intended to help the practitioner and others with an interest or connection to the profession of arms understand counterinsurgency and its important components. As such, it also offers a detailed examination of special operations forces (SOF), defined as "organizations containing specially selected personnel that are organized, equipped and trained to conduct high-risk, high value special operations to achieve military, political, economic, or informational objectives by using special and unique operational methodologies in hostile, denied, or politically sensitive areas to achieve desired tactical, operational and/or strategic effects in times of peace, conflict or war," are a key component to counterinsurgency.[24]

The book begins with a chapter written by Major Tony Balasevicius on Mao's theory of the "People's War." This insightful examination of Mao's philosophical and operational construct for conducting an insurgency provides a timeless, not to mention extremely relevant, foundation for any student or practitioner of insurgency. Throughout the chapter, Balasevicius examines Mao's principles, rules, operational tenets, and strategy. In the end, the author concludes that there is nothing startling or new about insurgency — it is an ageless human phenomena and success, as Mao demonstrated, always rests on one key dynamic — gaining the support and mobilizing the will of the people.

The second chapter by Dr. Peter Denton deals indirectly with insurgency by covering the issue of force disparity. Denton underlines that combat has always been asymmetrical, arguing that opposing forces tend to fight on equal terms only if battle cannot be avoided. He argues that force disparity is an absolute disjunction between the forces available to the opposing sides. It is not just difference in degree, but also in kind. He explains that force disparity in the context of twenty-first century warfare recognizes that combatants may be so utterly different in the nature and makeup of their respective militaries that it is virtually impossible, if not completely useless, to even compare the two sides. The ironic outcome is that, today, force disparity renders more powerful weapons systems less important to the final outcome of warfare than ever before. Conversely, social and economic issues become the critical elements of battlespace operations before primary phase combat begins, and become even more critical during the secondary phase. In the end, understanding the dynamics of force disparity is critical to comprehending the difficulties of countering insurgency.

In chapter 3, Major Tony Balasevicius and Colonel Horn, Ph. D., discuss the importance of intelligence to irregular warfare. These authors explain that in the current security environment, particularly in the case of the insurgencies in Iraq and Afghanistan, the challenge of capturing or killing insurgents — who shrewdly embed themselves within the fabric of society — without creating collateral damage that alienates or disenfranchises the populace is a difficult task. As such, they argue that intelligence is the key to success. They further explain that accurate intelligence aids tremendously in the conventional fight by enhancing force protection by assisting in the identification of enemy activity whether planned ambushes, attacks on convoys or forward operating bases, or the laying of IEDs. Not only does the information save lives, it also provides the necessary details for prosecuting operations to capture or kill insurgents. Balasevicius and Horn make the case that timely accurate intelligence will keep the enemy off balance, separate insurgents from the population, and deny them sanctuary and staging bases. They conclude that accurate, timely intelligence enables the counterinsurgency forces to provide the stable secure environment to allow political, social, and economic reform to develop in today's complex environment.

In chapter 4, Dr. Emily Spencer provides a convincing argument for the importance of exhibiting high cultural intelligence for all participants involved in a counterinsurgency. Cultural intelligence, or CQ, is defined as the ability to recognize the shared beliefs, values, attitudes, and behaviours of a group of people and, most important, to apply this knowledge toward a specific goal. Not only can poor cultural intelligence alienate a host nation population, it can also have detrimental affects in relation to the Canadian public's support of the war effort, not to mention the international community. As such, good CQ is vital to counterinsurgency warfare.

In chapter 5, Colonel Horn defines terrorism and provides an overview of its relationship to insurgency. In many ways this chapter is a primer on terrorism that outlines its definition, purpose, and effectiveness. In short, terrorism is an effective tactic for the weak in their attempts to undermine, discredit, and overthrow the ruling authority. Horn also examines the evolving nature of terrorism and the implications all of this has on insurgency. In the end, he concludes that to comprehend insurgency it is important to understand terrorism as they are inextricably linked to each other.

The next chapter, written by Captain Andrew Brown, examines the role of special operations forces and intelligence in the counterinsurgency battle using the context of the British campaign in Northern Ireland to show that the two are mutually supporting. Brown demonstrates how SOF, specifically the Special Air Service (SAS), was instrumental in assisting with the development and maturation of intelligence collection and application in the early years of the insurgency. He further develops the analysis to show how SOF also evolved to become the "action arm" of the intelligence apparatus. Working together, the attributes, special skill sets, and capabilities of SOF combined with timely, accurate intelligence formed an effective combination that allowed the government to prosecute precision strikes against insurgent leadership, operatives, and operations that eventually turned the tide and forced the belligerents to a political solution.

In chapter 7, Major Tony Balasevicius and Lieutenant-Colonel Greg Smith examine the lessons learned from the Soviet counterinsurgency in

Afghanistan in the 1980s. They clearly point out that the Soviet counter-insurgency campaign, contrary to popular misconception, was actually well thought out and tactically, as well as operationally, sound. Nonetheless, resources constraints, the complexities of Afghan culture, geography, and politics led the Soviets to exercise a policy of brutality and retaliation. They conclude by asking if the North Atlantic Treaty Organization (NATO) learned from the Soviet experience.

Chapter 8 retains the focus on Afghanistan and explores the successful American campaign to oust the Taliban from power in the fall of 2001, in the aftermath of 9/11. The author examines the unconventional warfare (UW) campaign prosecuted by both the Central Intelligence Agency (CIA) and U.S. special forces and how they effectively leveraged Afghan resistance forces to provide the ground manoeuvre forces required to defeat Taliban and Al Qaeda military forces on the ground. As such, the chapter describes the role of SOF in a UW campaign, as well as the lessons that can be extracted with regard to UW operations from the initial stage of Operation Enduring Freedom.

In chapter 9, Colonel Horn comments on the evolution of operations from the Cold War to the current contemporary operating environment. Specifically, he examines the major theoretical constructs that framed operations during this time period and still have relevance in the current security environment. In addition, the chapter outlines a number of leadership lessons for preparing leaders for the contemporary operating environment, specifically within the context of the Canadian counterinsurgency engagement in Afghanistan.

The tenth chapter, written by Dr. Christopher Spearin, takes an asymmetric approach to the book's theme of insurgency. In this chapter the author discusses the use of private military corporations (PMC) to replace SOF in the conduct of operations in insurgencies and other operational areas in today's complex security environment. As the "Long War" drags on and the militaries of all participating nations are stressed to meet the recurring requirement of troops to task, particularly in specialized areas such as SOF where numbers are small, force generation long, and missions in overabundance, Spearin notes that the default to PMCs is natural. However, he also warns that there is a paradox, or perhaps more accurately a vicious circle. The more popular and successful the PMCs, the more SOF organizations are bled dry as scarce, highly trained operators quit the military to accept more lucrative contracts with PMCs that are retained to fill the positions SOF have just vacated.

In the final chapter, Colonel J. Paul de B. Taillon, Ph.D., discusses the importance of coalition operations in the Long War, namely the international efforts against terrorism and the global insurgency. He specifically focuses on coalition SOF and their effectiveness and importance to winning this struggle. Taillon examines the attributes, skill sets, and characteristics that make SOF the force of choice in the current security environment. He also provides a strong case for why coalition SOF are critical to American counterinsurgency efforts and he underlines this thesis by specifically highlighting coalition SOF operations in both Afghanistan and Iraq.

NOTES

1. John Geddes, "This Means War," 20 June 2006, *Maclean's, www.macleans.ca/topstories/canada/article.jsp?content=20060626_129652_129652* (accessed 18 July 2006).
2. Lieutenant-Colonel Omer Lavoie, interview, 8 October 2006.
3. U.S. Army Combined Arms Center, *Counterinsurgency FM 3–24* (Washington, DC: Department of the Army, December 2006), 1–1.
4. *Ibid.*, Foreword.
5. Bard E. O'Neill, *Insurgency and Terrorism. Inside Modern Revolutionary Warfare* (Dulles, VA: Brassey's Inc., 1990), 13.
6. *Counterinsurgency FM 3–24,* 1–1.
7. Montgomery McFate and Andrea V. Jackson, "The Object Beyond War: Counterinsurgency and the Four Tools of Political Competition," *Unrestricted Warfare Symposium 2006 Proceedings,* 150.
8. Major-General Robert Scales, presentation at "Cognitive Dominance Workshop," West Point, 11 July 2006.
9. Michael Ignatieff, *Virtual War: Ethical Challenges* (Annapolis: United States Naval Academy, March 2001), 7.
10. Major-General Robert Scales, presentation at Cognitive Dominance Workshop, West Point, 11 July 2006.
11. Interview, Lieutenant-Colonel Omer Lavoie, 13 October 2006.
12. Ignatieff, 8.
13. Declan Walsh, Richard Norton-Taylor, and Julian Borger, "From Soft Hats to Hard Facts in Battle to Beat Taliban," *The Guardian,* 18 November 2006, 5.

14. Paul Koring, "The Afghan Mission — A Thin Canadian Line Holds in Kandahar," *Globe and Mail*, 6 December 2006, A26.

15. Walsh, and others, "From Soft Hats to Hard Facts," *The Guardian*, 18 November 2006, 5.

16. Mitch Potter, "The Story of C Company," *Toronto Star*, 30 September 2006, *www.thestar.com/NASApp/cs/contentserver?pagename=thestar* (accessed 27 October 2006).

17. Quoted in John Ferris, "Invading Afghanistan, 1836–2006: Politics and Pacification," *Calgary Papers in Military and Strategic Studies, Vol. 1, Canada in Kandahar*, 19.

18. Robert Kaplan, *Warrior Politics: Why Leadership Demands a Pagan Ethos* (New York: Vintage Books, 2002), 118.

19. Brigadier-General David Fraser, presentation at the Canadian Infantry Association Annual General Meeting, 25 May 2007.

20. Adnan R. Khan, "I'm Here to Fight: Canadian Troops in Kandahar," *Maclean's*, 5 April 2006, *www.macleans.ca/topstories/world/article.jsp?content=20060403_124448_124448* (accessed 18 July 2006).

21. U.S. DoD, *Afghan Cultural Field Guide*, MCIA-2630-AFG-001–04, November 2003, 24.

22. Adnan R. Khan, "Prepare to Bury Your Dead," *Maclean's*, 20 March 2006, *www.macleans.ca/topstories/world/article.jsp?content=20060320_123593_123593* (accessed 18 July 2006).

23. Brigadier-General David Fraser, presentation at the Canadian Infantry Association Annual General Meeting, 25 May 2007.

24. Canada, *Canadian Special Operations Forces Command: An Overview* (Ottawa: DND, 2008), 6.

I

MAO ZEDONG
AND THE PEOPLE'S WAR

Tony Balasevicius

INCREASINGLY, CANADA'S MILITARY IS being called upon to deploy into complex operational environments where it must deal with highly adaptive adversaries seeking to destabilize society through a variety of asymmetric means. In articulating this new paradigm, the Canadian Army's *Land Operations 2021: Adaptive Dispersed Operations* has identified a future security environment in which "the likelihood of large force-on-force exchanges will be eclipsed by irregular warfare carried out by highly adaptive, technologically enabled adversaries … intent less on defeating armed forces than eroding an adversary's will to fight."[1] Assuming this vision of the future battlespace is correct, the Canadian Army has a responsibility to understand its dynamics and complexities. To do so it must first define the concept of irregular warfare, understand its genesis and then identify the foundations on which its success depends. Only then can an effective strategy be developed to counter the threat.

The idea of irregular warfare, referred to within the framework of the army's notion of the future security environment, is little more than a modern adaptation of the classic insurgency strategy developed and refined by Mao Zedong. In the most basic terms, Mao's insurgency, commonly referred to as the People's War, can be viewed as an uprising against an established form of authority such as a government or occupying force.[2]

Historically, insurgencies have been successful because they have evolved to meet the specific conditions of their environment and circumstances.[3] Mao's contribution to this process was to integrate political, social, and economic elements into what had been essentially a military activity. Moreover, Mao was able to solidify and refine his core ideas regarding insurgency during a period of almost continuous conflict between 1927 and 1949, where he fought wars against the Kuomintang, China's Nationalist Party and the Japanese.[4]

In order to better understand Mao's success with regard to insurgency this chapter will explore the theory of the People's War. To do this it is necessary to look at the different components that make up the theory and how each has been integrated into the overall construct. However, before this can be done, it is prudent to examine Mao's key ideas on the topic of war and conflict.

Mao's thinking on warfare developed over time and from a variety of sources. In fact, his early research into the subject included a number of the great Western commanders such as Napoleon and military theorists like Clausewitz, Jomini, and Sun Tzu. However, Mao derived much of his influence about the conduct of war from practical experience.[5] In fact, his ability to develop a simple theatrical concept and constantly adjust it to meet the requirements of a particular situation became the hallmark of Mao's approach to the development of the People's War.[6] In this respect, the basic concept behind the doctrine was simple — it was all about gaining and maintaining the support of the population while slowly wearing away the will of the enemy through a series of terrorist attacks and military actions.

The genesis of this idea derived from Mao's realization that the methods of revolution that had proven successful in Russia were not working in China. He correctly reasoned that this was because the Kuomintang (Nationalist) army had the means to crush the uprisings long before it could reach the needed momentum to achieve success. As a result, Mao concluded that a new course of action was needed if the Communist Party of China (CPC) was to overthrow the established authority.[7]

Thus, in seeking to adjust the idea of revolution to the specific conditions within China, Mao's influence became enmeshed with the very essence of the People's War. Unlike Marxist-Leninist theory, where the urban proletariat was seen as the main source of revolution, Mao recognized that the peasantry in the countryside must be the instrument of change. Moreover, unlike other political ideologues, Mao believed that military strategy had to be directly connected to the economic and political ideology it was seeking to establish. However, Mao's greatest influence on the development of modern insurgency lays in his innovative solution for overcoming his position of weakness.[8] Mao understood that he did not have the matériel resources to defeat the Nationalist government so he redefined the rules for political and military success.

In redefining these rules Mao "argued that there was a broader set of resources available on which to build power — the most important of them being the will of man."[9] Mao reasoned that victory could be attained as long as the struggle remained within the parameters of what the "human will" was capable of achieving. In this respect, Mao was able to shift the centre of gravity from possessing military capability to controlling the people. Major William L. Cogley, the former chief of Asian Studies at the U.S. Air Force Special Operations School, explains, "Failure to recognize, or refusal to accept, [this] different nature of armed struggle ... has been the major stumbling block for those attempting to counter it."[10]

MOBILIZATION

Within this new construct, the key to success was the development of the human potential. This was done through a process of political mobilization. As Mao explained, "To wish for victory and yet neglect political mobilization is like wishing to 'go south by driving the chariot north,' and the result would inevitably be to forfeit victory."[11] To mobilize the masses, Mao needed to first gain their support. To this end, he promised the peasants a number of reforms with the centrepiece being land redistribution. He wrote, "to bring the people on side prominence must be given to land reform; only through it could the ample support of the peasants be achieved, only through land reform could mass organizations be built, recruits be found, and leadership talent reared up from the masses."[12] In essence, political mobilization within the context of the

People's War became a process devoted to winning over and then preparing the people for conflict.

Western literature has often referred to this idea as winning the "hearts and minds." However, this phrase is extremely misleading. Within the context of the People's War, the idea is really about control and using that control to achieve specific goals. As author Edward Rice points out, the concept of land reform is little more than a simple but extremely innovative motivator for controlling the people. He explains, "They [the Communist] would mobilize the peasants of the countryside against the status quo authority with such things as the seizure and redistribution of the land. They would arm the peasants, who would [then] have to fight if they were to protect their gains."[13] To efficiently mobilize the people Mao needed some way of harnessing the process. The only organization big enough for such a task was the army.

Mao concluded that the army would need to have two roles, fighting and party work. As he stated: "We have an army for fighting as well as an army for labour.... they do a dual job, warfare and production."[14] Mao believed that this dual function could only be achieved by close co-operation between the party, the soldiers, and the people. To attain this unity Mao carried out a number of important and novel reforms within his military force.

First, he reduced the basic fighting formation from a division into smaller regimental-sized units for better control. He then established a party cadre in every organization starting at the company level. This cadre was commanded by a political commissar, who was responsible for looking after the party's interest, and providing political instruction. Mao believed the political department within the military was the "lifeline of all work as it would control the political indoctrination process of both the soldiers and the people."[15] Party control over the army was further strengthened when Mao designated the political officer and military leader as co-commanders. [16] The actual exercise of control was done through what appeared to be democratic organizations called the people's councils.

These councils were initially established as a forum for administration and a method of understanding and dealing with local disputes and issues. More important, the system also created an opportunity for the party to educate the people in such things as reading and writing, understanding the revolution, and the evils of foreign aggression.[17] However, over time, the councils evolved and developed a much darker side to them.

Mao found that the councils were an ideal method of monitoring the "proper development" of the people. They could also be used by the party to manipulate public opinion. As Han Suyin, an authority on Mao writes, "the most powerful educational method consisted of the conference — debate." This is where, "All rank disappeared [and] soldiers had full rights to free speech." During the conference "not only were battles and campaigns discussed, but the individual conduct of any commander or fighter could also be criticized."[18] This public criticism allowed CPC officials to manipulate the downfall or rise of specific individuals.

Under this new system the councils became the platform by which the party's cadres would do their work but they would only succeed if the people trusted the army and the party. To ensure this trust developed, Mao imposed a regime of harsh discipline on his troops and cadres. He put into practice a simple but effective code known as "Three Rules and the Eight Remarks." These were:

> **Rules:**
> All actions are subject to command,
> Do not steal from the people, and
> Be neither selfish nor unjust.
>
> **Remarks:**
> Replace the door when you leave the house.
> Roll up the bedding on which you have slept.
> Be courteous.
> Be honest in your transactions.
> Return what you borrow.
> Replace what you break.
> Do not bathe in the presence of women.
> Do not, without authority, search those you arrest.[19]

As these types of behaviours were unusual for military forces during the period as they tended to work on the theory "to the victor go the spoils," it is not surprising that the implementation of the "Three Rules and Eight Remarks" quickly won over the peasants. As the bond of trust developed, Mao took every opportunity to encourage the people to believe that the Red Army was their army, one that was devoted to their interests.[20]

Although the councils and the army were important for control, Mao also used a number of other less intrusive techniques to achieve the same effect. These included providing firm and fair governance, building confidence by developing sound social policies, and creating a solid propaganda campaign.[21] In fact, propaganda was embedded into the very idea of the People's War through a program of indoctrination. As Mao explained, indoctrination was a two-part process, "First, it means telling the army and the people about the political aim of the war." Mao believed that it was necessary for everyone to understand why the war was being fought and how it concerned them. For example, during the Second Sino-Japanese War the political aim was "to drive out Japanese imperialism and build a new China of freedom and equality."[22] Mao realized that before an effective anti-Japanese backlash could be created everyone had to understand the aim of the war. Second, he thought that it was not enough merely to explain the aim but that "the steps and policies for its attainment must also be given." [23]

Practically, the process of indoctrination was achieved through "word of mouth, by leaflets and bulletins, by newspapers, books and pamphlets, through plays and films, through schools, and through the mass organizations." Mao stressed, "Our job is not to recite our political programme to the people, for nobody will listen to such recitations; we must link the political mobilization for the war with developments in the war and with the life of the soldiers and the people, and make it a continuous movement." On this point he emphasized, "This is a matter of immense importance on which our victory in the war primarily depends."[24]

THE STRATEGIC FRAMEWORK OF THE PEOPLE'S WAR

To provide a strategic framework for his fight against the established authority Mao laid out the fundamental steps that were necessary to achieve victory. These included:

a.   Arousing and organizing the people;
b.   Achieving internal unification politically;
c.   Establishing bases;
d.   Equipping forces;
e.   Recovering national strength;
f.   Destroying enemy's national strength; and
g.   Regaining lost territories.[25]

The resource limitations within the CPC would not allow these objectives to be accomplished simultaneously; therefore, Mao proposed to achieve them in three phases.

Mao described the first phase as the *strategic defensive* in which the insurgents were on the defensive. He emphasized that during this phase the insurgency should not become involved in direct military action with the enemy, but it should harass it by engaging in such things as espionage, terrorist attacks, and/or civil unrest.[26] Mao stated: "Phase I is devoted to the organization of an underground resistance movement for the purpose of spreading propaganda and eliciting support for the movement." He highlighted the fact that "the purpose of this support is to lay the ground work to overthrow the existing authority." Whether or not that was the current government or, as in the case of the Japanese, an occupying power was irrelevant.[27]

The second phase was viewed by Mao as the *strategic stalemate* stage. At this point the enemy still retained the upper hand but both sides had reached some state of equilibrium. Mao explained that this period was characterized by small-scale combat operations. Activities during this stage included terrorism and guerrilla warfare.[28] Once the insurgent forces had obtained local superiority, the insurgency could then proceed to the third phase, which Mao referred to as the *strategic counteroffensive*. This last stage was characterized by extensive large-scale mobile operations that were carried out with the view of completing the final destruction of the enemy.[29]

MILITARY OBJECTIVES AND THE PEOPLE'S WAR

The strategic objective of the People's War was to reverse the power relationship within China. This was achieved at the operational level by wearing down the Nationalist's strength, while the CPC attempted to build up its own through sustained efforts at mobilizing support from the population.[30] Achievement of these operational objectives meant Mao needed to establish and maintain certain tactical conditions throughout his campaign. As a minimum he had to have "a cause to fight for, support from the local populace, bases, mobility, supplies, and information."[31]

These conditions allowed Mao to meet the operational objective of building strength through mobilizing support. This in turn, provided the foundation for achieving his other operational imperative — creating a base of operations. He realized that before he could move the insurgency forward, he needed a place where he could establish the necessary tactical conditions. For him, this place was in the mountainous areas in Jiangxi where he set up his first base in 1927.[32]

THE INSURGENCY BASE

During the insurgency, the concept of a *base* became Mao's political, economic, and military hub. It was used to provide protection for his forces, house his supplies, and serve as a platform from which he could expand his power. To be effective, in determining the placement of the base(s) one had to consider a number of factors such as the geographical conditions in the area, the enemy's situation, the population, the ability to develop political power and mass and the party organization in the area.[33] Most important, each base had to be strong enough to withstand large-scale attacks without having to draw on the resources of other bases.[34] Once the primary base had been established Mao sought to use it as a springboard for expansion into the surrounding regions.

This method of expansion is often referred to, by Western analysts, as the "Oil Spot Strategy." This is a tactic used by both insurgent and counterinsurgent forces, because it recognizes that neither side has sufficient resources to secure the entire country during the initial stages of an insurgency. As a result, each side attempts to consolidate the areas that will protect their core support as they attempt to increase their authority outward from their bases.[35] In Mao's case, once the primary base was firmly established this growth could begin with the conduct of military operations that were focused on expansion.

With regard to military operations, Mao believed that the "object of war is simply to preserve oneself and to annihilate the enemy. To annihilate the enemy means to disarm him or to deprive him of the power of resistance, and not to annihilate him completely in a physical sense."[36] In general, military operations of the People's War were based on Mao's "Ten Principles of War" or what he referred to as his directives. These were:

1. Attack isolated enemy forces first, attack strong enemy forces later;
2. Take towns and rural areas first, take big cities later;
3. Wiping out the enemy's strength is the main objective, not seizing territory;
4. Only attack enemy forces that can be completely overcome;
5. Fight no battle you are not sure of winning;
6. Have courage in battle and no fear of sacrifice or fatigue;
7. Attack the enemy when he is on the move;
8. In cities, seize all weakly defended battlements; wait before attacking strong enemy lines;
9. Use captured arms and personnel to reinforce; and
10. Rest, train and consolidate in short intervals. The enemy should be permitted scant breathing space.[37]

Over time these directives were distilled into a slogan, which became known as the famous four:

> When the enemy advances, we retreat. When the enemy halts and encamps, we trouble them. When the enemy seeks to avoid battle, we attack. And, when the enemy retreats, we pursue.[38]

Initially, Mao's small army did not have the numerical or matériel resources to take on the Nationalist forces directly. To overcome this problem Mao created a flexible, multi-tiered force structure that was based on regulars (the Red Army) and irregulars (guerrillas). These forces were trained to carry out different types of warfare based on the quality of the soldiers and equipment that was available. In the end, they practised guerrilla, mobile, and positional warfare.[39]

GUERRILLA WARFARE

Guerrilla warfare was a form of combat where small groups of irregulars used mobile tactics that were primarily based on ambushes and raids to attack larger less mobile forces. Guerrillas often attempted to draw larger enemy units into unsuitable terrain to minimize their superior firepower and then used the ground, and the elements of surprise and mobility, to attack their vulnerable points. Mao viewed guerrilla warfare as the war of the local population. He suggested, "Because guerrilla warfare derives from the masses and is supported by them, it can neither exist nor flourish if it separates itself from their sympathies and co-operation."[40]

Mao appreciated the guerrilla's ability to wear down the enemy and accepted the value of guerrilla units in providing local security, acting as scouts or watchers, and gathering intelligence. However, within the construct of the People's War, the main operational roles of guerrilla units were confined to deterrent and harassment missions. Mao stated: "In concrete terms, and especially concerning military operations, when we talk of the people in the base area as a factor, we mean that we have an armed people. That is the main reason why the enemy is afraid to approach our base area."[41]

This attitude stemmed from the realization that despite their benefits guerrillas could not achieve decisive results on the battlefield. Mao asserted, "Guerrilla warfare does not bring as quick results or as great renown as regular warfare, but a long road tests a horse's strength and a long task proves a man's heart, and in the course of this long and cruel war guerrilla warfare will demonstrate its immense power."[42] That being said, Mao did integrate guerrilla warfare into the overall concept of the People's War because he understood that the main advantage of guerrilla warfare was that it could be carried out by the people with very little training or equipment. However, to compensate for this weakness guerrillas were expected to be "cunning" in their operations. In this regard, Mao noted that the essential requirements for successful guerrilla operations included the "retention of the initiative, alertness;

carefully planned tactical attacks in a war of strategical defense, tactical speed in a war strategically protracted."[43] As a result, he suggested that guerrilla strategy "must be based primarily on alertness, mobility, and attack."[44]

Mao recognized the importance of forming guerrilla units as early as possible. Ideally this process would start during the initial stages of the political mobilization process.[45] To this end he suggested that such units could develop in the following ways:

a. From the masses of the people;
b. From regular army units temporarily detailed for the purpose;
c. From regular army units permanently detailed for the purpose;
d. From the combination of a regular army unit and a unit recruited from the people;
e. From the local militia;
f. From deserters from the ranks of the enemy; and
g. From former bandits and bandit groups.... In the present hostilities, no doubt, all these sources will be employed.[46]

Mao understood that creating guerrilla units was one matter, but having them carry out effective operations was something quite different. He realized that success with poorly trained and equipped peasants would be based on the quality of leadership that could be developed at the grassroots level.

In this respect, Mao believed that "since each guerrilla group fights in a protracted war, its officers must be brave and positive men whose entire loyalty is dedicated to the cause of emancipation of the people."[47] He pointed out, "An officer should have the following qualities: great powers of endurance so that in spite of any hardship he sets an example to his men and be a model for them; he must be able to mix easily with the people; his spirit and that of the men must be one in strengthening the policy of resistance." More important, "If he wishes to gain victories, he must study tactics." Mao insisted, "A guerrilla group with officers of this caliber would be unbeatable."[48]

Despite the emphasis on leadership, cunning, and detailed planning, the fact remained that successful guerrilla operations depended on two critical factors. First, they needed the full support of the population and, second, they needed to have intimate knowledge of the terrain they were fighting on. When Mao began to expand his base these advantages were no longer available to the guerrilla.[49] As a result, guerrilla units always remained a local resource, but they did have what Mao referred to as strategic potential.

Mao pointed out that "the strategic role of guerrilla warfare is twofold, to support regular warfare and to transform itself into regular warfare." He stressed, "Considering the unprecedented extent and duration of guerrilla warfare in China's War of Resistance, it is all the more important not to underestimate its strategic role."[50] In the end, the limited employability of the guerrilla had to be overcome. This was done with the Red Army, and, although it could be used to carry out guerrilla warfare when necessary, its primary military focus was on mobile and positional warfare.[51]

Mobile Warfare

Mao viewed mobile warfare as the conduct of operations by large forces operating as self-contained organizations. Interestingly, the key characteristic of these operations was the absence of fixed battle lines or any type of established front line. As a result, the Red Army's "lines of operation" were usually determined by the direction in which it was moving. Mao believed that in a revolutionary war, there could be no set battle lines, which he pointed out had also been the case in the Soviet Union following the 1917 Russian Revolution.[52]

Mao broke mobile warfare down into a series of distinct operations. These included active and passive defence, preparations for combating "encirclement and suppression" campaigns, strategic retreat, and strategic counteroffensive.[53] Mao acknowledged that such operations could create the conditions for victory but in and of themselves they could not achieve what he referred to as the reality of victory. He believed that "to bring about victory or defeat, a decisive battle between the two armies was necessary."[54] Mao held that the result of all mobile operations was the complete destruction of large enemy forces through a "war of annihilation," or what Mao viewed as the decisive battle.

In order to achieve decisive battle, Mao realized that mobile warfare must be based on quick decisions using offensives that operated on exterior lines within the framework of a strategy along interior lines.[55] Mao believed that to be successful such operations had to employ forces that could operate over an extended and fluid front. He stressed, "To achieve success, the Chinese troops must conduct their warfare with a high degree of mobility on extensive battlefields, making swift advances and withdrawals, swift concentrations and dispersals."[56] Although these concepts may appear familiar to Western soldiers, it is important to note that Mao's ideas about mobile warfare diverge from the "Western way of war" in many respects.

These differences are especially relevant in regard to Mao's emphasis on time and space. In Western military thinking, the purpose of manoeuvre is to capture and hold ground; however, as Mao had no interest in holding territory outside his base area, space and time became weapons rather than goals.[57] The idea was to use space to manoeuvre the enemy into a favourable position and then attack. In this respect, the principles of mobile warfare were similar to those of guerrilla operations. From a practical perspective, operational manoeuvre was not always possible, especially for a force that spent much of its time on the strategic defensive. This meant that the CPC forces would have to transition into what Mao termed positional warfare.

POSITIONAL WARFARE

Mao viewed positional warfare as a war of fixed lines similar in concept to the European "way of war" during the First World War. In general, he was not particularly fond of this type of fighting. He believed that if one concentrated forces on a narrow front for a war of attrition, then one would be throwing away the advantages of geography and economy of organization.[58] However, while Mao's thinking stayed away from positional warfare, he did not abandon the idea completely.[59]

He recognized that these operations were important to defending key points or positions. Moreover, they would become prevalent during the end of the third stage of insurgency where his forces would have to attack the cities and other strong points of the established authority.

Mao referred to this inevitability when he stated: "In this third stage positional warfare will undoubtedly play a greater role, for then the enemy will be holding fast to his positions, and we shall not be able to recover our lost territory unless we launch powerful positional attacks in support of mobile warfare."[60] It was for this reason that the concept remained an important part of the People's War.

Although the theory of the People's War sounds straightforward — much like all doctrine — its execution is far less so. For example, in reality the progress of the Chinese insurgency was extremely uneven. This was especially the case during the strategic counteroffensive (the third stage) when the unevenness of progress throughout the vast Chinese territory resulted in the third stage occurring in some areas, while the second or even first stage was happening in others. To overcome this problem, Mao used the flexibility that was inherent in his eclectic force structure and his operational methodology to optimize capabilities for each circumstance.[61]

COMPOUND WARFARE

This operational flexibility and how it was used by Mao is particularly important to understanding the underlying military success of the People's War. Mao believed that regular and irregular units were complementary. He stressed, "Considering the revolutionary war as a whole, the operations of the people's guerrillas and those of the main forces of the Red Army complement each other like a man's right and left arm, and if we had only the main forces of the Red Army without the people's guerrillas, we would be like a warrior with only one arm."[62] In fact, Mao often grouped his guerrilla units with his mobile forces creating a synergistic effect. This phenomenon of using conventional and irregular forces against an enemy has been defined within the Western military context as compound warfare.[63]

Within the construct of the People's War, guerrilla forces gave important advantages to Mao's mobile forces. These included developing intelligence information while suppressing intelligence gathering by the Nationalists. Guerrillas also provided supplies and quick passage through their territory, while denying this ability to their enemy.[64] On the other hand, Mao's mobile regular forces also provided certain advantages to the guerrillas. For example, they often pressured the Nationalists to withdraw or forced them into, or out of, areas where the guerrillas were operating, creating conditions for greater freedom of action. [65]

From a historical perspective, the synergy derived by combining regular and irregular operations makes compound warfare especially effective for smaller forces particularly when they are operating over large areas or in difficult terrain. In this respect, Mao had both of these advantages and used compound warfare as a combat multiplier to significantly enhance the overall flexibility and effectiveness of his forces.[66]

Concluding Remarks

In looking at the evolution of the People's War there can be little question that the success of Mao's concepts rested on gaining the support of, and then mobilizing, the people. This support was garnered with critical social reforms that were focused on giving the people what they wanted and then making them fight for what they had been given. Mao was then able to channel this potential into the conduct of military operations that benefitted from an innovative and flexible force structure. In the end, this combination proved to be extremely resilient.

It was this resiliency that has allowed the doctrine to become a model that can be adapted to the specific circumstances of the user. For example, few insurgencies have the luxury of starting a conflict with an army of any kind, which means they must rely solely on guerrilla-based forces that will eventually transform themselves into larger mobile armies. Such an evolution can be seen with Hezbollah's fight against the Israelis.[67] In this respect, Mao's ideas on insurgencies have withstood the test of time.

However, despite its success, the concepts of People's War have not resonated within the Western military establishment that often seeks a quick fix solution to every problem. Key to understanding Mao's concept of the People's War is the realization that its complex nature belies any type of quick fix. Victory for either side can only be achieved by gaining and maintaining control of the people and this is a long and difficult process.

In attempting to find a solution to the problem one must follow Mao's lead. The established authority must provide the people with a simple but innovative motivator that has general appeal. However, it must be something that the people are willing to defend. Once this has been accomplished the people must be armed and organized so they can fight to protect their gains. This will give them the incentive and the means they need to defend their area and, more important, it will provide the means of extending the counterinsurgency's control.

Western literature has called this the fight for the villages, which is an accurate way of describing the conflict. With this formula the established authority can eliminate the support insurgents receive from the local populace, as well as their bases and mobility, and, consequently, their supplies and information. That being said, in the end, even the simplest of theoretical solutions are difficult to execute. For this reason the question for counterinsurgency forces is always what price are they willing to pay for security?

NOTES

1. Department of National Defence, *Land Operations 2021: Adaptive Dispersed Operations. The Force Employment Concept for Canada's Army of Tomorrow* (Kingston: Directorate of Land Concepts and Design, 2007), 2.
2. Bard E. O'Neill, *Insurgency & Terrorism: Inside Modern Revolutionary Warfare* (Washington, DC: Brassey's Inc., 1990), 13. Bard E. O'Neill, a recognized expert on the subject, articulates this concept as a "struggle between a non-ruling group and the ruling authorities in which the non-ruling group consciously uses political resources (e.g., organizational expertise, propaganda and demonstrations) and violence to destroy, reformulate, or sustain the basis of legitimacy." It should be noted that over the past few years Western nations have come to recognize the transnational nature of modern insurgencies and now refer to insurgency as, "a competition involving at least one non-state movement using means that include violence against an established authority to achieve political change (Definition as developed by a COIN study group during United States Marine Corps (USMC) Joint Urban Warrior 2005. Taken from National Defence, *Canadian Army Counterinsurgency Operations* (Draft) (Kingston: Land Force Doctrine and Training System [henceforth LFDTS], 2005).
3. The concept of insurgency is not new to military operations. In fact, insurgencies have been around for almost as long as organized warfare. Examples of such struggles can be found in ancient Egypt and China, while the Roman, Ottoman, and Napoleonic empires each had to deal with various types of insurgencies throughout their

histories. More recently, there have been many insurgencies in response to European colonial expansion into Asia and Africa. Interestingly, conventional military forces have also used elements of insurgency doctrine through the use of special forces in support of conventional operations since primarily the Second World War.

4. C.P Fitzgerald, *Mao Tse-tung and China* (New York: Holmes & Meier Publishers, 1976), 16, 26, 38. Also see Jung Chang, and Jon Halliday. *Mao: The Unknown Story* (New York: Knopf, 2005.), 350-365.

5. Suyin Han, *The Morning Deluge; Mao Tse-tung and the Chinese Revolution, 1893–1954* (Boston: Little, Brown, 1972), 47.

6. Philip Short, *Mao: A Life* (New York: Henry Holt, 2000.), 99. See also Han, 4–5.

7. William J. Pomeroy, *Guerrilla Warfare and Marxism; A Collection of Writings from Karl Marx to the Present on Armed Struggles for Liberation and for Socialism* (New York: International Publishers, 1968.), 167.

8. Mao Zedong, *Problems of Strategy in China's Revolutionary War* (December 1936), *Selected Works*, Vol. 1, 190–91. Quoted in *www.marxists.org/reference/archive/mao/works/red-book/ch08.htm* (accessed 21 December 2007), 190–91.

9. William L. Cogley, "A New Look at People's War," *Air University Review* (July-August 1977), *www.airpower.maxwell.af.mil/airchronicles/aureview/1977/jul-aug/cogley.html* (accessed 12 January 2008).

10. *Ibid.* Cogley also states "Convinced that power is defined primarily in material terms that weapons are the decisive factor in war, professional military officers and civilian leaders have concentrated on military action and neglected or ignored political action."

11. Mao Tse-tung, "On Protracted War," Reference Archive (marxists.org) 2000, *www.marxists.org/reference/archive/mao/works/1938/guerrilla-warfare/index.htm* (accessed 10 March 2008) (page 36 of PDF).

12. Mao Zedong, *On Practice: On the Relation Between Knowledge and Practice, Between Knowing and Doing* (July 1937) in *Selected Works of Mao Tse-tung* (Beijing: Foreign Languages Press, 1967), 299. On the other hand, it is important to note that Mao believed knowledge also came from what he refers to as indirect experience, or "all knowledge from past times and foreign land." That being said, he was quick to point out that it was only reliable if during the course of their direct experience the requirement of "scientific abstraction" had also been fulfilled. Mao validates this theory by suggesting "the reason why Marx, Engels, Lenin and Stalin could work out their theories was mainly that they personally took part in the practice of the class struggle and the scientific experimentation of their time." He asserts, "Lacking this condition, no genius could have succeeded." The saying, "without stepping outside his gate the scholar knows all the wide world's affairs," was to him merely empty talk.

13. Edward E. Rice, *Mao's Way* (Berkeley: University of California Press, 1972), 55.

14. "Get Organized! (29 November 1943)," *Selected Works*, Vol. 3, 153. Accessed at *www.marxists.org/reference/archive/mao/works/red-book/ch09.htm* (accessed 15 March 2008).

15. Han, 197. This control was absolute; to oversee army-political indoctrination it was decided that a ratio of one party member to two non-party in the army would now be the norm. As a result, "Mao would always consider the Red Army as the training ground for Party cadres, since armed struggle [not combat operations] was the dominant factor in the Revolution in China."

16. Short, 211.
17. *Ibid.*, 197. The officers also often taught reading, writing, and arithmetic to their soldiers.
18. *Ibid.*, 197.
19. Mao Tse-tung, "On Guerrilla Warfare," Reference Archive (marxists.org) 2000, *www.marxists.org/reference/archive/mao/works/1937/guerrilla-warfare/index.htm* (accessed 24 March 2008).
20. Han, 175–76.
21. Julian Paget, *Counter-Insurgency Campaigning* (London: Faber and Faber Limited, 1967), 168.
22. Mao Tse-tung, "On Protracted War" (page 67 of PDF).
23. *Ibid.*, 67.
24. *Ibid.* (page 17 of PDF).
25. Mao Tse-tung, "On Guerrilla Warfare" (page 2 of PDF). Within the context of today's military campaign planning process these steps would be referred to as "Deceive Points."
26. *Ibid.*
27. Mao Tse-tung, "On Protracted War" (page 21 of PDF).
28. *Ibid.*
29. *Ibid.* Mao understood that it is only through this phase that the enemy can ultimately be defeated.
30. John J. McCuen, *The Art of Counter-Revolutionary War: The Strategy of Counter-insurgency* (London: Faber and Faber, 1966), 30. Part of McCuen's quote was taken from Mao Tse-tung, "Strategic Problems in the Anti-Japanese Guerrilla War," *Selected Works*, Vol. 2 (New York: International Publishers, 1954), 125.
31. Paget, 23.
32. Fitzgerald, 26.
33. Clearly, as the insurrection grows, or if the geographical area to be covered is extensive, many bases would be established.
34. A report, entitled "How to Hold Onto and Consolidate the Anti-Japanese Democratic Base Areas," carried in *Party Life*, published by the Northern Bureau of the CPC Central Committee on January 15, 1943, *http://english.peopledaily.com.cn/dengxp/v011/text/a1070.html* (accessed 10 December 2007). It is important to note that Mao distinguishes the difference between defending and securing an area or base. The task of defending was the responsibility of the Red Army. On the other hand, securing the area was the task given to the Red Guards, all of whom were drawn from the local inhabitants and formed the backbone of the Communists' guerrilla forces.
35. McCuen, 196–206. Within the construct of the People's War it is important to note that there is a difference between defending and securing a base area. The task of defending was the responsibility of the Red Army. On the other hand, securing the base was often given to the Red Guards, all of whom were drawn from local inhabitants, who formed the backbone of the Communists' guerrilla units. Only when such units were initially not available did the task would fall to the Red Army.
36. Quoted in Michael Elliott-Bateman, *Defeat in the East: The Mark of Mao Tse-tung on War* (London: Oxford University Press, 1967), 124
37. Robert Taber, *The War of the Flea: A Study of Guerrilla Warfare Theory and Practice* (New York: L. Stuart, 1965), 52–53.

38. *Ibid.*, 48–49.

39. Cogley.

40. Mao Tse-tung, "On Guerrilla Warfare" (page 3 of PDF).

41. Mao Zedong, *Problems of Strategy in China's Revolutionary War,* 238.

42. Mao Tse-tung, "On Protracted War" (page 52 of PDF). Mao did go on to state, "The principle of the Eighth Route Army is, 'Guerrilla warfare is basic, but lose no chance for mobile warfare under favorable conditions.'"

43. Mao Tse-tung, "On Guerrilla Warfare" (page 37 of PDF).

44. *Ibid.*, 4.

45. Mao Tse-tung, "On Guerrilla Warfare" (page 37 of PDF). This emphasis was because such forces may be the only ones available to the insurgent during the initial stages of the conflict.

46. *Ibid.*, 21.

47. *Ibid.*, 30. Also see chapter 1.

48. *Ibid.*, 30. He went on to say, "I do not mean that every guerrilla group can have, at its inception, officers of such qualities. The officers must be men naturally endowed with good qualities which can be developed during the course of campaigning. The most important natural quality is that of complete loyalty to the idea of people's emancipation. If this is present, the others will develop; if it is not present, nothing can be done."

49. Cogley.

50. Mao Tse-tung, "On Protracted War" (page 51 of PDF).

51. Cogley.

52. Mao Tse-tung, "On Protracted War" (page 49 of PDF).

53. *Ibid.*, 49–53.

54. *Ibid.*, 38.

55. *Ibid.*, 38. In fact, most battles initiated by the Red Army usually lasted only a few minutes.

56. *Ibid.*, 38.

57. Peter Paret, Gordon Alexander Craig, and Felix Gilbert. *Makers of Modern Strategy: From Machiavelli to the Nuclear Age* (Princeton, N.J.: Princeton University Press, 1986), 839.

58. Mao Tse-tung, "On Protracted War" (page 24 of PDF)

59. *Ibid.*, 24.

60. *Ibid.*, 24.

61. Mao Tse-tung, "On Guerrilla Warfare" (page 30 of PDF).

62. *Ibid.*, 238.

63. Thomas M. Huber, ed., *Compound Warfare That Fatal Knot* (Fort Leavenworth: U.S. Army Command and General Staff College Press, 2002), 2.

64. *Ibid.*, 2.

65. *Ibid.*, 2–5. Huber does qualify this by stating, "Although the model of compound warfare (CW) offered here has been kept simple in hopes that it will serve as a convenient framework for analysis, readers should remember that enormous variety exists in the historical cases of compound warfare. As in most other realms of military thought, the theory is simple but the reality is complex. The CW model assumes that one side in a CW conflict uses CW methods and the other does not. In reality, both sides may use CW methods. In most historical cases of compound warfare, one side uses CW

methods predominantly; the other side deliberately uses them to the extent it is able. The model assumes two kinds of force, regular or conventional force, and irregular or guerrilla force. Several types of mobile regional militias may fall between these two poles and may contribute importantly to the leverage of the CW operator. In other words, various intermediate types of force are possible between the regular and irregular models promulgated here for simplicity."

66. Quoted in Huber, 92. For example, the number of irregulars operating with Wellington's forces during the Spanish campaign provides some insight into effectiveness of compound warfare. Huber states that "France had 320,000 troops in Spain at the height of its presence in 1810 and ... during their six-year campaign, French forces lost 240,000 men. Of these, 45,000 were killed in action against conventional forces, 50,000 died of illness and accident, and 145,000 were killed in action against guerrilla forces." By comparison, he estimates that "Wellington's army in Spain at its height had only about 40,000 troops, with some 25,000 Portuguese forces attached." Also see David G. Chandler, "Wellington in the Peninsula," 155–65, in David G. Chandler, *On the Napoleonic Wars* (London: Greenhill, 1994), 156–74; and David G. Chandler, "Wellington and the Guerrillas," 166–80, in Chandler, *Napoleonic Wars,* 172.

67. Council of Foreign Relations, *www.cfr.org/publication/9155* (accessed 2 December 2007). According to the Council of Foreign Relations, "Hezbollah was founded in 1982 in response to the Israeli invasion of Lebanon, and subsumed members of the 1980s coalition of groups known as Islamic Jihad. It has close links to Iran and Syria." The site goes on to say, "Hezbollah is a Lebanese umbrella organization of radical Islamic Shiite groups and organizations. It opposes the West, seeks to create a Muslim fundamentalist state modelled on Iran, and is a bitter foe of Israel. Hezbollah, whose name means *party of God*, is a terrorist group believed responsible for nearly 200 attacks since 1982 that have killed more than 800 people, according to the website Terrorism Knowledge Base (*www.tkb.org/Group.jsp?groupID=3101*). Experts say Hezbollah is also a significant force in Lebanese politics and a major provider of social services, operating schools, hospitals, and agricultural services, for thousands of Lebanese Shiites. It also operates the al-Manar satellite television channel and broadcast station."

2

THE END OF ASYMMETRY:

Force Disparity and the Aims of War

Peter H. Denton

SYMMETRY IS A CONCEPT commonly and mistakenly used to characterize twenty-first century warfare, yet it is as old in human terms as conflict itself and is clearly not unique to the contemporary defence environment. Like the biblical story of David and Goliath, ideally, combat has always been asymmetrical; opposing forces tend to fight on equal terms only if battle cannot be avoided.

"Symmetry" and "asymmetry" are opposite ends of a spectrum that assumes a common measure between comparable things. Whatever the measure used, something is more or less symmetrical or asymmetrical only when it is compared to something else. When the comparison is between apples and screwdrivers, or between oranges and circuit boards, however, there is little value in using asymmetry to describe their relation. Similarly, such comparative analyses of twenty-first century combatants are not fruitful. Thus, to better understand current and potential armed conflict, the term asymmetry must be replaced with the systems concept of *force disparity*.

Force disparity is an absolute disjunction between the forces available to the belligerent groups. It does not reflect just a difference in degree; it also highlights differences in kind. Force disparity in the context of twenty-first century warfare recognizes that the militaries of the combatants may be so utterly different in nature and in their equipment that nothing useful or meaningful is to be gained through a comparison of the two sides. Either the military forces are incommensurable — what value is there in comparing Hellfire missiles to pointed sticks? — or the disparity is so absolute that the two sides will never be fielding forces that are even remotely comparable in numbers, equipment, or training.

Force disparity alone is merely a descriptive term, stating what should be obvious to even the most casual observer. What is not so obvious, and what presents serious challenges for global peace in the twenty-first century, are the system implications of force disparity. Force disparity entails a non-linear method of combat on both sides for the accomplishment of war aims and emphasizes how in a systems environment individual actions can be leveraged to create disproportionate effects.

FORCE DISPARITY AND THE AIMS OF WAR

War aims are related to the means by which they can be achieved. In a conflict between two powers that can field an equivalent military force, war aims are likely to be complementary. One country may wish to acquire territory, another, to defend it. What makes the available forces comparable renders the war aims complementary. Even when there is a preponderance of force on one side (the inevitable asymmetries of combat), as long as there are comparable forces, war aims are complementary.

Force disparity in twenty-first century warfare, however, creates two distinct phases of conflict in which the overall war aims of both sides change significantly between phases. In the primary phase, the war aims of the dominant force are apt to be immediate, clear, straightforward, and territorial (in a classic or traditional sense of warfare). For the realization of these war aims, the direct application of military force to specific objectives is required, and success is easily measured by how quickly these objectives are attained while minimizing friendly casualties and maximizing those of the enemy.

Once these primary aims are accomplished, the war aims in the secondary phase concentrate on maintenance, systems change and disengagement. Maintenance involves maintaining force disparity and, therefore, force security in a post-combat situation. Systems change involves changing, replacing or rebuilding the political, economic, and social systems affected by primary phase conflict. Disengagement obviously is the result of these operations, in that the intention of the primary phase force members is to do their jobs and go home as quickly as possible. However, in the secondary phase of conflict, the dominant force will have fewer opportunities for the direct application of overwhelming force and the benchmarks for evaluating success (such as the war aims themselves) are necessarily more ambiguous than in the primary phase.

If we then turn to the war aims of the inferior side in a situation of force disparity, the war aims are not complementary with those of the dominant force in either conflict phase. In the primary phase of conflict, conceding immediate and inevitable defeat, the war aim of the inferior side is to survive hostile contact with maximum military capacity still intact so that it can position itself for the secondary phase.

The secondary phase war aims of the inferior side depend on engagement and escalation, unlike those of the dominant side which lean toward stability and disengagement. The inferior side wants to deliver direct and focused violent activity that is clear in terms of short-term objectives. Conflict involves the local application of force intended to leverage system effects dangerous to the dominant force. The absence of clear long-term goals in the secondary phase for the inferior side has no effect on the identification and prosecution of local targets.

For the inferior side, whether the conflict is religious in motivation — or political, economic, or psychological — the "Cause" is used to discount the significance of casualties regardless of their rate. Moreover, the failure to achieve an end to hostilities is not something that alone undermines the will to fight of the opposition. Indeed, if the immediate secondary phase war aim is simply to hurt the invader, then (given the opportunities to lash out presented by multiple targets) every day can be judged a success. Force disparity creates a situation in which the inferior side cannot lose — when the dominant side inflicts casualties, it is to be expected; when the inferior side inflicts casualties, it is a victory for the rebels.

Although this is not a new phenomenon — after all, it could easily be described as classic guerrilla warfare — in the context of global economic, political, and social systems, and thanks to the immediacy of electronic communications, local actions are undertaken primarily to leverage a variety of effects at a distance from the combat zone. Such immediate secondary phase war aims, understood in terms of complex and interrelated systems, allow for the choice and use of leveraged weaponry — like box cutters on passenger jets — that have system effects far out of proportion to their initial impact.

FORCE DISPARITY AND THE WEAPONS OF WAR

The system effects of force disparity in twenty-first century warfare require a reconsideration of the weapons of war and the dimensions of the battlespace. The conundrum posed by force disparity is that superior firepower may be the means of tactical victory, while guaranteeing long-term strategic defeat. To this point in history, the side with the technical advantage — whether the larger guns, longer pikes, faster chariots, better ships, or more skilled sailors — has tended to be victorious. Today, this relationship between victory and technical advantage is no longer the case.

Not only have the parameters of victory changed in both present and potential conflicts within global culture, but without a consideration of the "softer side" of contemporary warfare, defeat may result from an inability to manage the system of conflict, especially if there is a fundamental force disparity in play. However spectacular the successes in the primary phase of conflict, defeat in the secondary phase (especially when the secondary phase war aims of the dominant force are ambiguous) results, not from a shortage of force, but from its misapplication.

The misperception that superior firepower wins wars as well as battles is a consequence of a larger misperception common in Western culture that technology is "primarily about widgets." A different conclusion emerges from an understanding of technology as instrumental knowledge, meaning knowledge used to a purpose. It is actually the knowledge, and the use to which the knowledge is put, that are of primary importance, not the tool itself. For instance, in the absence of certain widgets, the same goals can be accomplished by other means.

The realization that subtleties rather than firepower win secondary phase conflicts changes the potential means by which war aims may be achieved, and even what war aims can be realized. This is not merely a case of preferring "spin doctors" to A-10 close support aircraft. The global economy presents a multitude of examples of how the manipulation of non-physical entities can lead to concrete consequences. Investor confidence, consumer behaviour, and public opinion are all "unreal," but changes in these things lead to real social, political, and economic consequences.

For example, the psychology of all combatants is increasingly significant because warfare in the post-modern age inevitably involves whole populations and the leveraging of effects translates a local defeat or victory into something that affects a much larger group of people. For example, suicide bombings are not intended to inflict damage or casualties in the first instance — unless used for directed assassination — but to leverage their effects in a global political context. The primary force multiplier is the message sent to a larger public that is not so much at risk from the physical threat of future attacks as from the psychological implications of their future possibility.

Were there to be an absolute ban on reporting about either the event or, particularly, those claiming responsibility, then, although their frequency might not be reduced, the leveraged effects would at least be minimized, if not eliminated. Arguably, the reason these attacks are most frequently aimed at democratic societies is self-evident given the apparent influence that public opinion and a free press has on decision-making by government or other entities.

The dominant side must use the system effects of force disparity to leverage positive effects in order to prevail in the secondary phase of conflict. Providing the inferior side with some tangible reasons for hope of a better future tempers the less rational dimensions of their secondary phase war aims and permits the construction of some means of realizing that hoped-for future. Building schools, digging wells, repairing roads and bridges, is more than humanitarian aid, which is how the work is portrayed; it is also a pragmatic extension of the dominant side's combat superiority.

If improved living conditions soften the resolve of the inferior side, then, to stay in the fight in secondary phase warfare, it must, paradoxically, deny such things to its own population under the guise of resisting the enemy. This tactic, in the longer term will, of course, inevitably undermine the opposition's popular support.

SYSTEM EFFECTS OF FORCE DISPARITY

Force disparity must be recognized as a dominant dimension of conflict in the post–Cold War period. The successful resolution of conflict in the twenty-first century requires a response that is much more sophisticated than will result from merely buying new and more advanced primary phase military hardware. In fact, by investing scarce resources this way, the dominant side denies itself funds for other initiatives that could be used to resolve secondary phase conflict or prevent local conflicts from being leveraged into larger ones.

Technological enhancement of weapons systems, while it allows for the exciting prospects of casualty-free conflict for the dominant side, is anything but cheap, and it creates the modern equivalent of the knight in expensive technological shining armour. Given the increasing rapidity of change in technological systems, the current knight will maintain superiority only for as long as it takes a much weaker opponent to find the chinks in his armour. While the traditional view would encourage the advent of the longbow or the gunpowder weapon as the reason for the demise of the mounted knight, "slipping his horse a mickey" would have accomplished the same result.

Further, such technological enhancement does not improve the circumstances of the dominant force in the primary phase of combat. In a situation of force disparity, the dominant side was going to win anyway — a few more gadgets, a few less casualties, makes little difference outside the confines of a video game perception of combat in which the goal is a higher score. If the dominant side cannot continue its advantage into the secondary phase of conflict, then none of the gadgetry is of real value, and the resources expended on developing that gadgetry might have been put to better use at both tactical and strategic levels.

The tactical and strategic implications of force disparity therefore require a focus not on one's strengths, but on one's weaknesses. They require an emphasis on exploring the vulnerabilities of whole systems, not narrowly defined battlespace systems, to identify what the assaults might resemble that would leverage or multiply the initial hit into something more deadly.

The tactical and strategic implications of force disparity require an emphasis not on primary combat systems — which are already overwhelming — but on secondary combat systems, to deal with the ambiguities of the secondary phases of conflict. There is a critical distinction between primary phase warfare, intended to obtain direct results, and secondary phase warfare, where the intention of the conflict is to leverage indirect effects in terms of the social, cultural, political, or economic systems involved.

In a situation of force disparity, the primary phase of combat is likely to be short. There is no obvious limit, however, to the length of the secondary phase, which (combined with the ambiguity of the war aims of the dominant force) leads to the troubling prospect of perpetual attrition. Consequently, force disparity must be factored into assessments of war aims, both one's own and those of an enemy. Setting unachievable or unrealistic goals makes victory in secondary phase conflict impossible. The inability to respond effectively in the secondary phase of conflict can either lead to perpetual conflict or to Goliath's humiliation and defeat.

To avoid this quagmire, one must understand the nature and implications of force disparity in complex systems and recognize the multivalent character of conflict scenarios in global culture. It is ironic that the creation of force disparity renders more powerful weapons systems less important to the final outcome of warfare in the twenty-first century than ever before. Instead, global peace and security depends on the successful resolution of secondary phase conflict using "weapons" not traditionally seen to be part of the spectrum of military operations. Given that the traditional battlefield has been replaced by the much less distinct "battlespace," we need to realize that the conditions for secondary phase conflict are established on both sides before the first shot is ever fired.

The ongoing decline of foreign aid as a percentage of gross national product among Western nations is therefore a much more dangerous indicator of global instability than an increase in military expenditures. Rather than spending more resources to widen the unbridgeable disparity between forces engaged in primary phase warfare, we should be using those resources to leverage system effects in areas where — should war break out — the secondary phase might prove to be the most dangerous in the long term. The realization that foreign aid serves security as well as humanitarian interests makes it possible to build a social coalition working toward a common end, even if for very different reasons.

Social justice issues have traditionally been associated with pacifist positions and sidelined by the military objectives of taking or defending territory. In a global culture such as we now enjoy, however, ensuring people have food, shelter, education, employment, and a sense of personal security has necessarily become part of the war aims of the dominant culture, both at home and in whatever theatre a conflict breaks out.

Accordingly, in a world where the disparity between rich and poor countries continues to increase, the provision of genuine aid can become a means of reducing the possibilities of conflict, before it occurs, and minimizing the leveraged effects of secondary phase conflict when it does occur. Social and economic issues are therefore critical elements of battlespace operations before primary phase combat begins and become even more critical during the secondary phase. The linkage between these issues and military operations already exists. What is needed is a unified doctrine that establishes the explicit intention to leverage positive social and economic effects by whatever means, military or otherwise, are required.

Such a statement, of course, can be construed as twenty-first century imperialism, the intention that accompanied European military, economic, and religious expansion in earlier times. When force disparity leads the dominant side into conflict for its own sake, or for the sake of its own citizens, this kind of criticism is merited. One would hope, however, that our developing global culture might eventually reflect the humanitarian concerns upon which the United Nations was founded and that force disparity might instead be used to leverage justice, peace, and hope.

Force Disparity and the Future of Canadian Forces Abroad

The existing force disparity between Western and other militaries suggests a possible niche for the Canadian Forces in its deployment to future conflict zones abroad and a possible unified focus for Canadian defence and foreign policy in effectively managing and resolving secondary phase conflict:

The CF will never have the money, personnel, or equipment to engage effectively in large-scale primary phase combat operations. We therefore should not even attempt such a structuring of the future CF for primary phase conflicts either on our own or in terms of interoperability with other militaries. We should make this decision part of a public linkage between Canadian defence and foreign policy that is intended to leverage the maximum humanitarian benefit in secondary phase conflict.

The CF should restructure its future operations, equipment procurement, and recruiting around task force units able to be deployed in secondary phase conflicts, in which the combat capability (ground, air, and sea) is focused on force protection of CF deployments. By establishing such doctrine first, we would have the grounds on which to decide what new technology is required and to lobby more effectively in both political and public spheres for the necessary resources.

The CF should commit itself to providing medical treatment; infrastructure development; and peacekeeping support to enable affected populations to recover rapidly from the loss of existing community systems as a result of primary phase conflict, natural disaster, or civil war.

The CF should therefore develop the capacity to mobilize rapidly, deploy, and sustain task forces comprised, as required, of a field hospital, combat engineers, and a peacekeeping force. Having the CF independently capable of all aspects of deployment, supply, and maintenance while in the field, including the protection of its deployed forces, would minimize interoperability issues.

There is a role for a small number of elite "high-tech" troops to engage in domestic counterterrorist operations or targeted strikes abroad. These troops would need to be prepared for immediate domestic deployment, rapid deployment overseas, and the ability to self-sustain short-term independent operations in the field.

Such an intentional focus on secondary phase conflict operations gain support from a larger segment of the Canadian population, while guiding defence expenditures in a specific direction at manageable and sustainable levels. Adopting such a policy for the CF abroad would also enable the identification and efficient delivery of directed aid from both government and non-governmental sources to affected populations.

A focus on secondary phase conflict operations could help resolve the existing dichotomy between peacemaking and peacekeeping in CF policy. It would also be in keeping with the role Canada has accepted for decades in support of United Nations initiatives for humanitarian intervention and the resolution of conflict around the world.

Asymmetry and its attendant ideas about high-technology warfare, however exciting or alarming, should not be used to guide Canadian defence policy into the twenty-first century. A more realistic, pragmatic, and fiscally responsible approach for Canada emerges from the systems implications of force disparity.

3

INTELLIGENCE AND ITS APPLICATION TO IRREGULAR WARFARE

Tony Balasevicius and Bernd Horn

I N THE IN THE AFTERMATH of the 11 September 2001 (9/11) terrorist attack on the World Trade Center towers in New York, Western military forces have been increasingly called upon to deploy into complex operational environments where they must deal with highly adaptive adversaries seeking to destabilize society through a variety of irregular or asymmetric means. With regard to insurgencies, Steven Metz, a renowned strategic analyst and research professor, argues that "rather than being discrete, conflicts between insurgents and an established regime are nested in complex, multidimensional clashes having political, social, cultural, and economic components." He goes on to assert, "In an even broader sense, contemporary insurgencies flow from systemic failures in the political, economic, and social realms. They arise not only from the failure or weakness of the state, but from more general flaws in cultural, social, and economic systems."[1]

In this respect, insurgencies, whether regionally based or globally focused, are a battle between the disenchanted and the ruling entity. The struggle is normally focused on influencing the population. Since 9/11, the current international security environment has become what can arguably be defined as a global insurgency. Within this paradigm the

West has been tested against a full range of sophisticated and complex threats and conflicts. Accordingly, Western countries have developed a myriad of capabilities to respond to what is being increasingly referred to in official military cycles as irregular warfare.

In short, "irregular warfare is a violent struggle among state and non-state actors for legitimacy and influence over the relevant population(s). Irregular warfare favors asymmetric approaches, through which it may employ a full range of capacities, in order to erode an adversary's power, influence, and will."[2] From an adversary's perspective, activities within the construct of irregular warfare can include everything from terrorism (e.g., suicide bombings; attacks on symbolic, economic, or political infrastructure; attacks on populations; and assassinations) to all out combat operations within the context of insurgencies such as those occurring in Iraq and Afghanistan.

Although the character of irregular warfare (e.g., extremist Islamic global insurgency, Iraq and Afghanistan) has changed in terms of the participants and tactics used, it is important to realize that it has not changed in its basic premise. In this respect, irregular warfare is still centred on a struggle to influence the people. As a result, the key to successfully countering irregular warfare will be the astute development of intelligence combined with the effective application of military force. In fact, many analysts believe that intelligence-driven operations are the only way for security forces to be successful when fighting insurgents that have sought refuge among the civilian population. In simplest terms intelligence is critical to success in irregular warfare operations.

Since an insurgency is the crucible from which other activities within the irregular warfare construct will eventually derive, the basic structure of an insurgency must be examined to understand the role intelligence can play. At the heart of any insurgency, as is the case with the current insurgencies that are raging, one will find the manifestation of conflict that started as a local grievance and over time evolved to take on a larger context. For example, according to an American strategic assessment, transnational networked organizations, many involved in the various insurgencies that are now being waged, have emerged from localized movements and evolved into major threats to the world order.[3] The assessment warns, "These organizations are also becoming increasingly sophisticated, well-connected, and well-armed. As they better integrate global media sophistication, lethal weaponry, potentially greater cultural awareness and intelligence, they will pose a considerably greater threat than at present."[4]

Although the many insurgencies underway today have become extremely sophisticated and far-reaching in their influence, they are still largely viewed as uprisings against an established form of authority such as a government or occupying military force.[5] In this respect, they are still seen in the traditional framework of an insurgency, which is defined as a "struggle between a non-ruling group and the ruling authorities in which the non-ruling group consciously uses political resources (e.g., organizational expertise, propaganda and demonstrations) and violence to destroy, reformulate, or sustain the basis of legitimacy of one or more aspects of politics."[6]

Not surprisingly, insurgencies are often the preferred method by which the disaffected attack the will and motivation of the status quo authority.[7] This is because the insurgents have an assortment of means at their disposal (ranging from civil unrest and terrorism to all-out combat operations) to fight the conventional capabilities of the security forces whose military capability is almost always substantially greater. Notwithstanding the means at the disposal of insurgents, attacking the will of an enemy is an extremely difficult and time-consuming process.[8] Thus, to achieve any type of success the insurgent must establish and maintain certain conditions throughout the campaign. These conditions include "a cause to fight for, support from the local populace, establishment of bases, mobility, supplies and information."[9]

Conversely, counterinsurgency/terrorist operations are carried out by the established authority and seek to destroy the insurgent through the use of political, social, and economic reforms that focus on satisfying the same grievances the insurgents are attempting to exploit. These reforms must be carried out while simultaneously attacking the physical entities of the insurgents' military and political apparatus.[10] This is no easy task. After all, while counterinsurgency forces must deprive the terrorist of the basic operational and tactical conditions needed to sustain the insurgency, they must also limit collateral damage on the population. Attempting to achieve this balance is extremely difficult. Insurgents will try to embed themselves within the very fabric of the communities in which they operate so that they can create, nurture, and sustain the conditions needed for success. For that reason, any attempt to attack insurgents risks a spill-over of violence that has the potential to cause collateral damage (i.e., civilian deaths).

In the end, winning "hearts and minds," or, more simply, the support of the populace, is critical for both the insurgents and the established authority as it provides the basis for the long-term sustainment of the insurgency or its early demise. Both antagonists need popular support, because it is a key enabler in developing the other conditions essential for success. It is this battle for the population — for popular support — that forms the nexus between the importance of intelligence and success in counterinsurgency. It is access to the population that is all important for success in counterinsurgency.

Access provides the source of critical information central to developing the intelligence picture or conversely being denied the required information. For example, during the Soviet-Afghan conflict in the 1990s, the Soviets were unable to achieve any type of surprise over the mujahideen because the insurgents controlled the population and were able to obtain information about the security forces, while the Soviets could not do the same. Not surprisingly, the mujahideen's control of the population allowed them to develop an extensive network of observers and messengers throughout much of the country, which in turn enabled them to maintain an almost continuous watch over Soviet movements.[11]

In the end, the access to, or denial of, information that can be turned into intelligence, is all important. Ironically, although intelligence is critical to military success, it is a concept that is not well understood by many within the profession of arms. This is due in part to the secrecy of the process, but is also the result of a false assumption by many military practitioners that information is intelligence and, therefore, once you have received the information, nothing further is necessary other than to act on it. Unfortunately, this mistaken impression could not be farther from the truth.

From a military perspective, intelligence is characterized as the product of our knowledge and understanding of the physical environment. According to *Canadian Forces Joint Intelligence Doctrine*, "this knowledge should include weather, demographics, and, most important, the culture within the area that security forces and other agencies must operate within. More specifically, the idea includes the activities, capabilities, and intentions of an actual or potential threat."[12]

Within the context of irregular warfare this threat is very complex and can take many forms. Criminal elements, underground units, supporters, sympathizers, guerrillas, paramilitary forces, conventional military forces, as well as external state and non-state sponsors have all got to be considered. These threats, however, only capture a part of the required intelligence picture. The physical environment is also an important focal point that centres more on the demographics and cultural mosaic of the operational area, than on the physical geography of the country.[13]

The importance of having access to good and timely intelligence and a process by which it can be created in a systematic and reliable way cannot be overstated. This is because the consequences of intelligence failure in either not having the relevant information or not having a process to synthesize it in a timely manner can be devastating. In February 1973, a Libyan Boeing 727 airliner flying in the Sinai desert region had become lost in a severe sandstorm while en route from Benghazi to Cairo. The Israelis, not having any information on the airliner and fearing it had been hijacked and was about to be used for a suicide attack on their capital, made the decision to shoot it down with the resultant loss of 106 lives.[14]

Conversely, the same effect occurs when security forces exploit intelligence that is either faulty or incomplete. This was the case in December 2001, when the bombing of an Afghan wedding party killed 110 of 112 people. This tragic event occurred when an intelligence source stated that the event was a gathering of Al Qaeda terrorists. To the pilots flying the mission the large gathering of cars converging on the hamlet seemed to bear out the accuracy of the report, and a six-hour assault commenced with tragic results.

Similarly, on 24 January 2002, American special operations forces raided a compound in Uruzgan province killing 16 civilians, once again based on faulty intelligence. The victims were not Taliban or Al Qaeda. In this case, the Pentagon conceded the error.[15] Even so, the effect these attacks had on eroding support for the coalition effort in Afghanistan is not hard to calculate.

These various intelligence failures provide a clear picture of what can happen when the process is not working. Exploiting poor information or not acting on good intelligence can result in the death of many innocent people. To prevent, or at least minimize this problem, agencies must be able to collect the right information and then turn it into useful intelligence in a timely manner. In an attempt to do this, they focus their efforts on two components, organization and process.

The organizational establishment occurs during the early stages of any insurgency when some type of a joint chain of command is established that includes members of the host nation (HN) and assisting coalition forces. With this joint command comes a need for supporting intelligence capabilities that can provide timely, responsive intelligence to commanders.[16] Unlike a military or joint civil/military chain of command, which tends to be hierarchical in nature, intelligence organizations are by necessity extremely flexible as they are usually constructed on the basis of providing intelligence from wherever it is available to wherever it is required. As a result, the organizational architecture must be both flexible and scalable enough to be quickly linked into a series of new and expanding networks. As this process expands agencies will often bypass (or skip) various levels of command so that intelligence can reach the designated user as quickly as possible.[17]

This "skip-echelon" system is closely linked to a collaborative parallel planning process that ensures information is available on a "pull" rather than the "push" principle at the level of command that needs it most.[18] When dealing with an insurgency or terrorist event, the intelligence architecture becomes much more complex as it is forced to extend its areas of intelligence responsibility (AIR), which it allocates to various levels of command (which are often global in scope).[19]

In addition, the process also begins with specific direction coming from requirements that have fallen out of the campaign planning process. This direction usually comes in the form of questions that need to be answered either by the commander or his staff in the form of the Commander's Critical Information Requirements (CCIRs). Part of the initial direction also specifies the authority of each agency to task individual collection assets to get the specific information being sought. In some cases, it may also issue authority to those responsible for providing the intelligence reports. [20]

The quality of intelligence reports that are provided is directly linked to the value of information that will be given to the analyst. As a result, getting the right information early enough is critical to the success of the process. Within the AIR, the intelligence community attempts to set up a number of networks and it is from these networks that information is harvested.[21] From an intelligence perspective, this is one of the reasons control of the population is so important. Once the populace is under close supervision, security forces have the ability to develop networks of observers, informers, and messengers that can maintain watch and eventually infiltrate the insurgents' organization.[22]

The actual information needed by analysts to support this effort is different from that required for conventional operations. This is because the collection effort is focused on identifying and then destroying or at least disrupting insurgent groups. As such, collection is aimed at identifying insurgent members, their location, command structures tactics, and goals. Information is also collected that can help determine the relationships and interaction between and within the various groups involved in the insurgency.[23]

Although some of the broader information requirements can be assembled from public sources, the primary means of gathering day to day information within an insurgency is human intelligence (HUMINT). According to Seth Jones, a researcher with the RAND Corporation, the American experience in Afghanistan illustrates the importance of HUMINT in providing actionable intelligence, and the usefulness of civil-military operations as a means of gathering that information.[24] He states, "Locals were often so thankful for receiving health care from U.S. military forces that they became willing to assist in the fight against insurgents."[25] Jones goes on to point out that patients coming into health clinics often volunteered information to U.S. forces about enemy activity in the area.[26]

Jones also provides an excellent example taken from the U.S. Army's Training and Doctrine Command, Lessons Learned cell where "a local who had come to a U.S. firebase in the Bermel Valley for a shura told U.S. forces about foreign fighters laying landmines. U.S. forces followed him to the location, dismounted before they reached the suspected mine site, found the ambush team, and started an attack. U.S. forces killed or wounded the entire enemy mine-laying ambush party, gathered intelligence about insurgent techniques, and walked away with no casualties — instead of driving into a coordinated IED/rocket-propelled grenade ambush."[27]

This example highlights the importance of gathering HUMINT through the use of various activities that are normally part of the day-to-day activities security forces use to maintain control of the population. These include such things as the use of security forces, manned observation posts, checkpoints, roadblocks, mounted and dismounted patrols, routine searches, as well as ground reconnaissance activities. Moreover, security force units can and will be tasked by commanders to mount operations specifically designed to obtain information or possibility to give cover to other intelligence-gathering activities.[28]

Other sources of HUMINT information can include military, paramilitary, irregular, and/or auxiliary units from the HN army or security apparatus, as well as from direct or indirect questioning of friendly sections of the civilian population. Sources from HN forces or, specifically, from the local individuals are particularly important to coalition forces as they provide intimate knowledge of the local demographics and furnish a cultural reference specific to the local situation.[29]

A lack of a formal local HUMINT capability is extremely difficult to develop once hostilities begin especially if coalitions are not willing to rely on HN services. Anthony H. Cordesman, an analyst who drafted specific intelligence lessons from the Iraq War, states: "During most of the counterinsurgency phase of the 'war after the war,' the U.S. has tried to carry out the mission of developing effective human intelligence (HUMINT) on its own, rather than in full partnership with the Iraqis." He revealed, "This ignored one of the critical lessons of Vietnam. Rather than see the need for effective Iraqi intelligence collection and analysis — and to rely on Iraqis for the lack of area and language skills and understanding of local political and tactical conditions — the U.S. tried to create a network of informers and local contacts and carry out analysis on its own." Cordesman concluded, "The U.S. simply does not have the capability in terms of expertise and access to suddenly improvise a largely autonomous HUMINT effort as a substitute for partnership with an intelligence organization run by local allies."[30]

This criticism is insightful for if networks cannot be developed in any significant way, security forces are placed at a disadvantage, and are then forced to put much of their emphasis on getting their information through technical intelligence. This means the reliance on tools such as aerial reconnaissance and radio intercept. Unfortunately, these sources often failed to produce usable tactical intelligence in a timely manner. The inability of the Soviets to achieve surprise during many of their operations in the 1980s was the direct result of not having mature networks that could provide reliable and timely information. This limitation forced them to place a great deal of emphasis on their technical intelligence assets. Moreover, since the ground forces were always short of combat elements, reconnaissance forces that could have provided some of the badly needed human intelligence capability that the Soviets lacked were often used in close combat duties.[31] More recently, during the heavy fighting in the Pashmul area of Afghanistan in 2006, Canadian battle group commander Lieutenant-Colonel Ian Hope noted, "[I] never had more than 20 percent of the information, most often not even that much."[32]

Regardless of how it is obtained, as the information starts to come in it must be processed. The best intelligence results are usually obtained from organizations that are "fully integrated and work to a centrally-agreed collection plan, employing a host of fusion and database managers, analysts, and other intelligence specialists who approach their task in a structured, objective, and systematic way."[33]

To fuse information in the most efficient manner, intelligence organizations use what is commonly referred to as the intelligence cycle. This cycle, commencing with actual direction, includes a number of additional distinct steps for the collection, processing, and dissemination of information.[34] The cycle is viewed as the framework within which each of the four operations is carried out and, ideally, each phase is synchronized with the commander's decision-making requirements so that actionable intelligence can be produced in a timely manner to influence the outcome of a particular operation.[35]

The cycle used to process the information includes the collating, analyzing, integrating, and interpretation of the material. The processing staff for this stage of the cycle includes trained intelligence operators who are supported by a number of specialists in the collection disciplines. Where appropriate, specialists from other arms and services may also join the analytical staff. For example, engineer intelligence operators, with their specialist knowledge of terrain, explosives, and route construction, could likely be seconded to the staff.[36] This type of expertise comes into play, because insurgents and terrorists are able to adapt their tactics quickly, so specialist expertise, analysis, and advice is required to catch the evolution, transformation, and changes of enemy tactics as quickly as they occur. For example, Hezbollah perfected the use of explosives in well laid-out ambushes; however, it has been the Iraqis that have made extensive use of improvised explosive devices (IED) using existing mass stocks of old ammunition. In fact, the Iraqis absorbed the lessons Hezbollah learned in their protracted struggle against the Israelis, built on their successes, and pioneered the use of mixed threats and methods that have proven much more difficult to counter than the more consistent type of bombs and target sets security forces were use to dealing with.[37]

Nonetheless, nowhere is the need for specialists more critical than when dealing with the subject of IEDs. Quite simply, intelligence staffs require the expertise of ammunition technicians. "With their training in explosives, firing devices and weapon inspection they are able to develop weapons intelligence in conjunction with both the police and forensic scientists. This discipline, based on such techniques as weapon matching, will be able to trace weapons to their sources of supply, to rounds they have fired, explosives and detonators to their origin and so on."[38] When properly coordinated, the intelligence staff, in conjunction with the necessary specialists, can begin to develop a picture of bomb makers, facilitators, IED networks, areas of operations, and bomb factories.

Not all threats are as compartmentalized as IEDs. Other techniques that are used by analytical teams in fighting counterinsurgencies include social network analysis that attempts to understand the relationships between and within various insurgent groups. This area of analysis looks at various "pattern recognition techniques to reduce factors contributing to insurgent violence to a few indicators; or predictive and forecasting techniques to help determine likely sites of future violence."[39] Game theory can also be used to examine the relative strategies of various groups with respect to counterinsurgency objectives.[40] Other concepts include the use of change detection techniques that review "the effects of changes in security force operating patterns on insurgent attack activity."[41]

Insurgents will often carry out specific types of violence such as assassinations, bombings, and kidnappings, and investigations into these types of activities are normally carried out by law enforcement organizations. If the police are incapable of completing such tasks, however, they may have to be carried out by the military.[42] In these circumstances emphasis is placed on crime scene analysis and military intelligence activities will begin to resemble police investigations.[43] An example of this type of military civilian amalgamation is the creation of the Combined Explosives Exploitation Cell (CEXC) in Iraq and Afghanistan. In sum, all the various organizations have been created to "perform police-like investigations of remnants of violent acts — usually the detonation of improvised explosive devices."[44]

Critical to the collection and processing cycles is the ability to keep track of the huge volumes of information and to allow analysts to access it when needed. To achieve this, most intelligence organizations have developed and maintain many databases. These databases are designed to collate and cross-reference the plethora of small and unconnected data into some type of usable material from which the analyst can draw. From this assembled information the analyst can provide context and produce useful options. Only when this process has been completed and intelligence has been generated can it be released so that the necessary action can be taken.

When this system is working properly and security forces have access to timely, detailed, tailored, and fused all-source intelligence, operations can be undertaken with a good probability of success. Moreover, the success can often be stunning. For example, on 9 April 1973, a small team of Israeli commandos landed on the Lebanese coast where it met up with Mossad agents who drove them into Beirut. The operatives were armed with complete intelligence of their targets. They had full details on the leader of the Black September movement (who was responsible for the Munich massacre in 1972), the chief of operations of the Palestine Liberation Organization (PLO), and the PLO's spokesman in Beirut, as well as the apartments and neighbourhood in which they lived. As a result, the unit successfully carried out a number of raids against these targets, as well as destroying, with the assistance of Israeli paratroopers, PLO weapons factories and fuel dumps in the area of Tyre and Sidon.[45]

In another similar case, on 12 July 1993, the Americans conducted a successful raid on the Abdi House in Somali based again on "excellent intelligence." The building was identified as a key militia headquarters. Furthermore, the commander responsible for planning the raid was given details on daily meetings that occurred at the target house — time, place, and who was normally present. In addition, intelligence identified the Somali leaders who attended as those responsible for planting a mine that killed U.S. service personnel, as well as planning and orchestrating all the acts of violence against U.S. and U.N. forces up to that point. Importantly, the information given also included a five-day window during which a strike could be conducted without endangering any innocent civilians who worked or frequented the building. In the end, a potent threat was neutralized with minimum collateral damage.[46] More recently, from 2007–08, the Canadian special operations task force (SOTF) operating in Kandahar, Afghanistan, fuelled with timely, accurate all-source intelligence, was able to remove an entire generation of Taliban leadership from within their area of operations.

These types of operations were based on detailed intelligence derived from information that can only be obtained through the sophisticated development and employment of technical collection means, as well as the use of intelligence networks based on agents and informers. Significantly, the latter, specifically the use of networks based on agents and informers, can be used aggressively to undermine the insurgent influence while destabilizing their cohesiveness and operational effectiveness. This is achieved by infiltrating informers and agents into the insurgent's organization. An agent is a person specifically recruited and trained to be placed into a hostile organization in order to gather information.[47] It is important to note that an agent differs from an informant who is "a person who, perhaps uninvited, passes information to an opponent about his organization, in other words, an uncontrolled source."[48]

Historically, the employment of agents has been a specialized intelligence activity, which is often controlled at the highest levels. It is an attractive option as nations have found that a relatively small number of well-placed and reliable agents can provide critical information usually at the pivotal points within the insurgents' command. It is for this reason that the Canadian *Counterinsurgency Manual* concludes, "If agents are able to penetrate the top level of the insurgents' command and control organization, information may be provided on the development of their strategies, the identification of important leaders, the system of liaison between the military wing and the insurgent political leadership and the methods [they use] of acquiring resources."[49]

At lower echelons, informers are useful in providing information on, "personalities, tactical plans and weapon caches." The manual recommends that, "At these levels, if continuity is to be maintained, it is important that the agent network expands at a similar rate to that of the insurgent movement; otherwise their relative value will diminish."[50] Interestingly, during the Soviet occupation of Afghanistan in the 1980s, Soviet intelligence services attempted to disrupt rebel actions by carrying out a number of subversion operations using both Afghan agents and informers.

In attempting to exploit the fragmented nature of the country's population, the Soviets were able to persuade some villages to form a truce and reject rebel demands for logistic support. Such villages were often found near major population centres, and would form their own militia groups that protected the village and enforced law and order within the community.[51] In certain cases, rebel groups were bribed into switching allegiances, while tribal chiefs were bribed with land and money to renounce support for the mujahideen. These techniques of co-opting the population had the effect of creating "a stratum of people in the countryside that have a vested political and economic stake in the system and were likely to defend it."[52] The same technique was attempted by the Americans in 2001 during their campaign to oust the Taliban government after 9/11.[53]

Interestingly, subversion was particularly successful when used to spread conflict and division among the various resistance groups. Because Afghan society, and the rebel groups it produced, was inherently fragmented and fraught with disunity, the Soviets repeatedly attempted to exploit these divisions and turn the groups against each other.[54] Agents were infiltrated into these rebel organizations, and used to spread rumours between various groups to create conflict between bands or to discredit specific mujahideen leaders in the eyes of others. One mujahideen leader discussed the effectiveness of these techniques in some areas; stating, "the KHAD (Democratic Republic of Afghanistan's secret police) agents have rendered mujahedeen groups completely useless by getting them to fight among themselves." He added, "Why should the Soviets worry about killing Afghans if the Mujahideen do it for them?"[55] Clearly, the ability to undertake such initiatives relies heavily on the intelligence (as well as cultural intelligence) to both identify and exploit opportunities as they arise or become known and understood.

An important resource in exploiting intelligence provided by agents and informers are special operations forces. SOF are defined as "organizations containing specially selected personnel that are organized, equipped and trained to conduct high-risk, high value special operations to achieve military, political, economic, or informational objectives by using special and unique operational methodologies in hostile, denied or politically sensitive areas to achieve desired tactical, operational and/

or strategic effects in times of peace, conflict or war."[56] As such, they are key players in counterinsurgency activities.

As noted in the case of the raid on the compound in Uruzgan and the successful raid on the Abdi House, a major tactic in achieving effects with SOF is through the use of Direct Action missions. These missions are designed to capture/kill medium to high value targets that are instrumental to the planning and decision making capacity of an insurgent network. In essence, by removing these targets (e.g., key leadership, facilitators, experts such as bomb makers, financiers, and planners) SOF cuts off the "brains and nervous system" of an insurgency.

By their nature, these operations are intelligence driven. After all, to execute surgically precise operations with minimum collateral damage requires precise information. In this respect, intelligence provides identities, networks, locations, facilitators, financiers, rat lines, caches, and supporters. These targets are then carefully prosecuted and when captured create additional information that provides further intelligence allowing for more targets and better fidelity of targets. In the end, good quality intelligence allows counterinsurgency forces to employ SOF in the application of highly specialized techniques to find, prevent, deter, pre-empt or resolve insurgent or terrorist plans or incidents by empowering SOF to conduct the precision missions with the minimum possibility of collateral damage.

But, in reality, the fidelity of data or detailed information, while critical to the success of SOF operations, is, quite frankly, essential to the success of all security force operations. Moreover, it demonstrates the relationship that is needed between the intelligence community and security forces overall. This assessment is supported by the British experience. In a "lessons learned" memorandum issued shortly after the initial invasion of Iraq, it stated, "The tempo and effects produced by land, sea and air operations were directly attributable to the quality, availability and timeliness of the intelligence provided, which was significantly and critically enhanced by access to US and other coalition sources."[57]

However, complete situational awareness within the dynamics of an insurgency requires more than just processed information. It also demands a comprehensive understanding of all the factors that are at work within the area of operations. This includes the political, economic, social, cultural, and religious aspects of the environment. Moreover, the force commander must put his understanding of who will oppose stabilization efforts and what is motivating them to do so, into some type of cultural context.[58] Therefore, knowledge of the cultural dynamic is critical for both comprehending the environment that forces are operating in and putting that information into context.

As such, cultural intelligence, CQ, becomes another essential part of the intelligence/counterinsurgency nexus. CQ is defined as "the ability to recognize the shared beliefs, values, attitudes and behaviors of a group of people and to apply this knowledge toward a specific goal."[59] In the struggle to control and influence populations, it is critical to understand what is important to them; how they think; and their customs, values, and norms as this will empower security forces to better engage and win-over the people. Essentially, CQ, as university professor Dr. Emily Spencer explains it, in the simplest terms, "is the ability to see reality through the eyes of others."[60]

Interestingly, the military application of CQ is not a phenomenon of the twenty-first century battlespace. In fact, it has been widely used by intrepid warriors operating within the realm of both conventional and irregular warfare as early as the Peloponnesian War, in the fifth century B.C. In more recent times, CQ has been able to achieve some startling military successes with surprisingly few resources. For example, during the First World War, Colonel T.E. Lawrence, the infamous Lawrence of Arabia,[61] was able to use his understanding of Arab culture and his geographic knowledge of the Middle East to win the trust of Feisal, the third son of Sharif Hussein bin Ali. In so doing, he became a major force in organizing and sustaining the Arab revolt against the Turks.[62] In the end, the revolt forced the Turkish Army to tie down significant resources that could have been much better used elsewhere.[63]

Although not well understood at the time, clearly the success of this endeavour validated the idea that CQ could be used by individuals to facilitate relationships that could be leveraged to produce tactical or operational victory. Such enlightened CQ is particularly important when dealing with modern counterinsurgency operations such as the NATO mission in Afghanistan and the American-led coalition in Iraq. Notwithstanding its vital importance, exhibiting high CQ continues to be a problem for Western militaries that tend to see the world in a Western-centric ideological, cultural, and religious context. For example, according to Cordesman, the American intelligence community was not ready for the scope of the task given to them in Iraq. Although he acknowledged that "the full depth of the problems the U.S. intelligence community encountered in trying to staff the Iraq War is highly classified," he suggested that, "at the peak of the war, most of the analysts dealing with HUMINT activity had little or no experience in dealing with Iraq, and many had never dealt with the Middle East."[64]

Needless to say, when operating in alien cultures, success in counterinsurgency will only be achieved through coordinating the efforts of national, international, and HN entities who are responsible for providing security, as well as economic, political, and social reform in the pursuit of winning the hearts and minds of local populations. In these situations, progress is often based on understanding the cultural nuances that are at play within the target society and ensuring that the actions undertaken will actually support local beliefs, customs, and understanding, and will not alienate the people government or coalition forces are trying to help.[65] Only when the cultural issues nuances are well understood can security operations be targeted to achieve specific effects and, ultimately, the desired outcome.

The CQ component of the intelligence puzzle is vitally important. It provides a key enabler in determining the perennial problem in counterinsurgency — differentiating friend from foe. As noted earlier, insurgents will bleed into the population both to ensure cover and gain support (given freely by the population or acquired through coercion and intimidation). Infiltrating the network that is constructed becomes difficult if not impossible, unless one understands the cultural nexus — particularly, elements such as tribal/clan affiliations, societal beliefs, norms and values, the power relationship, and local decision-making networks.

This is where the complexity builds. To influence the population and succeed at counterinsurgency, it is key to attain information that can be distilled into intelligence on the insurgents from the local populace. But to do this, one must understand the society in which one is operating. With this understanding it then becomes important to separate insurgents from the local population as quickly as possible to deny the insurgents information and support, while gaining vital information for counterinsurgency operations.

Paradoxically, to achieve this separation of "friend from foe," security forces must focus on intelligence-driven operations that require information input from populations that may already be infiltrated with insurgents. As Warrant Officer Dominic Chenard explained, "There are farmers all around the area, but we don't know what they do or what they think. You can't tell the difference between a friendly and unfriendly. The guy standing at the side of the road could be holding a pitchfork today, then the next time you see him he could be pointing an RPG at you."[66]

As such, the only hope of achieving success is with an extensive knowledge of the population and the insurgents. American Major-General (Retired) Robert H. Scales Jr. summarized, "an intimate knowledge of the enemy's motivation, intent, will, tactical method, and cultural environment has proven to be far more important for success than the deployment of smart bombs, unmanned aircraft, and expansive bandwidth."[67] The reason is simple. It is that knowledge that will allow fissure points between the population and insurgents to be recognized, expanded, and exploited.

From an intelligence perspective, understanding the elements of culture that are at play within the HN allows security forces to take advantage of opportunities. For example, transgressions in value and belief systems can be exploited. Moreover, nuances in speech, gestures, and tribal affiliations can provide valuable clues as to the possible location or intentions of the belligerents, which can then facilitate the conduct of operations. To this end, experience has shown that good interpreters can to do far more than just relay verbatim translations to the security forces.[68]

In fact, seasoned interpreters in Afghanistan are able to explain nuances that are missed by those with only a basic understanding of the language and are able to translate these nuances into more meaningful messages. As a result, they provide coalition forces with excellent information. The message, through the means in which it is expressed (e.g., pauses, ambiguities, et cetera), might have less to do with what is being said and more to do with how it is being said.[69] In the end, such well developed CQ skills can sometimes help security forces to recognize that there is far more to many stories than what mere words are saying. All this adds to the information picture that can then be analyzed and distilled to provide the intelligence necessary to drive targeted operations.

As critical as intelligence is to counterinsurgency, unfortunately, the effectiveness of various intelligence activities during insurgencies or counterterrorist operations depends on the ability of different agencies with diverse priorities and mandates to work together on a centrally-agreed collection plan and to focus limited resources to achieve a specific end. Although relatively straightforward in theory, in reality this task is far more difficult. In fact, one of the main difficulties to effective intelligence production is the friction caused between competing agencies and in many cases different sections within the same agency.

This inability to work together even when national security is at stake was graphically illustrated in the aftermath of the 9/11 terrorist attack. Even before the dust had settled, a litany of accusations and revelations began to seep out. For example, by mid-2001 many of those in the know — intelligence, law enforcement, bureaucrats in a dozen countries — were aware and worried that a major terrorist strike was imminent.[70] By the summer of 2001, intelligence services were picking up enough chatter about a terrorist attack to prompt the U.S. Department of Defense to put its troops on full alert as early as 22 June. In addition, the department ordered six ships from the Fifth Fleet based in Bahrain to steam out to sea to avoid any possible attacks on them.[71] By early July, Ben Bonk, deputy director of the CIA's Counterterrorism Center, provided evidence that Al Qaeda was planning "something spectacular." The evidence was supposedly gripping.[72]

Interestingly, the first warning of a possible attack came from Phoenix, Arizona, on 10 July, when Ken Williams, an experienced international terrorism agent wrote a memorandum detailing his suspicions about some suspected Islamic radicals who had been taking flying lessons in Arizona. More captivatingly, Williams actually proposed an investigation to see if Al Qaeda was using flight schools nationwide. He submitted his report to headquarters and two other field offices, including New York City. It died in all three locations.[73]

A second warning arrived five weeks later on 13 August, when Zacarias Moussaoui, a Frenchman of Moroccan ancestry arrived at the Pan Am International Flight Academy in Minnesota for simulator training on a Boeing 747. He wanted to learn how to fly a Boeing 747 in four or five days, which raised suspicions, so one of the school's instructors contacted the FBI. Moussaoui was detained the next day. The next two weeks were spent trying to persuade headquarters to allow the field agents authority to search Moussaoui's computer.[74]

FBI whistle-blower Coleen Rowley revealed that agents at the Minneapolis field office became so frustrated with the inaction of their higher chain of command in regard to their investigation into Moussaoui, the alleged twentieth hijacker, that they attempted to bypass their bosses and alerted the CIA's Counterterrorism Center. They were subsequently chastised by the FBI hierarchy for going outside channels. Rowley revealed that the resistance to their warnings and pleas for warrants was so great that agents in her office joked that some FBI officials "had to be spies or moles ... who were actually working for Osama bin Laden."[75] In fact, one agent speculated in his notes that Moussaoui "may be planning to fly something into the World Trade Center."[76]

In a parallel development, another of the terrorists, Khalid al-Midhar, was identified well in advance. In January 2000 a group of Al Qaeda operatives met in Kuala Lumpur, Malaysia, to plot the attack on the USS *Cole*. The meeting was caught on tape by Malaysian authorities and it was turned over to the CIA. During the summer of 2001, the CIA identified one of the attendees as al-Midhar, a Saudi whom intelligence officials thought entered the United States shortly after the Malaysian meeting and left six months later. The CIA put his name on a terrorist watch list and eventually handed it over to the Immigration and Naturalization Service, but by then he had already slipped back into the United States. Within the next few days the CIA notified the FBI who started a frantic manhunt but with no success. On 11 September authorities believe he flew American Airlines Flight 77 into the Pentagon.[77]

Even with these types of graphic failures, getting different agencies with diverse priorities and mandates to work together in an effort to reduce the friction and open up the flow of information between agencies is a difficult task. The key to establishing a free flow of information and intelligence within a counterinsurgency environment is to centrally coordinate all intelligence staffs, starting with the creation of a single director of intelligence and then establishing a similar authority at each lower level of command. That being said, actual coordination would still be carried out by forming intelligence committees that would coordinate the collection, processing, and dissemination of information and intelligence.

In this situation, each committee would owe allegiance to the next higher level, which would be responsible for the effectiveness and coordination of the intelligence efforts of those below it. To improve coordination among agencies, each agency would become part of the committees and each committee would meet regularly to exchange and discuss both information and intelligence. The idea is to have the organization and process contribute to developing the necessary working relationship between the various agencies.[78]

The main issue is whether or not an intelligence committee is or can be actually established that encompasses all the players within the HN. After all, the greatest concern is infiltration by insurgents, particularly in alien cultures and societies where tribal/clan ties are all pervasive. In fact, the coalition in Afghanistan struggles with this now, as spectacular Taliban attacks are often followed by evidence of active complicity by senior Afghan government and/or security force officials. In addition, classified Afghan Army codes and frequencies were recently found on the body of a dead insurgent, once again showing the level of infiltration.

The counterintelligence (CI) challenge aside, the need for intelligence fusion that includes all players is vital. When this scale of coordination cannot occur, the normal focus for daily intelligence coordination becomes the all-source intelligence centre (ASIC) or, if a joint operation is being planned, as is increasingly the case, the joint ASIC (JASIC). The ASIC contains the entirety of the intelligence staff, which will include the necessary fusion and analysis personnel needed to conduct the transformation of raw information to processed intelligence. However, key to breaking down the barriers of information and intelligence stovepipes is having representatives from the various agencies working together in one organization or area.[79]

A good example of this type of arrangement working effectively began in the 1980s, when the CIA Counterterrorism Center, which was designed in 1986 as a means to get FBI and CIA agents working side by side, was established. Between 1989 and 2002, it broke up at least three planned attacks by the Hezbollah terror group outside of the Middle East.[80] It continues to function effectively today and is a group worth emulating.[81]

Although the character of modern irregular warfare, particularly insurgency, has changed somewhat in terms of its conduct, it has not altered its basic premise. In this respect, it is still very much a struggle to influence the people and the key to success in this conflict is the necessary detailed intelligence to drive target-specific, precise operations.

In the end, accurate intelligence will aid tremendously in the conventional fight. It will enhance force protection by assisting in the identification of enemy activity whether planned ambushes, attacks on convoys or forward operating bases, or the laying of IEDs. The information can save lives and provide the necessary details for prosecuting operations to capture or kill insurgents. In addition, intelligence can increase the security for the population by indicating where the enemy is; where the enemy will be/is massing, and as such, will be able to prompt the necessary security force reaction. This in turn will keep the enemy off balance, separate it from the population, and deny it sanctuary and staging bases. In addition, accurate intelligence will allow for the determination of ingress routes, rat lines, and support bases and once again provide targets for security forces to eliminate. In summary, accurate timely intelligence enables the counterinsurgency forces to provide the stable secure environment needed to allow political, social, and economic reform to transpire. In today's complex environment it is the key to success.

NOTES

1. Steven Metz, "New Challenges and Old Concepts: Understanding 21st Century Insurgency," *U.S. Army War College Quarterly: Parameters*, Vol. 37, No. 4, Winter 2007–08, 22–23.

2. Department of Defense, *Directive Number 3000.07 Irregular Warfare* (Washington, DC: DoD, 1 December 2008), 11.

3. Department of Defense, *The Joint Operating Environment (JOE)* (Suffolk, VA: U.S. Joint Forces Command, 2008), 46.

4. *Ibid.*, 46.

5. Department of National Defence (DND), *Canadian Army Counter-insurgency Operations* (Draft) (Kingston: LFDTS, 2005), chapter 1, 10–14.

6. Bard E. O'Neill, *Insurgency & Terrorism: Inside Modern Revolutionary Warfare* (Washington, DC: Brassey's Inc., 1990), 13. Over the past few years, Western nations have come to recognize the transnational nature of modern insurgencies and now refer to insurgency as, "a competition involving at least one non-state movement using means that include violence against an established authority to achieve political change." This definition was developed by a COIN study group during USMC Joint Urban Warrior 2005. Taken from *Canadian Army Counter-insurgency Operations* (Draft).

7. *Canadian Army Counter-insurgency Operations*, 11.

8. John J. McCuen. *The Art of Counter-revolutionary War: The Strategy of Counter-insurgency* (London: Faber and Faber, 1966), 30. Part of McCuen's quote was taken from Mao Tse-tung, "Strategic Problems in the Anti-Japanese Guerrilla War," *Selected Works*, Vol. 2 (New York: International Publishers, 1954), 125.

9. Julian Paget, *Counter-insurgency Campaigning* (London: Faber and Faber Limited, 1967), 23

10. Accessed at *http://earthops.org/sovereign/low_intensity/100–20.2.html* (accessed 20 October 2006).

11. General (Retired) M.Y. Nawroz, and Lieutenant-Colonel (Retired) L.W. Grau, *The Soviet War in Afghanistan: History and Harbinger of Future War?* (Fort Leavenworth, KS: Foreign Military Studies Office), 10.

12. Department of National Defence, *Canadian Forces Joint Intelligence Doctrine.* B-GJ-005–200/FP-000. J2 Plans Pol, 2003–05–21, 1–1. However, having the right type of information on a particular threat is of little value to the military commander that must make the decisions until some form of analysis is completed and useful deductions are drawn from it. More precisely, information on its own is little more than a fact or a series of facts and as such usually has limited or no value. However, when the information is analyzed and related to other information already known, or when it can be put into the context of a particular situation, it may be able to create a completely new set of facts and knowledge. This outcome is referred to as intelligence.

13. Adapted from the "Intelligence Notebook," online at the CF Intelligence Branch Association website, *www.intbranch.org/engl/intntbk/int03.html* (accessed 25 September 2004).

14. Peter Harclerode, *Secret Soldiers: Special Forces in the War Against Terrorism* (London: Cassell & Co., 2000), 346.

15. Massimo Calabresi and Romesh Ratnesar, "Can We Stop the Next Attack?" *Time,* 11 March 2002, 22.

16. *Canadian Army Counter-insurgency Operations* (Draft), Chapter 7, 5–6/30.

17. *Ibid.*, 6/30.

18. *Ibid.*, 7/30.

19. *Ibid.*, 7/30.

20. National Defence. *Land Force Information operations: Intelligence Field Manual* (Kingston: Director Army Doctrine, B-GL-357–001/FP-001, dated, 2000), 1.

21. *Ibid.*, 8/30.

22. Nawroz, 10.

23. Walt L. Perry and John Gordon, *Analytic Support to Intelligence in Counterinsurgencies* (Santa Monica, CA: RAND Corp, 2008), 15.

24. Seth G. Jones, *Counterinsurgency in Afghanistan,* Rand Counterinsurgency Study, Vol.4.(Santa Monica: RAND National Defense Research Institute, 2008), 99.

25. *Ibid.*, 99.

26. *Ibid.*, 100. Jones points out that "While intelligence gathered from locals can be useful, it should be taken with some caution. HUMINT sources may have other motives for supplying intelligence, such as tribal rivalries, and they may leak information to insurgent forces."

27. *Ibid.*, 100.

28. *Canadian Army Counter-insurgency Operations* (Draft), chapter 7, 15/30.

29. *Ibid.* 7: 15/30.

30. Anthony H. Cordesman, *The Intelligence Lessons of the Iraq War(s)* (Washington, DC: Center for Strategic and International Studies, 6 August 2004), 75.

31. Nawroz, 10–12.

32. Lieutenant-Colonel Ian Hope, presentation at the Canadian Infantry Association Annual General Meeting, 25 May 2007.

33. *Canadian Army Counter-insurgency Operations* (Draft), chapter 7, 23/30.

34. Colonel Gary D. Payton, ed., "The Art of Intelligence by the General," *Airpower Journal,* Winter 1993, 5; and Major L.H. Rémillard, "The 'All-Source' Way of Doing Business. The Evolution of Intelligence in Modern Military Operations," *Canadian Military Journal,* Vol. 8, No. 3, Autumn 2007, 23.

35. Department of National Defence. *Canadian Forces Joint Intelligence Doctrine,* (B-GJ-005–200/FP-000. J2 Plans Pol, 2003–05–21), 1–1.

36. *Canadian Army Counter-insurgency Operations* (Draft), chapter 7, 17/30. Intelligence will often be derived from information gathered during friendly force operations (i.e., troops in contact, tactical questioning of detainees, interface with the population, and host nation security forces).

37. Cordesman, 88.

38. *Canadian Army Counter-insurgency Operations* (Draft), chapter 7, 7/30.

39. Walt L. Perry and John Gordon, 53.

40. *Ibid.,* 53.

41. *Ibid.,* 53.

42. *Ibid.,* 15.

43. *Ibid.,* 16.

44. *Ibid.,* 16.

45. Harclerode, 289–91. In addition, in 1976, initial planning for the Entebbe operation included four options. The first three variations depended on the co-operation of the Ugandans for a successful withdrawal once the Israeli special operations forces had rescued the hostages. However, once Mossad produced information that indicated that Idi Amin was heavily involved in aiding the terrorists, detailed planning could begin on the fourth option — raid Entebbe airport and carry out rescue operations and withdraw to friendly territory.

46. "Ambush in Mogadishu — Interview with General Thomas Montgomery," *Frontline, www.pbs.org/wgbh/pages/frontline/shows/ambush/interview/montgomery.html* (accessed 9 July 2002).

47. *Canadian Army Counter-insurgency Operations* (Draft), chapter 7, 17/30.

48. *Ibid.,* 17/30.

49. *Ibid.,* 17/30.

50. *Ibid.,* 17/30.

51. In the case of Afghanistan this plays to the ancient tribal custom that has often been described as "my brother and I against my cousin. My cousin, my brother and I against the world." It also underscores the point that foreign troops will eventually go home but that the belligerents are already at home.

52. Alex Alexiev, *The United States and the War in Afghanistan* (Santa Monica: Rand, 1988), 4.

53. See Gary C. Schroen, *First In: An Insider's Account of How the CIA Spearheaded the War on Terror in Afghanistan* (New York: Presidio, 2006); and Gary Berntsen, *Jawbreaker. The Attack on Bin Laden and Al-Qaeda* (New York: Three Rivers Press, 2005).

54. E.R. Girardet. *Afghanistan: The Soviet War* (New York: St. Martin's Press, 1985), 36. The systematic applications of KGB-style subversion included "the use of psychological and economic pressures, informers, agents-provocateurs, financial pay-offs,

imprisonment, threats and privileges ... represents an ... effective weapon in the government's efforts to attract or split loyalties among the tribes, ethnic groups, exiled political parties and resistance fronts."

55. *Ibid.*, 129.

56. Canada, *Canadian Special Operations Forces Command. An Overview* (Ottawa: DND, 2008), 6.

57. Quoted in Cordesman, 92.

58. Quoted in George W. Smith, "Avoiding a Napoleonic Ulcer: Bridging the Gap of Cultural Intelligence," *A Common Perspective*, May 2006, Vol. 14, No. 1, 23.

59. Dr. Emily Spencer, *Crucible of Success: Applying the Four Domain CQ Paradigm* (Kingston: Canadian Forces Leadership Institute, Technical Report 2007–05, May 2007).

60. *Ibid.*

61. Stanley and Rodelle Weintraub, eds., *T.E. Lawrence. Evolution of a Revolt: Early postwar writings of T.E. Lawrence* (London: Pennsylvania State University Press, 1968), 9–29. Interestingly, Lawrence was not a soldier by profession. In fact, after graduating from Oxford in 1910 he was awarded a post-graduate scholarship at Magdalen College and spent much of his research time in the Middle East touring and conducting archaeological work. When the First World War broke out in 1914, Lawrence entered military service and was commissioned into the British Army as an Intelligence Officer.

62. *Ibid.* General Edmund Allenby used Lawrence as a liaison officer to the Arabs, who operated to the east of the British. He combined their efforts, pushing his mechanized forces north against the Turks with lightning attacks, while the Arabs hampered Turkish efforts to move troops and supplies.

63. *Ibid.*, 9–29.

64. Cordesman, 75.

65. David Kilcullen, "Counter-insurgency Redux," *Survival* 48, 2006–07, 122.

66. Doug Beazley, "Dig in, Stay Alive 60 Days Between a Rock and a Hard Place," *Winnipeg Sun*, 12 December 2006, 10.

67. Robert H. Scales Jr., "Culture-Centric Warfare," *Proceedings*, October 2004, 32.

68. Lorenzo Puertas, "Corporal Jones and the Moment of Truth," *Proceedings*, November 2004, 44.

69. Being savvy about picking up cultural cues can also help determine if an area is under the influence of the enemy and whether the locals are "willingly" supporting insurgents. Such information can establish how best to influence the thinking of locals. For example, in an area where insurgents are coercing locals to co-operate by threat of punishment, securing the area and assuring the locals of the government's long-term commitment to them can help them side with government forces. Cited in Colonel (Retired) W.N. Peters, *Shifting to the Moral Plane: The Canadian Approach to Information Operations* (Kingston: Canadian Forces Leadership Institute Technical Report, 2007), 20–21. The NATO definition for Information Operations is "Info Ops is a military function to provide advice and coordination of military information activities in order to create desired effects on the will, understanding and capability of adversaries, potential adversaries and other NAC approved parties in support of Alliance mission objectives."

70. Michael Elliot, "They Had a Plan," *Time*, 12 August 2002, 25.

71. *Ibid.*, 25.

72. *Ibid.*, 33. See also Hirsh and Isikoff, 32; Romesh Ratnesar and Michael Weisskopf, "How the FBI Blew the Case," *Time*, 3 June 2002, 21; and Michael Isikoff and Daniel Klaidman, "The Hijackers We Let Escape," *Newsweek*, 10 June 2002, 20–28.
73. Elliot, "They Had a Plan," 35. See also Elliot, "How the US Missed the Clues," 23.
74. Elliot, "They Had a Plan," 36.
75. Ratnesar and Weisskopf, 21.
76. Hirsh and Isikoff, 33–34.
77. Elliot, "They Had a Plan," 36.
78. *Canadian Army Counter-insurgency Operations* (Draft), chapter 7, 11/30.
79. *Ibid.*, 8/30.
80. Massimo Calabresi and Romesh Ratnesar, "Can we Stop the Next Attack?" *Time*, 11 March 2002, 22.
81. Gregory Treverton, a senior policy analyst at RAND, has pointed out, "Cold War intelligence was organized, on the collection side, around sources — signals (SIGINT), imagery (IMINT), and espionage (human intelligence, or HUMINT) — and, on the analytic side, around agencies, such as the CIA or the Defense Intelligence Agency (DIA)." He states, "The most sweeping change in the law created national intelligence centers under the authority of the DNI, which are organized around issues or missions. The centers, with the National Counterterrorism Center (NCTC) as the prototype, would both deploy and use the information, technology, and staff resources of the existing agencies — the CIA, DIA, National Security Agency, and others." He went on to suggest, "The centers would be intelligence's versions of the military's 'unified commands,' looking to the agencies to acquire the technological systems, train the people, and execute the operations planned by the national intelligence centers." Whether this type of a situation could be duplicated in a coalition where not everyone is treated equally is difficult to predict. That being said, intelligence is critical to success in modern operations and must therefore become responsive to the user not the organization producing the product. Gregory F. Treverton, *The Next Steps in Reshaping Intelligence* (Santa Monica, CA: RAND Corp, 2005), viii.

4

"THE PEOPLE PUZZLE":

The Importance of Cultural Intelligence to Counterinsurgency

Emily Spencer

"It's all cultural in the end."

— Lieutenant-Colonel Ian Hope,
Commanding Officer Canadian Battle Group
(Task Force Orion)[1]

AN AMERICAN VETERAN OF several foreign interventions once observed of the U.S. military, "What we need is cultural intelligence." He continued, "What I [as a soldier] need to understand is how these societies function. What makes them tick? Who makes the decisions? What is it about their society that is so remarkably different in their values, in the way they think compared to my values and the way I think?"[2] More recently, Brigadier-General David Fraser, the former commander of the International Security Assistance Force (ISAF) Multinational Brigade Sector South in Kandahar, Afghanistan, admitted, "I underestimated one factor — culture." He then elaborated, "I was looking at the wrong map — I needed to look at the tribal map not the geographic map. The tribal map is over 2,000 years old. Wherever we go in the world we must take into account culture. Culture will affect what we do. This is the most important map [i.e., tribal] there is." Fraser lamented, "I did not take that in up front. Not all enemy reported was actually Taliban — identification of enemy forces was often culturally driven."[3]

Specifically, in counterinsurgency warfare the seminal battle is primarily about influencing the population to support the governing authority and deny support and information to the insurgents. To have any hope of influencing the masses and, especially, winning their "hearts and minds," it is vitally important to understand them and their culture. Failure to understand their beliefs, values, and attitudes and how they *see* the world is tantamount to mission failure. Sorting out the "people puzzle" is critical to success. As such, cultural intelligence (CQ)[4] — or the ability to recognize the shared beliefs, values, attitudes, and behaviours of a group of people and, most important, to apply this knowledge toward a specific goal — is a, if not the, key mission enabler in counterinsurgency.

THE IMPORTANCE OF CQ TO COUNTERINSURGENCY

The non-linear and asymmetric approach of the contemporary defence environment, particularly with respect to insurgencies and counterinsurgencies, demands that soldiers act as warriors and technicians as well as scholars and diplomats. Kinetic solutions are no longer the panacea of warfare. Rather, individuals need to see "reality" through the eyes of another culture, specifically the one with which they are interacting. They need to adapt their own attitudes and behaviours so they can better influence their target audience and achieve their specific aims. Cultural knowledge contributes to this end, while an understanding of CQ and, in particular, the four CQ domain paradigm, provides the template for how to use this cultural knowledge to attain desired objectives.[5]

The conflicts in Afghanistan and Iraq underscore the importance of exhibiting high CQ in counterinsurgency campaigns. For example, in his retirement speech, U.S. Army General P. J. Schoomaker reminded his audience, "We must never forget that war is fought in the human dimension."[6] Similarly, Lieutenant-Colonel Ian Hope, a combat-tested Canadian battle group commander in Afghanistan remarked, "In combat, the power of personality, intellect and intuition, determination and trust, outweigh the power of technology, and everything else."[7] Moreover, the *Marine Corps*

Small Wars Manual warned, "Human reactions cannot be reduced to exact science, but there are certain principles that should guide our conduct." It went on to caution, "Psychological errors may be committed which antagonize the population of a country occupied and all the foreign sympathizers; mistakes may have the most far reaching effect and it may require a long period to re-establish confidence, respect, and order."[8]

Additionally, a common theme that surfaces in accounts by soldiers serving in conflict zones is the need for a deeper understanding of host nation peoples. "The pitfalls presented by a different culture and an ill-defined, poorly functioning (or non-existent) local judicial, administrative, and political systems are enormous," Major P.M. Zeman of the United States Marine Corps noted.[9] U.S. Army Major-General (Retired) Robert H. Scales Jr. echoed these sentiments while describing the vital "cultural" phase of the war where "intimate knowledge of the enemy's motivation, intent, will, tactical method, and cultural environment has proved to be far more important for success than the deployment of smart bombs, unmanned aircraft, and expansive bandwidth."[10] American Naval Reservist, Lorenzo Puertas, also aptly noted, "Every war is a war of persuasion.... we must destroy the enemy's will to fight." He continued, "Persuasion always is culturally sensitive. You cannot persuade someone if you do not understand his language, motivations, fears, and desires."[11]

Indeed, American General Anthony Zinni described the turbulent and chaotic environment modern military personnel would face on operations. He stated: "The situations you're going to be faced with go far beyond what you're trained for in a very narrow military sense. They become cultural issues; issues of traumatized populations' welfare, food, shelter; issues of government; issues of cultural, ethnic, religious problems; historic issues; economic issues that you have to deal with that aren't part of the METT-T [mission, enemy, troops, terrain and weather — time available] process necessarily. And the rigid military thinking can get you in trouble. What you need to know isn't what our intel[ligence] apparatus is geared to collect for you and to analyze and to present to you."[12]

After all, in this global age of media, decisions by soldiers in remote areas can have far-reaching consequences for home and host populations. Puertas illustrated this point by describing the potential consequences of one corporal and his decisions after being fired on in an alley in Iraq. "Without cultural training, his reaction will be a product of his personal experiences and beliefs," Puertas asserted. He added, "He might have cultural misunderstandings that lead to serious errors in judgement. He might fail in his mission — and he might find himself despised by one poor neighborhood, or by a billion horrified TV viewers." Puertas cautioned, "Cultural knowledge of the battlespace should not be left to on-the-job training."[13] Indeed, it has been noted that, "In the constant cross cultural exchange a simple mistake could become an obscenity without the 'guilty' party even being aware of the error."[14]

As Lieutenant-General Andrew Leslie, a former deputy commander of the ISAF revealed, "Individuals were sent home [from Afghanistan]. Immaturity and the inability to actually think outside the box made them ineffective." He continued, "What they tried to do was bring their usually limited experience from somewhere else and apply it the same way that it had been done somewhere else and that didn't work." Leslie explained, "each mission has got its own unique drivers, cultural conditions, local nuances, relationships with your other allies or other combatants." Moreover, he emphasized that the Afghan problem needed an Afghan solution.[15]

The fact of the matter is, in the current security environment, everyone down to the lowest ranking individual requires cultural intelligence. In the CNN era of 24/7 instantaneous news coverage that beams events as they happen into the living rooms of audiences around the world, the careless act of a single soldier can have strategic ramifications. With regard to the concept of the "strategic corporal," Canadian Colonel Bernd Horn observed, "The perception of the media, as well as that of defence analysts, right or wrong, for better or for worse, is critical." He explained, "They [the media] set the terms of the public debate. What they report becomes the basis of societal perception; it influences and forms the public's attitudes and beliefs. Repeated often enough or pervasively enough, perception becomes reality." Thus, Horn concluded that militaries "must always be attentive and responsive to the perceptions of others."[16] Therefore, in the bitterly contested counterinsurgency fight, which is almost always in the glare of international media, everyone who participates must be culturally savvy to ensure they do not purposefully or inadvertently offend or alienate audiences whether at home, abroad, or in the operational area.

Despite the obvious need for cultural knowledge and an understanding of how best to apply this knowledge to advance the mission, there a gap in training and application of these skills among military personnel.

As Major-General Scales pointed out, the U.S. military has a big gap in cultural intelligence. It is not just a matter of getting more linguists, he explained. Rather, and more important, there is a need to get your point across — including intent — and in order to do this cultural appreciation is paramount.[17]

To help fill this gap in knowledge, one must first understand what culture is, and appreciate how the concept of cultural intelligence came into being. Then, one needs a useful template on which to hang culturally specific knowledge so that it may be used to fulfill military objectives.

Understanding Culture

CQ is a concept that hinges on the idea of culture, thus to appreciate CQ one must first understand culture. The issue of culture itself is fraught with academic debate. Yet, to fully understand CQ one must find a way through this academic quagmire.

The literature is replete with descriptions of what culture is. It is a concept that anthropologists and other academics have long analyzed and debated, yet there remains no clear consensus as to its definition. As author Ralph Peters noted, "We need to struggle against our American tendency to focus on hardware and bean counting to attack the more difficult and subtle problems posed by human behaviour and regional history."[18] Indeed, the U.S. Department of Defense has identified that "culture will remain a source of friction and potential conflict among societies. The future operational environment must accommodate a significant trend in the growing significance of cultures and sub-cultures. Fed by globalization, regionalization, and information age capabilities, new groups are discovering (and sometimes rediscovering) a shared culture. This trend complicates our ability to define, understand, and influence future operational environment."[19] Notably, these challenges are not restricted to Americans.

The most important thing to understand about culture is its sheer complexity. As Lieutenant-Colonel Ian Hope states in the epigraph at the beginning of this report, "It's all cultural in the end." Moreover, our understandings of culture are limited by our understandings of the world and are thus susceptible to the fallacies of ethnocentrisms. Nonetheless, we need to map the minefield as effectively as possible.

When applying CQ as a force multiplier, the focus is on shaping the behaviours of the people in each of the four CQ domains — national, international, host nation, and enemy. Human behaviours are shaped by many things, including immediate situational factors. At their core, however lie basic beliefs, values, and attitudes about the way the world is. Without suggesting that beliefs, values, and attitudes are the only things that shape behaviour at a group level, appreciating some fundamental group attitudes that are comprised of belief-value pairings, provides insight into how certain groups of people "tick." This understanding helps to predict behaviours and shows fault lines that can be targeted to shift them. Notably, cultural change is slow and generally greatly resisted.

Culture refers to a set of common beliefs and values within a group of people that, combined, transform into attitudes that are expressed as behaviours.[20] (See Figure 1) Culture helps to create individual and group identity. Group identity, or culture, is formed when individuals who share common attitudes and behaviours identify with each other. Individuals may enter into the group already having bought into the shared attitudes and behaviours, or the group may instigate this commonality. Cultural values, beliefs and attitudes are generally long lasting and resistant to change. They are passed down through generations and are often unconscious in nature.

BELIEF + VALUE $\longrightarrow$ ATTITUDE $\longrightarrow$ BEHAVIOUR

FIGURE 1: *The Relationships Between Beliefs, Values, Attitudes, and Behaviours.*[21]

Beliefs represent perceived "facts" about the world (and beyond) that do not require evaluation or proof of their correctness.[22] For example, Pagans believe in many gods, Christians believe in one God, and Muslims believe in Allah. None of these competing religious "beliefs" has been unequivocally proven correct. Some beliefs may even continue to be held within a group of people in spite of refuting "facts." This can lead to attribution errors in which a cause and effect relationship is misconceived because of the rigidity of a certain belief. For instance, if you believed without question that technology improves quality of life, then, as technology advanced, you would either take it for granted that quality of life was also on the rise, or, faced with blatant evidence to the contrary, you would assume that it was not technology that caused this decline. Despite the limitations that certain beliefs place on an individual or group's ability to fully evaluate their surroundings, common beliefs remain at the core of cultural identity. For example, the vast majority of Afghans and Iraqis believe their religious and tribal leaders with regard to the motives of Westerners in their land. As American military strategist Edward Luttwak explained, "The alternative would be to believe what for them is entirely unbelievable: that foreigners are unselfishly expending blood and treasure to help them. They themselves would never invade a foreign country except to plunder it, the way Iraq invaded Kuwait, thus having made Saddam Hussein genuinely popular for a time when troops brought back their loot. As many opinion polls and countless incidents demonstrate, the Americans and their allies are widely considered to be the worst of invaders, who came to rob Muslim Iraqis not only of their territory and oil but also of their religion and even family honor."[23]

Associated with beliefs, values place a moral and/or pragmatic weight on beliefs.[24] For instance, Christians do not simply believe in God, they use this belief to build an understanding of what is important in life. In this sense, "Christian values," provide a moral shorthand for determining "right" from "wrong." From a pragmatic perspective, if you believe that university education enables individuals to earn more over the course of a lifetime, and economic advancement is something that you deem important, then you will attach a high worth, or "value" to university education.

The relationships between beliefs and values are complex and dynamic. Values are generally attached to beliefs, yet adhering to certain values can also strengthen beliefs or create new ones. Paradoxically, individuals and groups can simultaneously have competing beliefs and values. Often, the weight attached to a certain belief will determine the course of action. For example, a moderate pacifist may at once be against all forms of violence and also believe strongly in self-preservation and the right to self-defence. In a situation in which the alternatives are shoot or be shot, this pacifist might choose to kill his/her attacker. In the same situation, someone with strong pacifist beliefs may rather be shot than go against his/her beliefs. Thus, what may appear as irrational to some may be completely sane and logical to others based on their beliefs and values. This is a particularly important point to recall when dealing with foreign cultures.

In combination, beliefs and values create attitudes. Attitudes reflect a consistent emotional response to a belief-value pair.[25] To change an attitude, either the belief or its associated value must be altered. To return to a previous example, if you believe that university education increases lifetime earnings and you value economic incentives, then you will have a positive attitude toward higher education. For your attitude toward higher education to change, either you must no longer believe that education leads to higher earnings, or the value that you place on economic incentives must be altered. Notably, many belief-value pairs may combine to form, strengthen or weaken an attitude. To continue with the university education example, besides higher earnings, you might also believe that a university education allows for more career flexibility, something that you consider to be important to quality of life. Your positive attitude toward higher education would thus be strengthened.

It is important to see attitudes as distinct from a combination of beliefs and values because once formed they may not be easily broken down into their component parts, and it is attitudes, rather than beliefs and values that predict behaviours. For example, Afghans believe warfare is a contest of endurance over time. They value displays of courage while leading an attack more than holding terrain or capturing an objective. For many Afghans, the purpose of warfare is to obtain glory and recognition for one's tribal clan.[26] An Afghan's primary loyalty is to family, kin group, clan, or tribe. Moreover, moral attitudes are often strict and inflexible, and they stress honour and an individual responsibility to fulfill expected roles.[27] That being said, however, the best way to alter attitudes is to target their core belief-value pairs with the understanding that there could be several pairs in operation at once. Notably, information and knowledge can help create a shift in attitudes.

Behaviour is the way in which individuals express themselves and, for the purposes of our discussion, can be verbal or non-verbal. In addition to being influenced by attitudes, motivation plays a role determining behaviour. Motivation can be influenced by the strength of beliefs and values that form attitudes (internal motivation) or it can be external, such as bribery, yet the applicability of external influences will also be influenced by beliefs, values, and attitudes. For example, bribing someone with money to motivate a certain behaviour would only work if that person valued money.

Culture is expressed through shared behaviours that include language, religion, work habits, recreation practices, et cetera. It helps people to classify their experiences and communicate them symbolically. Generally, our daily lives reflect our beliefs, values, and attitudes in a multitude of ways. They shape our lives and contribute to our sense of identity. Culture influences what we do and who we think we are; our beliefs, values, and attitudes, as demonstrated through our behaviours, also shape how others see us.

As the above discussion suggests, the complexity of culture cannot be overstated. Not only do cultures comprise many intertwining layers of meaning, they are living organisms that are paradoxically, given their static appearance, continuously in a state of change. The U.S. Marine Corps handbook on operational culture for deploying personnel to Afghanistan notes, "The study of culture is never 'finished.' What was true yesterday is slowly changing. And it's not an exact science."[28]

CULTURAL ROOTS

Besides helping individuals make sense of the world, cultures developed as a means of survival.[29] In this way they have geographic and geopolitical roots.[30] Beliefs, values, and attitudes that comprise cultural identity take root in perceptions of the world that are formed based on perceptions about geographic and climatic realities. In his contentious, yet thought-provoking, book about the impending clash of civilizations, political scientist Samuel P. Huntington was perhaps being overly simplistic when he stated: "the major differences in political and economic development among civilizations are clearly rooted in their different cultures."[31] Surely, the African continent at large did not choose a culture of poverty. Rather, geography and geopolitics contributed to the development of African culture. In fact, it is more accurate to examine the impact that geography and geopolitics have on culture and *vice versa*. (See Figure 2) Geography and geopolitics influence culture, which in turn shapes geopolitical dynamics and the degree to which geographic features are (or can be) manipulated.

Geography + Geopolitics ⟺ Culture

FIGURE 2: *The Relationship Between Geography, Geopolitics, and Culture.*

Geography and geopolitics help cultural groups distinguish themselves from others. Huntington wrote: "We know who we are only when we know who we are not and often only when we know whom we are against."[32] He explained, "People and nations are attempting to answer the most basic question humans can face: who are we?" Huntington continued, "People define themselves in terms of ancestry, religion, language, history, values, customs, and institutions. They identify with cultural groups: tribes, ethnic groups, religious communities, nations, and, at the broadest level, civilizations."[33]

Through this logic we in the West have come to see the world in terms of us versus them, or the West versus the rest. This at once presupposes a Western cultural commonality and simultaneously admits that "the rest" (as opposed to East) comprises several non-Western entities.

Even in the "West versus rest" paradigm, states remain the primary actors in the world.[34] This is an important factor to keep in mind because it represents a central paradox in the way that many people see the world. On one hand, nations are grouped according to broad belief-value systems to which the nation states contribute, but that extend far beyond the limits of national borders. On the other hand, our legal frameworks and default understandings remain at the nation-state level. For example, while it is clear that insurgents in the war in Afghanistan are of many national groups and some are finding refuge in Pakistan, the international community can take no legal action within Pakistan's borders.

With an understanding of culture and an appreciation of how it develops and continues to grow, individuals can subsequently learn how to apply high levels of CQ. Nonetheless, CQ is also a complex concept and thus requires further explanation as well.

DEFINING CULTURAL INTELLIGENCE

CQ is a new label that has been attached to an old concept and over the years has led to the creation of several definitions. Despite the plethora of descriptions for CQ, the term lacks a clear, concise definition. In this respect, it is important to establish a practical definition and conceptualization of CQ as it applies to the defence community in order to create a common language and understanding of the concept and its application.

Despite some basic differences between the academic and military literature pertaining to CQ, both the civilian and military schools of thought are inextricably linked and each requires further explanation. One of the leading authors on CQ in the civilian domain is scholar P. Christopher Earley. Earley, working with Elaine Mosakowski, in a 2004 *Harvard Business Review* article described CQ as an outsider's "ability to interpret someone's unfamiliar and ambiguous gestures in just the way that person's compatriots and colleagues would, even to mirror them." They continued, "A person with high cultural intelligence can somehow tease out of a person's or group's behaviour those features that would be true of all people and all groups, those peculiar to this person or this group, and those that are neither universal nor idiosyncratic. The vast realm that lies between those two poles is culture."[35]

In a more complex analysis of CQ, Earley and Soon Ang defined CQ as "a person's capability to adapt effectively to new cultural contexts." While slightly vague, they further explain that CQ has both process and content features that comprise cognitive, motivational, and behavioural elements.[36] Earley and Randall S. Peterson elaborated on this concept and build upon Earley and Ang's original concept that "CQ captures [the] capability for adaptation across cultures and … reflects a person's capability to gather, interpret, and act upon these radically different cues to function effectively across cultural settings or in a multicultural situation." Earley and Peterson added, "CQ reflects a person's capability of developing entirely novel behaviour (e.g., speech, sounds, gestures, etc.) if required." They surmised, "At its core, CQ consists of three fundamental elements: metacognition and cognition (thinking, learning and strategizing); motivation (efficacy and confidence, persistence, value congruence and affect for the new culture); and behavior (social mimicry, and behavioural repertoire)."[37]

Other researchers have also explored the idea of CQ being composed of cognitive, motivational, and behavioural domains or similar variations of this triplex system. For instance, James Johnson and a group of researchers defined CQ in terms of attitude, skills, and knowledge and another scholar in the field, David C. Thomas, emphasized knowledge, skills, and mindfulness.[38]

Most of this literature, however, prioritizes CQ as pertaining to other cultures and notably not one's own. Earley and Ang were clear when they stated: "CQ reflects a person's adaptation to new cultural settings and capability to deal effectively with other people with whom the person does not share a common cultural background."[39] Indeed, they even went so far as to suggest that individuals who are part of their own cultural in-group would find it particularly difficult to adjust to a new cultural setting as it may be one of the first times that they experience alienation from the in-group and lessons learned in one culture may not be useful in another.[40]

This argument, however, ignores the support of, and reactions from, the home population. Although this concept is something that may work for businesses, it is not acceptable for militaries that serve democratic nations. The ability of an individual to understand the behavioural patterns, beliefs, values, and attitudes of their own society must remain an important aspect of the definition of CQ as it applies to the Canadian Forces and other Western militaries. Most of the military literature that discusses CQ recognizes this fact.

Indeed, to help mitigate problems that arise from cultural misunderstandings and to maximize support for the war effort at home and abroad, Western militaries are starting to define CQ and underscore important aspects about culture that contribute to mission success. For example, the U.S. Center for Advanced Defence Studies, defined cultural intelligence as "the ability to engage in a set of behaviours that use language, interpersonal skills, and qualities appropriately tuned to the culture-based values and attitudes of the people with whom one interacts."[41] U.S. Army scholar and researcher Leonard Wong and his team describe cultural savvy, or in our terms CQ, for their report to the U.S. Army War College as enabling "an officer [to] see perspectives outside his or her own boundaries." They explained, "It does not imply, however, that the officer abandons the Army or U.S. culture in pursuit of a relativistic worldview. Instead, the future strategic leader is grounded in National and Army values, but is also able to anticipate and understand the values, assumptions, and norms of other groups, organizations, and nations."[42]

A further definition is provided by U.S. Navy Commander John P. Coles. He defined CQ as "analyzed social, political, economic, and other demographic information that provides understanding of a people or nation's history, institutions, psychology, beliefs (such as religion), and behaviours." He asserted, "It helps provide understanding as to why a people act as they do and what they think. Cultural intelligence provides a baseline for education and designing successful strategies to interact with foreign peoples whether they are allies, neutrals, people of an occupied territory, or enemy." Coles emphasized, "Cultural intelligence is more than demographics. It provides understanding of not only how other groups act but why."[43]

This chapter builds on both the civilian literature about CQ and the military concerns and definitions of CQ in order to establish a clear understanding of what CQ is. As mentioned, CQ is the ability to recognize the shared beliefs, values, attitudes, and behaviours of a group of people and, most important, to apply this knowledge to the fulfillment of a particular goal.[44] More specifically, CQ refers to the cognitive, motivational, and behavioural capacities to understand and effectively respond to the beliefs, values, attitudes, and behaviours of individuals and institutions of their own and other groups, societies, and cultures under complex and changing circumstances to effect a desired change. CQ, thus, has four principle components (see Figure 3): first, one must clearly understand his or her own national objective and/or goal for applying enhanced CQ; second, individuals require region specific knowledge and awareness; third, they need the ability, or skill set, and motivation to apply enhanced CQ; and finally, they need to exhibit the behaviour needed to achieve the desired objective.

CQ COMPONENTS

1. National objective and/or goal

2. Region specific knowledge/awareness

3. Ability (or skill) set and motivation

4. Appropriate behaviour

Figure 3: *CQ Components.*

Additionally, CQ must be applied in the context of the national, international, host nation, and enemy arenas to be effective. Similar to a picture on a puzzle box, the "four CQ domain paradigm" provides the framework for fitting individual cultural knowledge pieces into the global context. Specific culture, country, or area cultural awareness provides details for each piece of the puzzle. Without both the overarching conceptualization provided by the four CQ domain paradigm and the individual pieces established through country and even area specific cultural awareness, the puzzle cannot be put together.

THE FOUR CQ DOMAIN PARADIGM

CQ empowers individuals to see "reality" through the eyes of another culture, specifically the one with which they are interacting. This ability, in turn, provides individuals with the skills to be able to adapt their attitudes and behaviours to better influence the target audience to achieve specific aims. For example, for the CF, CQ requires an appreciation of the role of the CF within the broader spectrum of Canadian society, the role the CF plays in multinational alliances, the complexities that may arise when operating in an overseas environment, particularly with host nation institutions and populations, as well as an in-depth understanding of the "enemy." Additionally, interactions between these four domains must be recognized and understood. Indeed, CQ demands that all four domains (see Figure 4) are continuously balanced. This is no easy task and it is further complicated by the fact that each domain and the relationships between them are complex and dynamic.

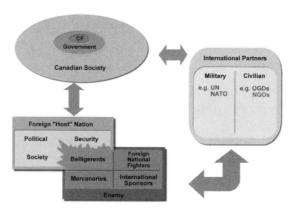

Figure 4: *The Four CQ Domains: National (i.e., Canadian Society), International, Host Nation, and Enemy*

NATIONAL DOMAIN

Winning and Keeping the "Hearts and Minds" of Canadians

For CF members, understanding the beliefs, values, and customs that comprise Canadian culture is important because the CF both represents and serves this culture. Applying this knowledge to maximize support for a mission from the Canadian public and within the CF is imperative for mission success. A military that serves a democratic nation cannot be fully successful if the will of the home population does not support the mission. The ever-present media in the twenty-first century with its ability to project "as it happens" events into living rooms around the globe exacerbates this point. As Colonel Fred Lewis, a former deputy commander of Task Force Afghanistan asserted, "The will of the Canadian people is our center of gravity. So, define center of gravity as our strength. If our strength fails, we lose."[45]

Therefore, part of applying CQ for CF leaders is to understand the behavioural patterns, beliefs, and institutions of Canadian society and to act according to these culturally acceptable norms and customs with the aim of retaining public support for the mission. An example that specifically indicates the Canadian public's desire to have their beliefs, values, and attitudes reflected in the behaviour of their soldiers is the media attention paid in the spring of 2007 to the alleged beatings of Afghan detainees that had been captured by Canadians and released to Afghan authorities. Licia Corbella, a reporter with the *Toronto Sun* remarked on the irony in the fact that "the Afghan authorities beat prisoners is hardly surprising when one understands the culture a bit better." Corbella asked, "Isn't that what being a good multiculturalist means? Understanding cultural differences?" She concluded, "Perhaps, thanks in part to Canada, prisons will be one of the first places in Afghanistan where beatings are not the norm. How's that for irony?"[46] Indeed, the reaction to the detainee situation suggests that many Canadians do not want to support a mission that does not continuously uphold Canadian beliefs, values, and attitudes, even in areas that clearly have different and opposing beliefs and values.[47]

Public polls show that support of the war effort also diminishes as the number of Canadian casualties increases.[48] For example, a 2006 Strategic Counsel poll found that 62 percent of Canadians oppose sending troops to Afghanistan; Ipsos Reid found a nation divided with 52 percent feeling that Canadian troops are performing a vital mission, but 48 percent saying the troops should be brought home as soon as possible.[49]

One way to try to sway public support for the war effort is to underscore the benefits of having CF members deployed to Afghanistan. Certainly, the mission needs to be judged as valuable by CF personnel and the civilians they serve. As Michael Ignatieff has noted, "A military force in a democracy can only retain its legitimacy, its self-confidence, and its public support if it plays by the rules, if it refuses to fight dirty, but all the wars and challenges that you face are coming at you from people who definitely and most emphatically fight dirty."[50] In fact, American Lieutenant-General James N. Mattis warned American service personnel "not [to] create more enemies than you take out by some immoral act."[51]

While some people judge value in terms of geopolitical/strategic advantage, by and large, Canadians view it in terms of quality of life issues that are based on cultural beliefs and values and are generally less easily measured. People want to feel like they are making a difference. This sentiment was expressed clearly by a Canadian information officer stationed in Kandahar. He lamented, "I will say it until I'm blue in the face, and I ask you to spread the word: we [as in the International Community] are actually getting it right over here, although it will take time. Canada plays a significant role in the South [Kandahar Province] but we are not alone. The U.N./NATO [United Nations/North Atlantic Treaty Organization] partnership, when executed correctly with Afghan input, works." He concluded, "What most impresses me over here is the late writer Margaret Mead's old adage about never doubting a small group of dedicated people can change the world; indeed history has shown it is the only thing that ever has. If you are imaginative, articulate, and inspiring in how you deliver your thoughts, the masses will follow for the greater good. Utopian perhaps, but as a student of history, I have to believe it's true."[52]

The value of a mission is arguably most apparent to the CF personnel in theatre. Combat commanders, thus, have the responsibility to inform their superiors of the challenges and successes of a mission. Hosting senior officers and high-ranking civil servants in theatre, as well as ensuring transparent and open communications at all times, can help the combat commander bridge gaps that exist between what is happening in theatre and what is believed to be occurring. This is an important process because both peace operations and wars are generally measured in terms of political successes rather than simply military victories, with political and military aspects ideally falling into alignment. Additionally, this process assists senior military leaders and politicians in working together and to better explain and frame messages that assure public support.[53]

INTERNATIONAL DOMAIN

Playing with Others: Military Coalitions, Intergovernmental Organizations, Non-Governmental Organizations, and Host Nation Partners

Exhibiting CQ is becoming more important in today's operating environment as greater emphasis is being placed on coalition operations for a multitude of reasons. The complex security environment has necessitated the creation of international coalitions to share the responsibility of ensuring global stability. Nations contribute members to military coalitions and intergovernmental organizations. In addition, individuals from a variety of national backgrounds join non-governmental organizations. All operate in the same theatre and each culture can cause any number of problems. To facilitate co-operation and effectiveness, particularly mission success, participants at all levels require enhanced CQ. Organizationally, each group might have its own unique task in the region, however, the overarching theme is generally to bring peace and stability to an area. For that reason, although these groups are usually working to achieve the same goal, they nonetheless operate under a variety of national chains of command and caveats.

Unity of command, as defined by the overall command of an area by one individual or organization, is rarely possible in complex scenarios involving multiple players. Part of the problem is that some organizations are military, while others are civilian or a combination of both. For example, military organizations strive for uniformity, a clear plan, decisive decisions, speed, and acceptance of risk. Conversely, aid agencies and diplomats prefer a slower, long-term, more risk-averse, more dialogue-intensive and consensus-based approach. If one wishes to make progress, these differences are important to factor in. Additionally, organizational chains of command may seem to supersede even national command in theatre. For example, both the Department of National Defence and the Department of Foreign Affairs and International Trade have personnel serving in Afghanistan. Both departments are serving the Canadian government, yet each has its own separate chain of command, thus obscuring unity of command even between these two Canadian departments.

Unity of effort, however, meaning the co-operative alignment of agencies toward the same goal with minimal duplication of effort, can and should be achieved. Ensuring that redundant behaviour is kept to a minimum, that pertinent information is shared between organizations, and that everyone is working toward the same long-term goal contributes to unity of effort. Understanding and acting on the cultural beliefs, values, attitudes, and behaviours of other organizations and appreciating how your own may be viewed by others (i.e., enlightened CQ) facilitates the achievement of unity of effort.

Exhibiting enhanced CQ is particularly important considering the current defence environment in which, increasingly, the CF is called on to operate within intergovernmental organizations (IGOs), such as the U.N. and NATO as well as other coalition operations, and to work in co-operation with other Canadian governmental departments and domestic and international non-governmental organizations (NGOs). Additionally, CF members deployed overseas must often help train and work with host nation, HN, partners.

Working with IGOs and within coalitions, which in the case of the CF means other national military forces, can be challenging for a variety of reasons. Differing practices, work ethics, behavioural norms are challenging and, at times, frustrating. Moreover, different rules of engagement (RoEs) among coalition partners can be particularly frustrating.

Additionally, cultural nuances in speech and behaviour can be easily misinterpreted, even within groups who share a common language. For example, in August 2006, a young Canadian captain described his participation in the battle of Panjwayi in an email to friends and family. Many of the issues that CF members face while serving in Afghanistan, such as being part of a coalition and facing enemy fire, are apparent in this first-hand account of the battle. In one section, the young captain described a dialogue that occurred between himself and a member of the U.S. Army National Guard Embedded Training Teams (ETT) who was working with the Afghan National Army (ANA). The conversation occurred during a period of intense fighting. The Canadian captain was busy ensuring that his team was at a safe distance from the enemy in preparation for a friendly artillery strike when the American captain appeared to state "There are no ANA forward of us." The Canadian replied "Roger." It was only after the American called in the fire mission that the Canadian realized that the American captain had not announced that there were no ANA members in front of them; rather, he had been posing a question. With the torrent of gunfire, the intonation in the American's voice had been drowned out. In the aftermath, the Canadian reminded the American, "I have no idea where *your* ANA are, you're supposed to look after them!"

Working with other Canadian governmental organizations and agencies poses a completely different set of issues, yet demonstrating CQ can mitigate potential problems in this relationship as well. Canadian beliefs and values, as well as political directive at the national level, are common among Canadian governmental organizations. Specific directives and mandates, however, may not be so transparently parallel. This situation can be aggravated by the existence of different organizational cultures and even languages.[54] It is important in these instances to really emphasize the idea of unity of effort and to acknowledge similarities and differences in order to function as a cohesive national unit. The bigger picture of achieving national objectives, over particular departmental objectives, must be underscored. Understanding and embracing the different cultural nuances that exist in each department greatly contributes to unity of effort across Canadian governmental organizations and agencies. One senior army officer remarked on the challenge of working with other Canadian governmental departments, "the greatest problem is one of ignorance. None of the players fully understand who the other participants are. Other government departments and civilian agencies are normally not accustomed to military directness or command structure."[55] Not surprisingly then, the initial interface between military and civilian members of different departments is often fraught with conflict and misunderstanding.

Acquiring unity of effort while working with NGOs is, arguably, more difficult than working with IGOs or other governmental departments. Nonetheless, enhanced CQ in these instances can also help to facilitate the process. The 2006 American counterinsurgency manual noted that many NGOs "maintain strict independence from governments and belligerents and do not want to be seen directly associating with military forces." The final assessment provided in the manual was that "Establishing basic awareness of these groups and their activities may be the most commanders can achieve."[56] Given the general overlap in strategic objective that often exists between the Canadian government and NGOs, that of facilitating a stable and humanitarian HN state, unity of effort in these cases should also be achievable. However, as Colonel François Vertefeuille reflected, this is no easy task:

> Serving as liaison between a military coalition HQ [headquarters] and a group of individuals from diplomatic and international aid organizations was one of the most difficult tasks of my entire career. Persuading this group of individuals, some of whom were overtly hostile to the military, to discuss matters related to operations of the PRTs [provincial reconstruction teams] (which are military units with a humanitarian objective) was extremely laborious.[57]

HOST NATION DOMAIN

In the Land of Oz: Applying CQ in an Unfamiliar Environment

When operating in a foreign environment, it is essential to understand the culture of the HN population. As noted, "Situational understanding requires thorough familiarity with all of the dynamics at work within the joint area of operations: political, economic, social, cultural, religious. The joint stability force commander must have an understanding of who will oppose stabilization efforts and what motivates them to do so."[58] As one Iraqi general remarked, "If an Iraqi officer is talking to an American officer, he doesn't want to have a Kurd translating between them for many reasons. One, he finds it socially unacceptable. Two, he thinks it might be a security risk."[59]

There is no doubt that CF personnel serving in Afghanistan are operating in a foreign, and somewhat incomprehensible, culture. For example, Colonel Horn described the situation that a convoy in which he was riding faced in the spring of 2006. He wrote of the voyage, "The countryside was barren, desolate and harsh, yet held a strange beauty." He continued, "Similarly, the sentiments of the local population reflected a startling array of contrasts in stance and bearing. The old men gave the convoy scant attention or ignored it outright as if it did not even exist. They seemed to embody a stoicism, which radiated a resiliency and patience that carried a nuance that this too would pass." The Afghan children, Horn described, demonstrated a "carefree exuberance" as they ran by the road and waved to the passing convoy. In contrast, however, "the young and middle-aged men would glare — their hostility and resentment barely concealable." Yet, it remained, according to Horn, "virtually impossible to differentiate friend from foe…. the threat environment was extreme, yet non-existent." Without warning, the convoy was hit by a suicide bomber driving a Toyota sedan. There were no fatalities. In his discussion of the events, Horn aptly reflected that "It has long been recognized that culture is to insurgency what terrain is to conventional mechanized warfare. However, as already indicated, in the current defence environment it is sometimes difficult to breach the cultural barrier."[60]

Moreover, as Figure 4 illustrates, and as Horn observed, there are several different elements at play in the HN domain. HN populations can generally be divided into political, security, civilian, and belligerent elements. One of the goals of counterinsurgency operations is to remove the belligerents from the HN. Notably, as illustrated in the figure, belligerents can permeate the entire HN society including the political and security infrastructure. As Lieutenant-Colonel Shane Schreiber noted, "The Taliban have an excellent IO capability — they know what buttons to push; how to terrorize the people."[61] Politicians, security enforcement personnel, and locals can all be tempted to join the insurgency through intrinsic (sympathizing with the ideals/goals of the insurgents) or through extrinsic means (such as aligning with insurgents to protect yourself, family, clan, et cetera).

Understanding nuances in speech and gestures (helped by interpreters when necessary) can provide clues as to the presence of belligerents, which facilitates mobility on the ground. Good interpreters in Afghanistan are able to relay more than verbatim translations to the CF. They are also able to explain nuances that are missed by those with only a basic understanding of the language and are able to translate these into more meaningful messages. In fact, the message, through the means in which it is expressed (pauses, ambiguities, et cetera), might have less to do with what is being said and more to do with how it is being said.

Understanding cultural cues can also help you determine if an area is under the influence of the enemy and whether or not locals are "willingly" supporting insurgents. This can help you determine how to influence locals to appreciate your way of thinking. For example, in an area where insurgents are coercing locals to co-operate by threat of punishment, securing the area of operation and assuring the locals of your long-term commitment to them can help them side with you. But to accomplish this is a matter of building trust, which can only be earned through concrete action. If you lack a sound understanding of what is important and what behaviours will be seen as credible, their co-operation will be difficult to attain.

On the other hand, while national culture (often coupled with political directive) can sometimes supersede military culture, belief in a universal military ethos can help guide the training of HN militaries. Playing to this perceived commonality, or indeed establishing a shared cultural space based on membership in the profession of arms, aids in establishing unity of effort when training and working with HN forces. For example, most CF veterans of Afghanistan underscore the military potential of the ANA — an organization respected by the Afghan people — and recognize that the ANA is the future of Afghanistan; a well-trained and equipped ANA will allow foreign troops to withdraw and leave the stability of Afghanistan in capable hands.

Interestingly, when working with and training ANA members, CF members emphasize the shared cultural values of the profession of arms over unique national beliefs and values. A Canadian veteran noted of the ANA, "they're soldiers, they just want to soldier with you. It doesn't matter where soldiers are from, they're going to get together, they're going to try to communicate, they're going to break bread together. [Canadian] troops would be making friends with the Afghan troops … when people live together like that, they're bound to become friends."[62] Additionally, Afghan soldiers can provide unique assets. As U.S. Marine Corps Gunnery Sergeant Rilon Reall, a training adviser to an Afghan Kandak (infantry battalion), concluded, "They [Afghan National Army troops] are Afghans. They understood the language, the people and the religion. They hear things in the truest sense."[63]

Simply put, building trust and credibility take time and they are difficult tasks. As Lieutenant-Colonel Hope asserted, "You cannot win without the trust of the local people. And that is only done over time by sustaining a presence."[64] Additionally, to gain the trust of local populations you need to appreciate how others see you. Viewing yourself through the eyes of HN members while being aware of the environment (human and physical) will help you make good decisions when trying to influence HN peoples. Moreover, building trust and credibility for your mission will add support of the national government and can lead to stability and economic adjustment in the HN.

ENEMY DOMAIN

Knowing the Enemy

Unlike the Cold War where the enemy was predictable and easily identifiable, to the point where its behaviour, decisions, as well as its tactics, techniques, and procedures (TTPs) could be templated in time and space, today's enemy is an amalgam of opponents drawn from criminals, warlords, HN belligerents, radical religious extremists, idealogues, jihadists, mercenaries, and foreign state–sponsored combatants. As opposed to the symmetrical enemy of the Cold War, the new opposition relies on asymmetric means. They follow no standard organizational framework, abide by no international rules, and follow no standard doctrine. Rather they are decentralized, agile, and non-linear. They are networked and rely on advanced technology and the globalization of communications, specifically the internet and cell phone technology, to facilitate financing, planning, and the sharing of successful TTPs. As Major-General Scales pointed out, "the enemy we face is dedicated to TTPs unacceptable to Western nations. They are organized and networked, passionate and fanatical, committed, relentless and, by our standards, savage."[65] Moreover, their non-linear and asymmetric approach, in stark contrast to the symmetrical mind-set of the Cold War opponents, makes no distinction between civilian and military. As such, operations are conducted both among and against civilians and society at large. Lieutenant-Colonel Omer Lavoie described the situation in Afghanistan: "It's not a linear battlefield and it's much harder to measure progress. The enemy has all the assets of an insurgent. One minute he has a hoe in his hand, the next minute it's an AK-47."

Exacerbating the challenge of identifying "friend from foe" is the reality that in many cases, such as in Afghanistan, the belligerents permeate the entire society. Sympathizers, as well as active combatants, can actually exist within the security and political apparatus of a HN country. Additionally, as Lieutenant-Colonel Hope observed, "Taliban have amazing regenerative ability. You only really destroy them when you diminish them in the eyes of an Afghan."[66] Thus, attempting to operate within such an environment in a collaborative manner is difficult.

Moreover, conducting operations in an environment in which the enemy actively seeks to blend into the population and use this to their advantage places additional strain on coalition forces. Captain Matthew Dawe, killed by an improvised explosive device, had expressed feelings of anger and frustration about the mission at times. He felt betrayed by some of the people he was trying to help, describing some local Afghans as "farmers by day and Taliban or killers by night." Dawe further lamented, "That is what is particularly frustrating about this mission — it's a guerrilla war." He finished, "You don't really know who your enemy is."[67] Another veteran explained Afghans "could pretend to be eager and co-operative ditch shovellers [sic] to your face and turn into mine-planting Taliban insurgents behind your back."[68]

Certainly the Taliban will use every weakness of the coalition to their advantage, particularly to enhance their information operations (IO) campaign.[69] Every friendly fire incident, every civilian death or incident of collateral damage plays to the opposing side — namely, more evidence of the callous oppressive foreign invaders. As Major-General Scales commented, "The enemy clearly understands the war that he's involved in: win and hold cultural high ground — that is his objective — we're playing catch up."[70] In the case of Afghanistan this plays to the ancient tribal custom that has often been described as "my brother and I against my cousin. My cousin, my brother and I against the world." It also underscores the point that foreign troops will eventually go home; most insurgents are already home.

In essence, enhanced CQ offers one of the few possible solutions to this complex operating environment. Success in counterinsurgencies, specifically in locations such as Afghanistan, depends on winning the hearts and minds of the populace. In fact, the HN population is the centre of gravity for success in theatre (although an equally compelling case can be made for domestic support in regards to maintaining a respective national contingent in Afghanistan to prosecute the mission). As such, kinetic operations are not the answer. Although they are capable of killing opponents, the enemy has proven itself capable of quickly regenerating numbers to continue the fight. Therefore, it is the credibility and local support of the opposing forces that must be destroyed. This can only be achieved when the HN population shift their full support toward the national government and its coalition partners. However, this will only be achieved when they feel the national government and coalition are in a position to provide security and basic governmental services.

Nonetheless, winning hearts and minds is not the only important function of exhibiting high CQ when dealing with enemy forces. The enemy forces, as noted earlier, are not homogeneous. They all have disparate beliefs, motives, incentives, and rationales for fighting or opposing government authority and coalition forces. Therefore, CQ becomes essential for understanding the enemy whether it is used in conjunction with an IO campaign designed to discredit a particular opponent with a specific target audience; a targeting campaign that aims to understand how decisions are made and by whom; or an attack on alliances or support along tribal lines that takes advantage of historic tensions and animosities. A Canadian lieutenant commenting on the fight with Taliban said they are a worthy opponent because they are fighting on their "home turf," and, even more difficult to deal with, "they have the belief that they're doing the right thing. You're combating that ideology, so you can't underestimate them."[71]

Clearly, enlightened CQ is essential if a military force wishes to successfully defeat opposing forces, particularly in a complex security environment as is found today in places like Afghanistan or Iraq. Only by understanding the attitudes, beliefs, behaviours, motives, and values (to name but a few factors) of the enemy can a military be successful. With this knowledge friendly forces can begin to target enemy IO campaign, as well as kinetic and other operations, to erode the enemy's support and gain that of the host nation population.

BALANCING THE BALLS

Interactions Between the Four CQ Domains

Balancing the four CQ domains so that CQ can be an effective force multiplier is important. This does not mean that people should be cultural chameleons as they jump between each domain; rather, individuals need to balance the knowledge that they acquire of each domain and apply it in a manner that allows them to further their goals and to achieve the necessary and desired national objectives. For the CF, these goals should ultimately align with those of the Canadian government and population and should be reflective of Canadian cultural values. Balancing the four CQ domains is of critical importance because behaving appropriately in each cultural domain is essential for mission success.

IMPLICATIONS FOR LEADERSHIP

The ability for military leaders to be able to recognize what CQ is and to apply this knowledge as a force multiplier has many implications for mission success. CQ facilitates winning the *hearts of minds* of home and HN populations, as well as the co-operation of military allies, other IGOs and NGOs. Moreover, it can also help retain the support of military members.

CQ can be applied at the tactical, operational, and strategic levels. It is important when planning at any of these levels to be aware of the four CQ domains — national, international, host nation, and enemy — and to appreciate how they interact and contribute to mission success. Different levels of leadership may need to prioritize the attention paid to specific domains; however, a balance between all four is always necessary.

The CQ domain paradigm allows leaders to consciously address cultural gaps in knowledge with specific information concerning the various cultures they may face on operations. This can be done through a combination of strategies and methodologies such as programmed cultural awareness training; designated reading lists tapping scholarly studies, travel books, sociological and anthropological studies, and literary works; discussions among peers and veterans with specific country experience; and through role-playing. Notably, when learning cultural-specific information, it is important to try to see the world through the eyes of the group that you are examining. This skill will help leaders make appropriate decisions and will contribute to their ability to shift others to their way of thinking.

CONCLUSION

Today's complex security environment demands that soldiers are warriors and technicians as well as scholars and diplomats. Kinetic solutions are no longer the panacea of warfare. CQ, on the other hand, offers one of the few possible solutions to this new and complex operating environment.

In sum, CQ is the ability to recognize the shared beliefs, values, attitudes, and behaviours of a group of people and, most important, to apply this knowledge toward a specific goal. More specifically, CQ refers to the cognitive, motivational, and behavioural capacities to understand and effectively respond to the beliefs, values, attitudes, and behaviours of individuals and institutions of their own and other groups, societies, and cultures under complex and changing circumstances in order to effect a desired change. In particular, CQ must be applied in the context of the national, international, host nation, and enemy arenas and the focus must be on its ability to be a force multiplier.

Balancing the four CQ domains (i.e., national, international, host nation, and enemy) so that CQ can be an effective force multiplier is of paramount importance. This does not mean that people should alter their own beliefs and values as they jump between each domain; rather, individuals need to balance the knowledge that they require of each domain and apply it in a manner that allows them to further their goals and to achieve the necessary and desired national objectives. Indeed, enhanced CQ requires that individuals know their audience so that they may exhibit appropriate behaviours that achieve the desired objectives.

As such, CQ is a, if not the, key enabler to mission success in counterinsurgency. A particularly decisive point of counterinsurgency is the ability to influence both home and host nation populations to support the ruling governing entity and/or coalition and to deny the same support to the insurgents. In essence, it is a struggle to win the hearts and minds of the people. To do so, it is necessary to understand the various audiences and fully appreciate their attitudes, beliefs, customs, and values so that the attitudes, behaviours, and actions of the government and coalition forces do not alienate the population, and instead win their trust and support. This is easier said than done. However, CQ is a critical enabler in this process of solving the "people puzzle." Consequently, it is a vital attribute for military personnel in today's complex security environment.

Notes

1.   Lieutenant-Colonel Ian Hope in a professional development presentation for the Canadian Forces Leadership Institute at the Canadian Defence Academy, Kingston, Ontario, November 2006.

2.   Cited in Frank G. Hoffman, "Principles for the Savage Wars of Peace," in Anthony McIvor, *Rethinking the Principles of War* (Annapolis: Naval Institute Press, 2005), 304.

3.   Brigadier-General David Fraser, former commander, ISAF Multinational Brigade Sector South, Kandahar, Afghanistan, presentation at the Canadian Infantry Association Annual General Meeting, Edmonton, 25 May 2007.

4.   There are several different terminologies used to express the advantageous use of cultural knowledge. These terms include, but are not limited to, cultural savvy, cultural astuteness, cultural literacy, cultural appreciation, cultural expertise, human terrain, cultural awareness, cultural competency, and cross-cultural competence. There are also many different proposed acronyms for cultural intelligence, for example, CI, CULTINT, and CQ.

CQ draws parallels to the more commonly used term Intelligence Quotient, or IQ. IQ is based on the early twentieth-century findings of German psychologist William Stern that the mental age to chronological age remains relatively constant throughout one's life. This suggests that an individual's IQ does not change throughout his or her lifetime. "What Does IQ Stand for and What does It Mean?" Accessed at *www.geocities.com/rnseitz/Definition_of_IQ.html* (accessed 14 July 2007).

The way that CQ is used in this chapter, however, does directly argue that individuals can increase their CQ with knowledge and the motivation to apply that knowledge toward a specific goal. Indeed, P. Christopher Earley and Soon Ang, the originators of the term, are also clear on this point. They write, "We use the shorthand label of CQ as a convenience to remind the reader that this is a facet of intelligence. However, we do not use CQ in a strict fashion as is implied by 'IQ'; that is, we do not mean to denote a mathematical relationship generated from normative data of capability. In this sense, our usage parallels that from the literature on emotional intelligence and their usage of 'EQ.'" P. Christopher Earley and Soon Ang, *Cultural Intelligence: Individual Interactions Across Cultures* (Stanford: Stanford Business Books, 2003), 4.

Cultural intelligence and the acronym CQ were chosen for this chapter for the same reason that Early and Ang chose to use the term: CQ stresses the intelligence component of cultural intelligence. Notably, however, CQ does not limit the concept to a strictly mathematical calculation of a static competency. Moreover, whatever the label one applies to the concept, in the end, the issue is to determine what enables people to function effectively in cultural settings.

5. Both CQ and the Four CQ Domain Paradigm will be further explained later in this chapter.

6. Farewell Message, U.S. Army Chief of Staff General Peter J. Schoomaker, thirty-fifth chief of staff of the U.S. Army.

7. Lieutenant Ian Hope, "Reflections on Afghanistan: Commanding Task Force Orion," in Bernd Horn, ed., *In Harm's Way: The Buck Stops Here, Senior Commanders on Operations* (Winnipeg: Canadian Defence Academy Press, 2007), 211.

8. George W. Smith, "Avoiding a Napoleonic Ulcer: Bridging the Gap of Cultural Intelligence," *A Common Perspective*, May 2006, Vol. 14, No. 1, 23. Accessed at *www.dtic.mil/doctrine/jel/comm_per/common_perspective.htm*.

9. P.M. Zeman, "Goat-Grab: Diplomacy in Iraq," *Proceedings*, November (2005), 20.

10. Robert H. Scales Jr., "Culture-Centric Warfare," *Proceedings*, October (2004), 32.

11. Lorenzo Puertas, "Corporal Jones and the Moment of Truth," *Proceedings*, November (2004), 44.

12. Smith, "Avoiding a Napoleonic Ulcer," 11.

13. Puertas, "Corporal Jones and the Moment of Truth," 43.

14. Roger Noble, "The Essential Thing: Mission Command and its Practical Application," *Command Papers*, Australian Defence College, May 2007, 4.

15. Major-General Andrew Leslie (Deputy Commander ISAF, 2002), CFLI interview, 8 February 2006.

16. Bernd Horn (Ed.), *From the Outside Looking In: Media and Defence Analyst Perspectives on Canadian Military Leadership* (Kingston: Canadian Defence Academy Press, 2005), 1.

17. Major-General Robert Scales, presentation at Cognitive Dominance Workshop, West Point, 11 July 2006.

18. Smith, "Avoiding a Napoleonic Ulcer," 12.

19. Department of Defense. Joint Operating Environment. Trends & Challenges for the Future Joint Force Through 2030 (Norfolk, VA: USJFCOM, December 2007), 12.

20. Allan D. English, *Understanding Military Culture: A Canadian Perspective* (Montreal: McGill-Queen's University Press, 2004), 12. Notably, there is long-standing debate about the nature and definition of culture. The 2006 American counterinsurgency manual, for example, contrasts cultural and social structures. It explains: "Social structure comprises the relationships among groups, institutions, and individuals within a society; in contrast, culture (ideas, norms, rituals, codes of behavior) provide meaning to individuals within the society." It defines culture as a "'web of meaning' shared by members of a particular society or group within a society." The manual explains this definition in terms of people's identity, beliefs, values,

attitudes, perceptions, and belief systems. It also emphasize that cultural knowledge about insurgents, as far as the military is concerned, should be exploited to be used to further U.S. national objectives. *Counterinsurgency*, 3–6, 3–8.

21. Adapted from English, *Understanding Military Culture*, 12.
22. *Ibid.*, 11–12.
23. Edward Luttwak, "Dead End: Counterinsurgency Warfare as Military Malpractice," *Harper's*, February 2007, 35.
24. English, *Understanding Military Culture*, 11.
25. *Ibid.*, 12–14.
26. U.S. DoD, *Afghan Cultural Field Guide*, MCIA-2630-AFG-001–04, November 2003, 24.
27. U.S. DoD, *Afghanistan Country Handbook, DoD-2630-AFG-018–03*, October 2003, 31.
28. Center for Advanced Operational Culture Learning (CAOCL), *Afghanistan: Operational Culture for Deploying Personnel* (CAOCL: Quantico, August 2006), 8.
29. English, *Understanding Military Culture*, 24.
30. Geopolitics looks at the relationships between politics, economics, and geography, both human and physical.
31. Samuel P. Huntington, *The Clash of Civilizations: Remaking of World Order* (New York: Touchstone, 1996), 29.
32. *Ibid.*, 21.
33. *Ibid.*
34. *Ibid.*
35. P. Christopher Earley and Elaine Mosakowski, "Cultural Intelligence," *Harvard Business Review* October (2004), 139–40.
36. Earley and Ang, *Cultural Intelligence: Individual Interactions Across Cultures*, 59, 67.
37. Earley and Peterson, "The Elusive Cultural Chameleon," 105.
38. James P. Johnson, Tomasz Lenartowicz, and Salvador Apud, "Cross-Cultural Competence in International Business," *Journal of International Business Studies*, Vol. 37, No. 4 (2006), 525–44; and David C. Thomas, "Domain and Development of Cultural Intelligence: The Importance of Mindfulness," *Group & Organization Management*, Vol. 31, No. 1 (2006), 78–96.
39. Earley and Ang, *Cultural Intelligence*, 12.
40. *Ibid.*, 94.
41. Center for Advanced Defence Studies Staff, "Cultural Intelligence and the United States Military," in *Defence Concepts Series* (Washington, DC, July 2006), 1.
42. Leonard Wong, Stephen Gerras, William Kidd, Robert Pricone, and Richard Swengros, "Strategic Leadership Competencies," *Report*, U.S. Department of the Army, 7.
43. John P. Coles, "Incorporating Cultural Intelligence Into Joint Doctrine," *IOSphere: Joint Information Operation Center*, Spring (2006), 7.
44. This definition as well as the concept of the four CQ domain paradigm was developed by the author after consulting multiple sources that explore CQ.
45. Interview with Colonel Fred Lewis by Adam Day, *Legion Magazine*, November 2006.
46. Licia Corbella, *Winnipeg Sun*, 2 May 2007, 9.
47. A recent Department of National Defence Report states that the "standing [with the Canadian public] of the Canadian Forces has clearly risen since the Somalia scandal thanks to a general alignment between military values and Canadian values." Cited in Allan Woods, *Toronto Star*, 19 May 2007.

48. See for example, Horn, "Full Spectrum Leadership," 206–07; Sayed Salahuddin, "Airstrikes Kill Scores of Afghan Civilians," Yahoo News, *http://news,yahoo.com/s/ nm/20070707/wl_nm/afghan_violence_dc_3* (accessed 7 July 2007); and Greg Weston, "Battle for Public Opinion Desire to Have Troops Withdraw from Combat in Afghanistan Growing, Polls Show," *Winnipeg Sun,* 24 June 2007, 13; and "Opposition Leaders Unite as War Toll Mounts," *Edmonton Sun,* 5 July 2007, 38.

49. John Geddes, "Canada in Combat," *Maclean's,* 15 March 2006, *www.macleans.ca/ topstories/world/article.jsp?content=20060320_123596_123596.*

50. Michael Ignatieff, *Virtual War: Ethical Challenges* (Annapolis: United States Naval Academy, March 2001), 7.

51. Lieutenant-General James N. Mattis, *Ethical Challenges in Contemporary Conflict: The Afghanistan and Iraq Cases* (Annapolis: United States Naval Academy, March 2001), 11.

52. Captain Allan Best in an email to the author received 17 March 2007.

53. This point was mentioned by Lieutenant-Colonel Ian Hope in a professional development presentation for the Canadian Forces Leadership Institute at the Canadian Defence Academy, Kingston, Ontario, November 2006.

54. Elizabeth Baldwin-Jones, Deputy Director, Regional Security, Foreign Affairs and International Trade Canada, emphasized this point in an address at the 2007 Women Leading in Defence Symposium, "Gender Matters: Leadership and the Changing Defence Environment," held in Ottawa on 6 March 2007. Her talk dealt mainly with the relationship between personnel from Foreign Affairs and International Trade Canada and CF members who were working in Afghanistan in 2006.

55. Bernd Horn, "Full Spectrum Leadership Challenges in Afghanistan," in Bernd Horn, ed., *In Harms Way: The Buck Stops Here,* 197–98.

56. *Ibid.*

57. Vertefeuille, "Civil-Military Operations," 188.

58. Smith, "Avoiding a Napoleonic Ulcer," 23.

59. Michael Burnett, "Speaking the Language: Warfighters Listen for Translation Support," *Special Operations Technology,* Vol. 6, No. 3, April 2008, 14.

60. Colonel Bernd Horn, "'Outside the Wire' — Some Leadership Challenges in Afghanistan," *Canadian Military Journal* 7, No. 3 (Autumn 2006), 6–14.

61. Lieutenant-Colonel Shane Schreiber, ACOS, Multinational Brigade HQ, 1 CMBG briefing, 22 January 2007.

62. Interviews conducted by Dr. Emily Spencer at CFB Edmonton, January 2007.

63. Renata D'Alesio, "Afghan Troops Key to Victory," CanWest News Service, TF 3–06 BG Notable News, *http://veritas.mil.ca/showfile.asp?Lang=E&URL=/Clips/National/ 061023/f00860DN.htm* (accessed 23 October 2006).

64. Adnan R. Khan, "I'm Here to Fight: Canadian Troops in Kandahar," *Maclean's* , 5 April 2006, *www.macleans.ca/topstories/world/article.jsp?content=20060403_124448_124448* (accessed 18 July 2006).

65. Major-General Robert Scales, presentation at "Cognitive Dominance Workshop," West Point, 11 July 2006.

66. Lieutenant-Colonel Ian Hope, presentation at the Canadian Infantry Association Annual General Meeting, 25 May 2007.

67. Cited in Meagan Fitzpatrick, "Slain Son Believed in Mission: Family of Captain Dawe Describes His Commitment, His Frustrations," *National Post,* 12 July 2007, A4.

68. Cited by Don Martin, *Calgary Herald,* 14 July 2007, A17.
69. The NATO definition for information operations is "Info Ops is a military function to provide advice and co-ordination of military information activities in order to create desired effects on the will, understanding and capability of adversaries, potential adversaries and other NAC approved parties in support of Alliance mission objectives." Colonel (Retired) W.N. Peters, *Shifting to the Moral Plane: The Canadian Approach to Information Operations* (Kingston: Canadian Forces Leadership Institute Technical Report, 2007), 20–21.
70. Major-General Robert Scales, presentation at "Cognitive Dominance Workshop," West Point, 11 July 2006.
71. Interviews conducted by Dr. Emily Spencer at Canadian Forces Base Edmonton, January 2007.

5

DEFINING TERRORISM

Bernd Horn

THE TOPIC OF INSURGENCY has taken on dramatic importance in the Western world since at least 2004. The militaries, think tanks, and media pundits in the Unites States, United Kingdom, and Canada, for example, have focused on this methodology of conflict with a vigour that would make one think it was a new phenomenon.[1] Insurgency, however, defined by American military doctrine as "an organized movement aimed at the overthrow of a constituted government through the use of subversion and armed conflict,"[2] or what scholars have described as a "struggle between a non-ruling group and the ruling authorities in which the non-ruling group consciously uses political resources (e.g., organizational expertise, propaganda and demonstrations) and violence to destroy, reformulate, or sustain the basis of legitimacy," is timeless.[3]

It just so happens that, at the moment, insurgency affects us more directly. Our national blood and treasure and that of the United States and United Kingdom are inextricably caught up in waging a counterinsurgency in Afghanistan and, for the United States and United Kingdom, in Iraq as well. But there is even more involved. The conflict being waged in those countries is only one dimension of the greater confrontation. The terrorist attack using hijacked fully fuelled commercial airliners as munitions to strike the Twin Towers of the World Trade Centre in New York, and the Pentagon in Washington, DC, ushered in a new reality. It was the day the world changed, to paraphrase the words of the influential *Economist* magazine.

This dramatic description is not undeserved. Aside from approximately 3,000 deaths and billions of dollars in damages, 9/11 set off a chain of events that have changed the face of the global security environment. Its impact ranged from new threats, to clear responses to both the real and perceived perils that nations, particularly those in North America and Europe, faced. Although terrorist acts were not unknown, the sheer savagery and magnitude of the 9/11 attack, as well as its complex planning indicated that terrorists were prepared to use new and innovative weapons of mass destruction. Moreover, the suicide bomber now provided the ultimate smart munitions — capable of deciding how, when, and, particularly, who to strike.

The Americans reacted by unleashing a Global War On Terror (GWOT) that engulfed them and their international allies in a deadly struggle in Afghanistan, Iraq, and around the world. But the unchallenged military prowess of the United States and its allies dictated that hostile elements, in many ways representing an international insurgency, had to adopt asymmetric approaches.[4] Importantly, easily accessible technology, international communications, and information technology, fuelled well-financed, extremely mobile, and lethal terrorist networks capable of striking around the world.

Quite simply, terrorism became a tactic of choice both in the regional insurgencies in Afghanistan and Iraq, and in the larger global insurgency. However, this should neither be surprising, nor new, since terrorism has always been a favoured tool of insurgents. For the weak, terrorism is a core part of insurgency. Indeed, terrorism has become a centrepiece of attention for most western countries, particularly the United States. Much of this is because of the savagery and scale of attack, as well as the symbolic nature of the strike on North American soil that 9/11 presented. As such, international terrorism and the growing threat of homegrown terrorists has become a major agenda item. But what exactly is terrorism?[5]

This chapter is intended as primer on terrorism. Additionally, it will link the concept of terrorism to insurgency. Moreover, it will highlight how the definition and application of terrorism is evolving in today's security environment.

As such, the now largely defunct term GWOT was somewhat of a misnomer. Terrorism is not a cause. It is a tool, an instrument, a tactic to achieve specific objectives. For example, terrorist attacks, particularly suicide-triggered events, create fear and uncertainty within a population, and among counterinsurgency forces. These types of attack also garner high-profile media attention, which gives them an image, both within the theatre of operations and abroad, of an inflated insurgent capability. In this way, terrorism is used as a means to achieve an end. Arguably, however, many scholars are now arguing that terrorism is also a form of struggle, if not an ideology. Some analysts believe that terrorism is a tactic, a strategy, and a way of life — all at same time. Notably, Ariel Sharon, a former prime minister of Israel stated "there is no good terrorism or bad terrorism. There is only terrorism."[6]

The concept of terrorism itself has many definitions. Walter Laqueur, an internationally renowned expert on terrorism and insurgency, asserts that "terrorism constitutes the illegitimate use of force to achieve a political objective when innocent people are targeted."[7] Similarly Benjamin Netanyahu, a former special operations soldier and prime minister of Israel, defined terrorism as "the deliberate and systemic assault on civilians to inspire fear for political ends."[8] In a similar vein, Brian Jenkins stated: "Terrorism is the use or threatened use of force designed to bring about political change."[9] Finally, scholar Michael Walzer described terrorism as "the random killing of innocent people, in the hope of creating pervasive fear." He added, "The fear can serve many political purposes. Randomness and innocence are crucial elements in the definition."[10]

The American Federal Bureau of Investigation (FBI) definition states, "Terrorism is the unlawful use of force and violence against persons or property to intimidate or coerce a government, the civilian population, or any segment thereof, in furtherance of political or social objectives."[11] The U.S. Departments of State and Defense define terrorism as "premeditated, politically motivated violence perpetrated against a noncombatant target by sub-national groups or clandestine state agents, usually intended to influence an audience."[12] Within the context of NATO, terrorism is defined as "the unlawful use or threatened use of force or violence against individuals or property in an attempt to coerce or intimidate governments or societies to achieve political, religious or ideological objectives."[13]

Similarly the Canadian Criminal Code defines terrorism as:

> An act or omission, inside or outside Canada, that is committed for a political, religious, or ideological purpose, objective or cause, and with the intention of intimidating the public, with regard to its security, including its economic security or compelling a person, a government, or a domestic or an international organization to do or to refrain from doing any act, whether the public or the person, government, or organization is inside or outside Canada, and that intentionally causes death or serious bodily harm to a person by the use of violence, endangers a person's life, causes a serious risk to the health or safety of the public or any segment of the public, causes substantial property damage, whether to public or private property, if causing such damage is likely to result in the conduct or harm referred to above, or causes serious interference with or serious disruption of an essential service, facility, or system, whether public or private, other than as a result of advocacy, protest, dissent, or stoppage of work that is not intended to result in the conduct or harm referred to above, and includes a conspiracy, attempt, or threat to commit any such act or omission, or being an accessory after the fact or counseling in relation to any such act or omission.[14]

Clearly, there are many different definitions of terrorism. More important, these definitions all have core components that are essential to understand to fully comprehend the concept of terrorism:

- it is unlawful;
- it is politically (and ideologically) motivated (not criminal i.e., for personal financial gain);
- it is premeditated (not an impulsive act of rage);
- it is directed against innocents;
- it is meant to cause fear and terror;
- the violence is actually directed to impact others (i.e., not specifically the victims); and

- its actions are decidedly outside the accepted limits imposed on the use of force in warfare (i.e., the targeting of non-combatants). This gives rise to its asymmetric nature.

In the end, the general purpose of terrorism is to alter behaviour and attitudes of specific groups. However, this is not to rule out the use of terrorism to achieve immediate objectives that assist in achieving larger goals (e.g., taking hostages for ransom; to force the release of prisoners; to gain publicity; to instill fear and panic; to force the government into draconian and repressive actions that will alienate society and cause a loss of popular support; to create the impression of anarchy and a state incapable of protecting its citizens; and/or to coerce a government to taking policy decisions or actions against its will).

Examples of acts of terrorism abound. A Dutch court that examined pre-recorded martyr videos as part of a terrorist plot trial in that country concluded that the martyrdom operations were specifically intended "to strike fear into the Dutch people."[15] Moreover, the attack on four Spanish commuter trains on 11 March 2004, when 10 bombs exploded just before rush hour killing 190 people and injuring hundreds of others, had an enormous impact on that country's population. The terrorist attack, compounded by the effect of media coverage, effectively planted fear in the hearts of the Spanish people and forced a change of government, sweeping Spanish Prime Minister José Maria Azmar from office.[16] It also led to the withdrawal of Spanish troops from Iraq. Two years prior, in December 2003, an Islamic website had already predicted:

> We think that the Spanish government could not tolerate more than two, maximum three blows, after which it will have to withdraw as a result of popular pressure. If its troops still remain in Iraq after those blows, then the victory of the Socialist Party is almost secured, and the withdrawal of the Spanish forces will be on its electoral programme.[17]

More recently, the June 2006 capture of two American soldiers near Yusufiya, Iraq provided insurgents with an opportunity to terrorize the population and their enemy. Members of the Al-Hesbah forum encouraged the creation of videos capturing the beheading of the U.S. soldiers. "It is preferable that the slaughter process is slow so we can feel the joy of it and to put fear in the enemies' souls," they insisted.[18]

One final example is the use of night letters by the Taliban. A printed one-page missive distributed in southeastern Afghanistan in May 2008 in the name of the "Afghanistan Islamic Emirate Khost Jihadi Military Front" warned "all residents in Khost" that:

> Tribal elders should not consider the U.S. stronger than Allah and not give verdicts against mujahidin; otherwise you will soon regret it.
>
> Those who spy and work for the infidel government and military forces should quit their jobs by 20 June; otherwise they will see something which they have never seen in their lives.
>
> Do not get close to the infidel forces at any time or in any place.
>
> During attacks on government and infidel forces, you should keep yourselves safe and not provide support for them; if this rule is violated, your death will be the same as the death of the U.S. and their puppets.
>
> Our mines are live; we do not allow the killing of civilians, but you should not show them to the infidels and their slaves. We will show our power to those who show our land mines to them or inform them about us.
>
> When you see infidel forces on the street and roads, stop where you are and do not go forward.
>
> Those mullahs who perform funerals for those who are killed in the campaign — national army, national and border police and intelligence — will be killed with torture; and remember: such a mullah will never be forgiven.[19]

These examples demonstrate the intended, as well as the actual, impact of terrorist tactics. They show that terrorism is purposeful. Those agents practising it intend to achieve specific outcomes, which may follow a carefully designed campaign plan intended to meet short, mid, and long-term objectives. The end purpose, as already mentioned, is to change the political or decision-making framework of the target state or community. The use of terrorist tactics is a direct result of the imbalance in power and military means between the antagonists. As such, terrorism is intended to erode the psychological support of the targeted regime by instilling fear (if not terror) in the population, government officials, as well as domestic and international supporters. Consequently, it is often a core component and tool of the insurgent.

Terrorism in the new security environment, despite all the efforts to prevent it, has endless possibilities for insurgents. Globalization, particularly the explosion in communications, international travel, and financing, as well as easy access to information and information technology, has made it easier for terrorists to operate. At one point American intelligence estimated that Al Qaeda (AQ) had the support of approximately 7,000,000 radical Muslims across the globe with more than 100,000 martyrs prepared to die for the cause. Moreover, they believed that Al Qaeda had about 1,000 sleeper cells in the United States and Europe.[20]

Although terrorism is not a new tactic, many scholars now argue that the motives of terrorists have changed. Where before 9/11 many terrorist groups conducted acts to seek publicity and support for their cause, without necessarily trying to inflict massive casualties on civilians, actions in the new millennium have increasingly focused on exactly that. Arguably, a major motive for terrorists in the new security environment is not only to mobilize support for a cause but also to punish those deemed responsible for perceived injustices, whether economic, ideological, political or religious. "The primary motive now seems to be to strike major damaging physical and psychological blows against their enemies, not just to defeat a regime outright or to compel them to meet the terrorists' demands," insists Professor David Charters, "rather it is to punish the target for being wrong."[21]

More foreboding is the evolution that terrorism and those who practice it are taking. Counterterrorist experts explain that it is often difficult to determine who we are now fighting as there is not always a clear identification of the enemy. For example, AQ is morphing into an ideology, a virtual network of networks. In fact, AQ is now the face of over a dozen Jihadist organizations that act alike. They are like-minded terrorists and insurgents who have trained with AQ and developed bonds. Moreover, they aspire to be like AQ in terms of influence and impact.

The new terrorists are also extremely intelligent and conflict savvy.[22] They are well versed in information operations and the use of information technology. For example, AQ makes a new video every three days to assist in spreading their message, eliciting support, and attracting recruits. Some experts see the enemy much like a virus that continually changes and adapts — terrorist cells that divide and separate, always transforming in the process. Ominously, the new insurgents/terrorists have proven to be resilient and fully capable of maintaining both physical and virtual sanctuaries (e.g., internet and the Federally Administered Tribal Areas (FATA)).

Counterterrorist experts have attempted to delineate the new terrorists. They have found that the new generation of terrorists is largely composed of individuals or cells (without necessarily having command linkage to a larger organization such as AQ). They are fluid and independent and use a bottom up leadership approach. They meet on the internet (which provides them with motivation, inspiration, and means) and are often physically disconnected. Finally, the new generation of terrorists has shifted to an ideological global Jihad or insurgency. Mustafa Setmariam Nasar, an important radical Islamist ideologue promoting a global jihad, has argued, "The future generation of international jihadists will form a fluid, non-hierarchical movement of autonomous armed groups instigating simultaneous armed struggle."[23]

Another important point of note is the one resounding legacy that the AQ has imparted on the world: its redefinition of jihad. Where jihad had previously been identified with freedom fighters in combat areas such as Bosnia and Afghanistan, this type of holy war has more recently, largely as a result of Osama bin Laden, become synonymous with the use of terrorism against innocent targets. As mentioned earlier, terrorists are no longer content just to have many people watching — now they want many people dead. Quite simply, to prosecute their global insurgency, whether regionally or internationally, they see terrorism as the tool and binding ideology that will bleed the West to exhaustion by prompting intervention all around the world, and forcing it to create the necessary infrastructure, organizations, policies, and processes to safeguard homelands and international travel and commerce.[24]

Today, to understand insurgency and hope to counter it, one must comprehend terrorism and its central role in insurgencies, whether regional or global.[25] As distasteful as terrorism is, it is undeniably a pervasive tactic of the weak — one that stretches the capabilities, patience, and professionalism, if not humanity, of the counterinsurgency forces and governments in power. Understanding terrorism, its strengths and weaknesses, as well as the motives of those who use it, are the first steps to countering it.

NOTES

1. Scholars have identified four waves of terrorism: First, the anarchism of the late 1890s; second, anti-colonialism after the Second World War; third, the leftist wave of the 1970s; and forth, the religious wave that has replaced Marxism as the leading radical ideology today in the Arab world. See Angela Gendron, "Al Qaeda: Propaganda and Media Strategy," *ITAC Trends in Terrorism Series*, No. 2, 2007.

2. U.S. Army Combined Arms Center, *Counterinsurgency FM 3–24* (Washington, DC: Department of the Army, June 2006), 1–1.

3. Bard E. O'Neill, *Insurgency & Terrorism: Inside Modern Revolutionary Warfare* (Washington, DC: Brassey's Inc., 1990), 13.

4. American strategist Steven Metz explained that "In the realm of military affairs and national security asymmetry is acting, organizing, and thinking differently than opponents in order to maximize one's own advantages, exploit an opponent's weaknesses, attain the initiative, or gain greater freedom of action. It can be political-strategic, military-strategic, operational, or a combination of these. It can entail different methods, technologies, values, organizations, time perspectives, or some combination of these. It can be short-term or long-term. It can be deliberate or by default. It can be discrete or pursued in conjunction with symmetric approaches. It can have both psychological and physical dimensions." Steven Metz and Douglas V. Johnson II, "Asymmetry and US Military Strategy: Definition, Background, and Strategic Concepts," U.S. Army War College, Strategic Studies Institute, January 2001, 5–6. Doctrinally, an asymmetric threat is a concept "used to describe attempts to circumvent or undermine an opponent's strengths while exploiting his weaknesses, using methods that differ significantly from the opponent's usual mode of operations." See Colonel W.J. Fulton, DNBCD, "Capabilities Required of DND, Asymmetric Threats and Weapons of Mass Destruction," (Fourth Draft), 18 March 2001, 2/22. Dr. John Cowan explained that "the asymmetry arises in part from our lack of preparedness for such threats, but also because the asymmetric techniques

exploit fundamental freedoms in the target societies which are viewed in every other context as strengths, not weaknesses." Dr. John S. Cowan, "The Asymmetric Threat," unpublished paper presented to the Canadian Defence Scientific Advisory Board (DSAB), March 2003.

5. The word *terrorism* comes from the Latin word for *dread*. It was first used to describe the "Reign of Terror" during the French Revolution, 1789–94. Blair Shewchuk, "Backlash of Bigotry: Terrorism After the Attack," CBC News online, *http://cc.msncache.com/cache.aspx?q=522http+www+cbc+ca+news=indepth=wor*ds (accessed 2 September 2008).

6. Quoted in Andrew Sinclair, *An Anatomy of Terror* (London: Pan Books, 2003), 362.

7. Barry Davies, *Terrorism. Inside a World Phenomenon* (London: Virgin, 2003), 14.

8. Benjamin Netanyahu, *Fighting Terrorism* (New York: Noonday Press, 1995), 8.

9. Barry Davies, 14.

10. Michael Walzer, "Terrorism and Just War," *Philosophia*, Vol. 34, No. 1 (January 2006), 3.

11. Roger W. Barnett, *Asymmetric Warfare* (Washington, DC: Brassey's Inc., 2003), 16.

12. John P. Holms, *Terrorism* (New York: Pinnacle Books, 2001), 20.

13. NATO Allied Administrative Publication 6, 2002, quoted in "Countering Terrorism: The U.K. Approach to the Military Contribution," Joint Doctrine & Concept Centre (London: MOD, no date), 7.

14. *Criminal Code of Canada*, S. 83.01

15. Gendron, "Al Qaeda: Propaganda and Media Strategy."

16. Anthony H. Cordesman, *The Ongoing Lessons of Afghanistan: Warfighting, Intelligence, Force Transformation and Nation Building* (Washington, DC: Center for Strategic and International Studies, 2004), 127.

17. *Ibid.*

18. Jane's Information Group, "Fourth Generation Warfare and the International Jihad," *Jane's Intelligence Review,* 1 October 2006.

19. Quoted in International Crisis Group, *Taliban Propaganda: Winning the War of Words,* Asia Report No. 158, 24 July 2008, 20.

20. Quoted in Andrew Sinclair, *An Anatomy of Terror* (London: Pan Books, 2003), 367.

21. David Charters and G.F. Walker, *After 9/11: Terrorism and Crime in a Globalised World* (Fredericton: Centre for Conflict Studies, 2004), 15.

22. It should be noted that not all insurgents are terrorists, but all terrorists are insurgents.

23. Jane's Information Group, "Fourth Generation Warfare." It is interesting to note that Walter Laqueur, emphasized, "terrorists originated not in the poorest and most neglected districts but hailed from places with concentrations of radical preachers. The backwardness, if any, was intellectual and cultural — not economic and social." Walter Laqueur, "The Terrorism to Come," paper promulgated as co-chair of the International Research Council at the Center for Strategic and International Studies.

24. The previous three paragraphs are based on discussions and presentations at the International Special Operations Force conference in Tampa Florida, 22 May 2008 and include the presentation of ideas of such individuals as Dr. David Kilcullen, Sebastian Gorka and Dr. Rohan Gunaratna.

25. The way ahead is difficult. The experts state that 95 percent of strategic counterinsurgency is changing the environment we live in. There are a number of approaches:

- establish an ideological response (i.e., counter the beliefs of the deviant groups);
- develop an educational response (e.g., work with madrassas);
- media response;
- financial and economic assistance;
- partnerships (i.e., allied and whole of government approach);
- military approach (but with a small footprint — SOF approach);
- focus on Western asymmetric advantage — technology, intelligence/intellect, relationships; and
- patient-persistent responses (i.e., take the fight to the enemy, continuous pressure, exploit fissures, deny sanctuary (physical and virtual), prevent regeneration, and use an indirect and clandestine approach in coordination with a global network).

6

OPERATIONAL ALCHEMY IN NORTHERN IRELAND:

The Mutually Enabling Relationship Between SOF and Intelligence

Andrew Brown

COUNTERINSURGENCY (COIN) IS A particularly difficult form of warfare in which insurgents frequently have the advantage of dictating when and where the fighting occurs. Indeed, as these irregular soldiers typically fight from a position of military inferiority, insurgents have little choice but to try and impose the terms of battle, at least during the beginning of an insurrection. After all, insurgency is a struggle of the weak against the strong.

Insurgent campaigns seek to weaken an established political power's legitimacy and control with a view toward establishing a new political authority. Because of their relative military weakness, insurgents mobilize concurrently on as many lines of operation as possible. These include: political campaigns; appeals to the religious and/or ethnic attitudes and values of the target society; economic levers; and military operations. Moreover, as is witnessed by their callousness to collateral damage such as non-combatant deaths, insurgents are not constrained by such codes as the Laws of Armed Conflict or the semblance of human decency. They willingly strike wherever they feel they can achieve their tactical and strategic ends, with little concern for those caught in the crossfire. In fact, insurgents most often hide among the population, their ability to do so being their greatest advantage, emerging to attack vulnerable points only when prospects for success are high. All of this occurs on an extended timeline, the logic being that the established political power can neither afford, nor justify, military operations indefinitely and can therefore be worn down. Insurgents recognize that time is on their side.[1]

For their part, COIN forces seek to use all elements of national power to uphold the established political structure and squash the insurgency. To this end, COIN may include "military, paramilitary, political, economic, psychological, and civic actions taken by a government to defeat insurgency."[2]

Key to the local government's success is maintaining or winning the centre of gravity of an insurgency: the people. This goal requires that the established political authority ensures the population's welfare and security through a comprehensive program that synchronizes a wide spectrum of political, social, and military means. In addition, the local government's military forces are obliged to exercise a great deal of discretion in the application of force so as not to cause collateral damage and thus alienate the local population by causing unintended harm or by seemingly legitimizing insurgent claims that the governing power is callous to the well-being of its citizens or, at a minimum, unable or unwilling to ensure the safety of its people.

As such, to retain the local population's support, COIN forces must engage insurgents in ways that minimize collateral damage and avoid draconian measures. Given the complexity of COIN activity, it stands to reason that the highly focused and precisely controlled effects produced by special operations forces are a logical part of the solution.

Nonetheless, SOF is not a silver bullet. Its effectiveness is entirely dependent on being able to determine precisely in time and space where the enemy should be engaged and to make these predictions a reality. Therefore, high-quality intelligence plays a vital role in enabling SOF COIN operations.

Conversely, just as SOF depends on high-quality intelligence from outside sources, there are times when SOF personnel are the best suited to ascertain sensitive information. For example, SOF expertise and training can be invaluable in facilitating intelligence collection in theatres where the consequences of being compromised may be deadly for those collecting intelligence.[3] Moreover, SOF is an ideal intelligence sensor that can be deployed in high-risk areas for extended periods, providing reliable observation and surveillance services to intelligence fusion centres.

In short, finding and striking elusive insurgent targets with fine precision that avoids incurring civilian casualties is made possible when a close relationship between intelligence and SOF exists. This was certainly the case in Northern Ireland after 1969, where the often invisible but fiercely determined Irish Republican Army (IRA)[4] created a difficult tactical situation for British forces. Indeed, the conflict in Northern Ireland demonstrated that SOF and intelligence are mutually enabling elements that, when working in conjunction, play a critical role in defeating insurgency. As such, the nature of the mutually enabling relationship between SOF and intelligence is worth examining in the context of Northern Ireland.

Although the British Army had the benefit of much experience fighting insurgents abroad before the restarting of the "Troubles" in 1969, the campaign in Northern Ireland was fought on British soil where operations were even more carefully examined by the government and under the close scrutiny of the judicial system. Moreover, intensive domestic media inquiry further complicated the situation by making military mistakes, which are inevitable to some degree in any major campaign, look far worse than they actually were.[5] Additionally, British forces, including the Special Air Service, SAS, were restrained in their use of force and bound by the rules of engagement articulated on the "yellow card" issued to all soldiers. These rules demanded that only minimum force be employed. Soldiers were authorized to fire only if fired upon first, or if they believed beyond all reasonable doubt that their lives were in danger — and, even then, if possible, a warning shot was to proceed any type of engagement.

Although such rules were designed to protect the public from irresponsible shootings, they were a burden on soldiers who had to abide by them in the most ambiguous of circumstances.[6] The difficulty of the situation was further underscored because the effective British tactic in Third World nations of separating the insurgents from the population by moving entire communities into protected areas, thus leaving the insurgents exposed in "free-fire zones," was for obvious reasons not possible in Northern Ireland.[7]

The IRA, meanwhile, used all manner of weapons available to them without restraint, including heavy-calibre machine guns, mortars, and huge explosives. They had access to weapons and financing from abroad and enjoyed an easily accessible safe haven across the border in the South.[8]

They were aggressive and well-organized, and enjoyed significant support within Northern Ireland and from sympathetic Irish groups abroad, especially in the United States. Moreover, they matched their military campaign with a sophisticated and well-funded political effort.

IRA "soldiers" lived and hid among the population, only picking up weapons and donning uniforms when conducting operations. Additionally, in their extraordinary efforts to ensure the population's support, the IRA strove to be seen defending the interests of the Catholic community.

IRA propagandists and sympathizers used any opportunity to portray British forces as unpopular, brutish, indiscriminate thugs whose job it was to keep Northern Ireland under London's boot heel. Concomitantly, they also asserted that English civil rights were not extended to the Catholic community.[9]

Within this volatile and complex environment, the SAS played a significant role in assisting intelligence establish itself during the early period of the Northern Ireland campaign, from circa 1969–76. During this period, the intelligence architecture in Northern Ireland was undersized, undeveloped, and/or uncoordinated, and was therefore ineffective in fulfilling the critical role intelligence plays in defeating insurgency.[10] In fact, in the early days of the British deployment, the military intelligence architecture consisted of only one Intelligence Corps captain and one sergeant.[11] This situation hardly provided a solid base for the COIN fight that was materializing.

Through its standard program of searching and questioning, the British Army managed to create a large database on the population of Northern Ireland and it discovered thousands of weapons and hundreds of thousands of rounds. Nonetheless, its efforts were hampered because they ran counter to the notion that the acquisition of good intelligence is largely dependent upon gaining the population's goodwill and confidence.[12] These challenges were exemplified in the 1970s because the cooperation between the various British intelligence collection agencies was uncoordinated and at times antagonistic. MI5, MI6, the Royal Ulster Constabulary (RUC) Special Branch, and the British Army each ran their own operations. There was competition for control, conflicting analyses being produced, and refusals and counter-refusals to share high-quality intelligence between agencies.[13] In short, during the early 1970s the overall

British intelligence effort in Northern Ireland was schizophrenic and characterized by a complex web of uncoordinated, stovepiped efforts.

It was within this dysfunctional milieu that the SAS proved its value. The "Regiment" has always been highly regarded for its competence in, among many other things, its thoroughness in planning and organizing. As such, beginning in March 1972, SAS soldiers were deployed to individual positions in the intelligence community to act as a catalyst for bringing unity to the overall effort. Officers were posted to key military intelligence positions at the brigade level and at army headquarters in Northern Ireland. In 1974, more SAS officers were added, again to help bond the disjointed intelligence system, and to control agents.[14] The SAS continued to provide such support to the burgeoning intelligence machine until at least 1976 when the architecture finally blossomed and began to evolve on its own, allowing the SAS to take on the more traditional role of targeting insurgents.[15]

While bringing excellent staff work, and inventiveness and cohesion to a flagging organization are hardly traditional SOF roles, the fact of the matter is that the SAS were superb in whatever missions were assigned them. To this end, when tasked to assist the intelligence effort, the SAS, according to established SAS authority Tony Geraghty, "provided some of the most innovative minds in the Intelligence game."[16]

Another manner through which the SAS assisted in enabling intelligence activities was by providing specialist training to intelligence collectors. Covert collection, such as close surveillance, in both rural and urban environments, against an enemy that hid among the population and emerged with surprising speed to attack those intelligence collectors unfortunate enough to be discovered, was a particularly hazardous duty. Collectors, therefore, needed excellent fieldcraft skills if they were to be successful in amassing information effectively while avoiding detection and its grim consequences. They also required a robust ability to defend themselves in situations that could escalate in mere seconds into life-or-death scenarios.

For example, one unit that required such skills was the Military Reconnaissance Force (MRF), which was established as part of the army's effort in the early 1970s to create an effective intelligence gathering capability. The MRF was responsible for running IRA prisoners who agreed to identify their colleagues while driving around in unmarked cars, a job so dangerous that few IRA turncoats survived to see the eventual return to peace. Importantly, the MRF handlers received their training in covert operations from SAS instructors in an intensive course that was run with the Regiment's assistance.[17] Consequently, the SAS was instrumental in empowering the unit to provide the necessary information gathering required to fuel the intelligence machine.

Another intelligence gathering unit that required expertise in covert operations was the RUC's "E4" department, which was solely dedicated to collecting intelligence on the IRA. "E4A," a sub-unit, was assigned the most dangerous roles, such as conducting man-to-man surveillance, and was backed up by RUC Special Support Units that provided "firepower, speed, and aggression" when necessary. Once again, the SOF was a critical enabler. The E4A agents acquired their skills sets from SAS instructors who provided training in England.[18]

The SAS also played a role in providing specialist training to the famed 14 Intelligence Company when it was formed, a unit that was to play an especially important role in collecting intelligence. A deliberately obscure outfit, 14 Intelligence Company, or 14 Int, was broken down into small, highly secretive units whose operations were run directly from London. So secretive was the unit that the name 14 Intelligence Company was not acknowledged until 1988, over a decade after its establishment.[19]

As they were at the forefront of intelligence collection in dangerous areas, 14 Int's members needed to possess unusual skill sets, such as the ability to work alone in IRA-dominated urban areas and to exercise close-quarter shooting skills if and when compromised.[20] Unit members were tasked with close observation of known IRA terrorists, which sometimes meant sustaining observation for days or weeks, sometimes only feet away from armed, violent individuals.[21] Indeed, the price of compromise was high, as any 14 Int agent captured by the IRA would be subject to vicious torture to reveal all the victim knew about the unit and its members.[22]

Naturally, the SAS was called upon to provide 14 Int with expertise. When the company was first established, its training officer was a serving member of 22 SAS who taught recruits the skills they needed to operate and survive, such as how to use a vehicle as a base of operations and how to avoid confrontation when questioned by suspicious locals.[23] Training for at least the first 50 14 Int members was conducted in part by the SAS near the Regiment's base in Hereford. They were instructed in basic covert warfare skills, such as surveillance, communications, and the running of agents. The course itself was designed by the SAS, and because 14 Int members employed SAS tactics, the Regiment occasionally sent advisers to Northern Ireland to check on how their protégés were doing.[24]

Once operational, the first detachment deployed to Armagh in the spring of 1974, 14 Int soldiers operated in unmarked cars and used non-standard weapons, such as silenced Ingram sub-machine guns. That the members of 14 Intelligence Company were well trained in self-defence became evident when one member fought his way out of an IRA ambush, entirely on his own, killing two terrorists and wounding a third.[25]

Although SOF was instrumental in training and advising nascent intelligence units and organizations, which in turn assisted the maturation of intelligence operations in Northern Ireland, this was not their only intelligence contribution. Yet another way SOF acted as an enabler for intelligence was by providing specialist training to units in conventional line battalions that were assigned complex intelligence collection duties. By the mid-1980s, the British Army had determined that regular troops could and should be used to conduct covert operations if provided the proper training. Once again, the SAS was called upon to provide expertise, this time providing the greater army with both a centre of excellence and a training entity that enabled line units to conduct covert operations.[26] With the benefit of SAS training, the army soon formed its own "close observation platoons" that went on to conduct effective operations, some of which led to the successful ambush of terrorists.[27]

Another major step forward, which reinforced the emerging link between SOF and intelligence organizations/operations was in 1980, when a new organization was created within the army known as the Intelligence and Security Group (Int and Sy Group). This unit placed 14 Intelligence Company and the SAS under a single commanding officer.[28] Drawing recruits from the regular army, it was designed to conduct surveillance and intelligence gathering. The SAS trained Int and Sy group members at its Hereford, England base, providing trainees with a regime in covert surveillance and intelligence collection before they deployed to Northern Ireland.[29]

Finally, the SAS also enabled intelligence collections efforts in Northern Ireland by actually acting as an intelligence sensor itself. In the early 1970s, the army grew frustrated over the RUC Special Branch's ineffectiveness in providing quality intelligence on the IRA. Its extreme unpopularity in the Catholic community rendered it unproductive. Consequently, as previously outlined, the army set out to create its own intelligence gathering capability that was to be based in part on reconnaissance and observation, skills that SAS members were expert in.

The subsequent overall expansion of intelligence collectors, including army, secret service, and police services, saw the fielding of many HUMINT collectors. Unfortunately, however, their efforts were largely uncoordinated. It took years for the different organizations to mature and develop tactics, techniques, and procedures that would be fully effective.

Fortuitously, in the interim, the SAS began to collect intelligence by conducting surveillance and helped to fill the gap that existed. Border crossing points were monitored, as were the homes of known IRA figures. The SAS also kept close watch on the roads around communities that had a strong IRA presence.[30] Also, of particular value was the Regiment's ability to maintain close observation of individuals, an inherently difficult task that was carried out in neighbourhoods where outsiders stuck out and were bound to be quickly compromised.[31]

Clearly the government's use of the SAS as an intelligence sensor was especially useful because it occurred at a time when there were few other organizations capable of doing this specific task. As always, SOF is summoned when there is a crisis and no one else can provide the necessary skill sets.

While SOF in Northern Ireland did much to enable the intelligence function, it is equally true that intelligence enabled SOF. Indeed, the eventual growth of effective intelligence-gathering organizations meant that high-quality intelligence was available that enabled SOF to bring its potent, focused effects to bear. Quite simply, the SAS became the action arm for intelligence.

By 1976, the British intelligence apparatus in Northern Ireland was maturing and becoming more effective. At this time, strategists also became aware that their COIN strategy required a review.

As part of this review, intelligence planners studied Britain's successful COIN campaign in Malaya. They quickly recognized that the cornerstone of their success in that campaign was the separation of the population from the insurgents. Whereas this separation was accomplished through the population's resettlement into highly secure villages, which left the insurgents exposed and vulnerable, this would not be possible in

Northern Ireland. The plan for Northern Ireland was aimed to achieve the same effect through different means. Here the British Army would use a robust intelligence system to isolate IRA terrorists.

Consequently, as previously noted, the various British intelligence agencies were expanded and improved. This ushered in an era in which SOF was no longer required to gather information to process into intelligence. Now it was needed to act on the intelligence being produced.

Intelligence often shed light on hardcore IRA terrorists who were on their way to an attack and whose surrender to interdicting forces was improbable. In such confrontations, situations could escalate extremely quickly. Moreover, the obligation to use minimum force, yet in circumstances that clearly called for the necessity to use precise deadly force, created a complex, if not ambiguous, operating environment for security forces. Such circumstances were unsuited for conventional forces and called for the superbly trained, covert-capable soldiers of the SAS.[32]

Indeed, this was an operating environment in which acting on intelligence meant pitting soldiers who were restricted to using minimum force against a ruthless enemy that took advantage of the soldiers' strict rules of engagement and killed without hesitation. Conventional soldiers were at a clear disadvantage with potentially fatal consequences, as a number unfortunate soldiers were to demonstrate. For example, on 16 March 1978, Lance-Corporal Jones, a Parachute Regiment soldier on duty with 14 Int, emerged from a hidden position to challenge three IRA terrorists. Without hesitation, the trio's leader shot Jones in the stomach, fatally wounding him, and shot and wounded Jones's partner.[33]

SOF skills were clearly an asset in complex situations like these. Not surprisingly, the SAS, as an action arm, soon proved critical to RUC's Special Branch, which lacked both the training and equipment to act on the intelligence that was gathered. In fact, when the SAS first deployed in strength to Northern Ireland in early 1976, they learned that the Special Branch had good intelligence on significant IRA figures, but did not possess the skill and resources to act on it. The SAS stepped into this capability void and forged a relationship with the Special Branch that saw the Regiment being called to act when quality intelligence was acquired.[34] By the late 1980s, this partnership had matured to the point that the RUC Special Branch's Tasking and Coordination Group (TCG) formally assigned missions to the SAS.

With time, the TCG also assigned tasks to other specialist military and police units based on which organization was the most appropriate unit for the task. However, the special relationship between the TCG and the SAS remained strong. In fact, the close relationship between the SAS and TCG grew to the point that the latter had authority over the Regiment's operations, and when operational decisions had to be made, such as whether or not to change the scope of an operation based on the tactical situation, the SAS deferred to the TCG.[35]

Notably, SAS also developed a working relationship with 14 Intelligence Company that was based on the co-operative intelligence gathering and precision action. When the SAS first deployed in 1976, it relied primarily upon the RUC for the actionable intelligence needed to identify and target key IRA members. However, the RUC's credibility began to wane because suspicion developed that it was co-operating with Protestant extremists. Consequently, the British chief of the general staff, Field Marshal Sir Michael Carver, directed that the army start using intelligence generated by the military. The result was a relationship in which 14 Int became "a silent partner" to the SAS.[36] The terms of this relationship were that 14 Int gathered and collated intelligence on the IRA, and when action was required, the SAS was brought in to strike.[37] The SAS, with their extensive experience in conducting dangerous covert operations and their unmatched weapons handling skills, brought soldiers to the fight who were capable of delivering precision effects and provided a solution to the complex problem faced by the British Army and government.

The profitable partnership between intelligence and the SAS, which produced excellent and often significant results in situations that were extremely dangerous, can be best appreciated by examining some notable operations. Operation JUDY, which took place in May 1987, provides a good case study.

In May 1987, British security forces had received excellent intelligence indicating that the IRA was planning to attack the police station in Loughgall, North Armagh County, with small arms and a huge bomb that was to be placed in the shovel of a mechanical digger that would be driven up to the station. Fortunately or unfortunately, depending on which side you were on, the IRA's entire plan was compromised. British Security Forces were aware of the plan's details, roughly when it would occur, and that the men involved included some of the most dangerous in the IRA.

Consequently, on 7 May, a force of nearly 40 SAS troops, plus supporting signallers and others, was assembled for an intelligence briefing during which the IRA's plan was revealed. The SAS deployed shortly after with a large force hidden in the trees next to the police station, another group actually inside the targeted building, and other teams along the IRA's anticipated ingress/egress route.[38] They believed such a robust security force was required because of the unusually large group that the IRA was sending, which included some of its fiercest characters, men who were well known for their violence.

The IRA team was led by Patrick Kelly, the officer commanding of the Tyrone IRA organization and a man directly associated with the IRA's Northern Command and its chief of staff. Another was Jim Lynagh, who was the IRA member most-wanted by security forces. He was a ruthless and feared individual whose violent tendencies were considered excessive, even in senior IRA circles. Lynagh was also one among a handful of IRA members who travelled to Libya in 1986 for training in handling the weapons that Qaddafi was then shipping to Ireland. A third member of the team was Padraig McKearney, who had served two jail sentences for blowing up a factory and for weapons offences. He was a prison escapee from a startling 1983 break from Long Kesh prison. Another was Gerard O'Callaghan, who with Lynagh and McKearney, was a senior member of the IRA's East Tyrone Active Service Unit (ASU). Finally, Declan Arthurs, Seamus Donnelly, Tony Gormley, and Eugene Kelly were the younger, though nevertheless experienced, members of the team.[39] Together, they represented a group of extremely dangerous men. The intelligence pointing toward their pending attack, however, gave security forces a rare opportunity to deal the IRA a devastating blow.

The SAS, with the assistance of the RUC, took full advantage of the opportunity. At 1915 hours on 8 May, a van carrying five of the IRA men approached the police station to conduct a quick reconnaissance. They then turned back. Shortly after, the van returned accompanied by the mechanical digger. Both vehicles drew up to the station. Three IRA exited the van, and one, Patrick Kelly, began to fire on the police station with an automatic rifle. The SAS opened up on the party, killing the three men in the open and the two who remained in the van (both of whom were wearing body armour). The three men who rode on the digger were shot and also killed, though not before one had time to light the bomb's fuse. Its detonation created a huge blast that destroyed part of the station and a neighbouring telephone exchange. In the end, however, all eight well-armed IRA were killed in circumstances that were fully justified and could not be exploited by IRA propagandists, while the security forces suffered no casualties.[40]

The operation was a stunning success and demonstrated the beneficial partnership between intelligence and SOF. The intelligence that forewarned of the attack was nothing less than superb. Intelligence personnel had briefed the SAS on the probable route the IRA would take, how the bomb would be constructed, and what the IRA's backup team would consist of. Intelligence also determined exactly how the men would be armed. The SAS were warned that there would be three Heckler and Koch 7.62 mm assault rifles, two 5.56 mm FN automatic rifles, one shotgun, and a Ruger revolver, all of which were prepositioned in an arms cache that the RUC had placed under continuous surveillance.[41] Although precisely how this intelligence was acquired remains unclear, at least in the public domain, the intelligence was highly accurate and cued the SAS to act, resulting in a tremendous victory.[42]

Indeed, the remarkable success of the British security services at Loughgall achieved considerable effect in undermining the IRA's strategic campaign. The operation accomplished much more than simply removing eight notorious insurgents from the field. Operation JUDY virtually eliminated the IRA's East Tyrone Brigade in what was the greatest death toll experienced by the insurgents since 1969. As such, the IRA lost some of its most experienced, determined, and irreplaceable members. Moreover, the sudden loss of these men also dealt a blow to the morale of IRA members and supporters. What's more, some of the killed insurgents were to have played a role in the IRA's so-called "Tet Offensive,"[43] an ambitious plan to use huge stores of weapons acquired from Libya to escalate the conflict and wear down Britain's resolve to continue its COIN effort. In fact, the IRA's disaster at Loughgall was the first in a series that forced the organization to abandon its Tet Offensive.[44]

Furthermore, as a consequence of the success of Operation JUDY, the IRA turned in on itself and became fixated on determining if they had been betrayed from within. Throughout the Tyrone area, the IRA and its supporters were gripped in a state of "near paranoia" that caused organization to cease operations and scrutinize itself for leaks.[45] Finally,

Operation JUDY struck such a blow to the IRA's capability and morale that it was eventually seen as having shoved the IRA toward the peace process.[46] Having achieved such deep and lasting effects, the operation provided an outstanding example of the potential that exists when capable intelligence and SOF organizations work together.[47]

Another high-risk, intelligence-led, and SOF executed operation that dealt a significant blow to the IRA was Operation FLAVIUS, which resulted in the interdiction of an IRA team sent to Gibraltar to conduct a devastating attack against the local British garrison. Shortly after the disaster at Loughgall, the IRA's Army Council decided that a revenge attack was needed to raise shattered morale and shock the British people. The British garrison in Gibraltar was selected as the target, as it had relatively lax security and it was very symbolic (i.e., there was much British pomp and ceremony with the local unit marching daily in full regalia through the streets). As such, the IRA believed that an attack there would generate significant international media coverage. The IRA was drawn to the fact that the Royal Anglian Regiment held a daily Changing of the Guard outside the governor general's home, during which 70 soldiers paraded. The attack was to occur at a quiet square used as a parade dispersal point, where the IRA would place a car bomb designed to kill as many soldiers as possible. The IRA Army Council ordered that a Special Active Service Unit be formed for the critical mission.

As with the plan for Loughgall, some of the IRA's top talent was chosen for the job. In charge of the operation was Mairead Ferrell, a tough, educated, and fiercely determined woman who had served 10 years in prison for conducting a hotel bombing and who had demonstrated unquestionable dedication to the Republican cause. Also recruited was Danny McCann, an extremely violent individual with whom the RUC had associated 26 murders. He was assessed to be the IRA's authority on conducting close-quarter killing. The third member was Sean Savage, a younger but enthusiastic individual who was chosen for his technical expertise. Finally, an unidentified woman was used to scout Gibraltar and the target ahead of the others. In short, the IRA had once again assembled a collection of particularly dangerous members, this time with the intent of conducting a symbolic, shocking mass casualty attack.[48]

The level of information acquired warning of the attack was detailed and indicated a threat so serious that SAS support was deemed necessary.

In November 1987, intelligence services learned that McCann and Savage had travelled on false passports from Spain's Costa del Sol to Belfast, raising suspicions that the IRA was planning an attack in Spain. Gibraltar was assessed as the mostly likely target. Security services immediately launched a comprehensive investigation to ascertain the IRA's intent and to create a counter-plan. On 23 February 1988, and again on 1 March, a woman travelled to Gibraltar on a fake passport under the name of Mary Parkin. During both trips she was tracked by MI5 as she followed the parade route for the Changing of the Guard ceremony. She was assessed as conducting a reconnaissance for an attack.

On 2 March, the British government's Joint Intelligence Committee received other information from Northern Ireland indicating that an attack would soon occur. The decision was therefore made to deploy a 16-man Special Projects Team from the SAS to Gibraltar. In short order, the intelligence services had pieced together a comprehensive understanding of the threat. All three members of the ASU, including Ferrell, McCann, and Savage, were identified. The names on their false passports were known. British authorities were fairly certain that the attack would take place on 8 March. They knew the target was the Changing of the Guard and they knew the attack would involve a massive remote-detonated car bomb.[49] The few intelligence gaps that remained were filled by reasonable analysis of the IRA's *modus operandi* since 1969. For example, the SAS knew that they would face IRA members renowned for their violence. It was therefore assumed that they would all be armed. It was also reasoned that they would use their weapons if confronted, and similarly, that they would remote detonate their bomb immediately if challenged.[50]

Indeed, it was this detailed intelligence picture that led the Gibraltar police to request SAS support. Gibraltar's Special Branch had the lead for Operation FLAVIUS but, owing to the extremely violent nature of the terrorists and the fact that they were assessed to have been in the final stages of planning for a devastating attack, the SAS were to be ready to assist as required.

In the days leading up to 8 March, the police/SOF/intelligence team was at heightened readiness in anticipation of the terrorists entering Gibraltar. Then on 5 March, Savage was spotted in Gibraltar by an alert intelligence operator and followed to a Renault car that was parked exactly where the daily parade ended. He was observed entering the vehicle for a few minutes to adjust something inside. It was assessed that he had delivered the car-bomb and was preparing it for detonation. After Savage left the vehicle, an SAS soldier was sent to conduct a hasty examination of the Renault. Though he had insufficient time to examine it, he noted that the new vehicle had a rusty antenna, so he reported that the car may have contained a bomb. Then, within minutes, Farrell and McCann were observed crossing the border into Gibraltar. With all three terrorists spotted almost concurrently, and with Savage's activity in the Renault, concern rose sharply that their attack was imminent.

With all three terrorists under close surveillance by the SAS, Farrell and McCann walked until they linked up with Savage. Shortly after, the commissioner of police signed a document giving the SAS power to attempt an arrest. Savage then broke off from Farrell and McCann and went on his own way. At this time a police siren sounded, prompting McCann to look over his shoulder and make eye contact with his SAS followers. The SAS troops, well aware that McCann was the IRA's foremost expert in close battle, saw him make a gesture with his arm that was interpreted as a possible move for a weapon or bomb trigger, and he was shot and killed. Farrell too reportedly made a similar gesture, pulling a purse across her body, and was also shot and killed. The sound of gunfire prompted Savage to turn, upon which an SAS soldier yelled "stop," while Savage reportedly moved his right hand toward a pocket. Again, out of concern that he would either bring out a weapon or trigger the bomb, he was shot and killed. The SAS later claimed that they were acutely concerned that any of the three would start shooting if confronted and that they would detonate the bomb by remote control.[51]

The effect achieved by the intelligence-SOF team was significant. There is no doubt that the three dead IRA members were setting up a massive bombing that targeted the Royal Anglian Regiment in a public area. As such, Operation FLAVIUS was immediately seen as a huge success, having prevented an attack that would have caused scores of dead and badly maimed soldiers and probably civilians as well. And, once again, key IRA members were removed from the field. But, more significantly, the Gibraltar bombing was to have been one of the IRA's opening moves of the Tet Offensive on the European continent. Its disruption caused the IRA's Army Council to conduct an internal inquiry to determine how the plan could have been ruined so effectively. Their finding was that the ASU members themselves had probably compromised the mission with careless talk. Curiously, the Army Council did not find that the IRA was possibly penetrated in its upper echelons, despite the disasters at Loughgall and Gibraltar, both of which clearly indicated high-level betrayal.[52] Nevertheless, the Gibraltar affair contributed to a sense of growing paranoia in the IRA that obstructed the Army Council's ability to ignite the hapless Tet Offensive.[53]

Still, the IRA managed to salvage the situation in Gibraltar from a public relations perspective when the British government failed to report the facts of the incident accurately in the days following the operation.[54] Nonetheless, intelligence had once again cued SOF in an operation that dealt a significant blow to the insurgency.

The operations in Loughgall and Gibraltar serve as excellent examples of the effects that can be achieved when high-quality intelligence is acquired and exploited by SOF operating in high-risk environments. There were many other operations that received far less public attention but nevertheless demonstrated the effectiveness of this partnership and are therefore worth mentioning in brief. For example, in January 1977, intelligence sources learned that the IRA was going to use a car that was parked on a road in Culderry, Armagh County, in an operation. The SAS deployed a four-man patrol to conduct close surveillance of the car and, if necessary, interdiction. As suspected, a car soon approached the parked vehicle and stopped just short of the SAS surveillance team. An IRA man, Seamus Harvey, got out dressed in combat clothing, a black hood, and a belt full of shotgun shells. Two SAS soldiers approached him with intent to arrest. However, a hidden IRA cover team opened fire on the SAS. The two SAS dove for cover, while their own cover team returned fire. In the end, Harvey was killed in the exchange, two of the 13 rounds that struck him were actually fired by his own team, in circumstances that were legally and ethically unassailable, even by the notorious IRA propagandists who used any opportunity to accuse the SAS of being murderers.[55]

Another excellent example of the efficacy of the intelligence-SOF partnership occurred in the summer of 1988, when security forces learned that the IRA had plans to assassinate a retired Ulster Defence Regiment (UDR) officer as part of a campaign to terrorize RUC and UDR supporters. British security forces determined that the best, and only, option was to catch the IRA red-handed in the act of attempting the assassination. Capturing the assassins any other way, for example while moving to their weapons cache in preparation for the operation, would be easily manipulated by propagandists. The SAS plan then was to place a soldier in the target's truck when intelligence warned the assassination was imminent and then have the truck "break down" on a road where an SAS team would hide in waiting for the assassins. The plan was, of course, extremely dangerous, as the SAS driver would be precariously exposed. In addition, the IRA hit team was to include three extremely dangerous men who between them were associated with at least 32 murders. In fact, one of the IRA men, Gerard Harte, had only weeks before, detonated a road-side bomb that flipped a troop-carrying bus, killing eight soldiers and wounding 27 in an appalling scene of carnage. In any event, the SAS plan was carried out with great success.

Intelligence warned that the hit team had removed weapons from its cache and that the operation was on. The SAS moved into position and staged the truck's breakdown. The IRA soon learned that their quarry was stationary by the side of the road and moved in to execute him. They drove up to the broken-down vehicle and confronted the SAS soldier posing as the UDR target. They then opened up with automatic rife fire. The SAS man leapt out of the line of fire, with bullets impacting all around him. The hidden SAS team then engaged the IRA team, killing all. In so doing, they caught the IRA team red-handed in the act of attempting an assassination and used lethal force in circumstances that were wholly justified and removed three radical and violent IRA men.[56] In the end, the IRA was ultimately ground down by an intelligence network that made it impossible for the organization to operate.

In the years after the latest round of "Troubles" broke out in 1969, the British intelligence community in Northern Ireland slowly developed into an extremely sophisticated, remarkably capable machine that increasingly reduced the IRA's ability to operate until the organization had little freedom of action.[57] SOF became, in many instances, the natural partner for intelligence, initially even fulfilling both roles. It is important to note that SOF was not the only, or always the best, partner for intelligence. Nor was SOF the decisive factor in the IRA's eventual defeat.[58] However, SOF certainly played an important part in the early years assisting with the growth and development of the intelligence battle in Northern Ireland and later became an important part of using hard-won intelligence to conduct high-impact operations. Furthermore, successes by SOF cast a shadow over the IRA. They quickly knew they faced a persistent and disturbing threat and that any of their planned operations could be compromised and subsequently interdicted by the SAS. Notably, the SAS achieved this dramatic effect with a relatively small number of soldiers. After 1976, the SAS presence in Northern Ireland usually consisted of a troop of just 30 men, with reinforcements from England available when required.[59]

It must also be pointed out that the SAS experience in Northern Ireland demonstrated that SOF intelligence-led COIN operations can be manipulated by an enemy who is adept at information operations. To this end, insurgent propaganda can be effective in undermining the effects produced by the SOF-intelligence team. The very nature of SOF operations in Northern Ireland, which pitted extremely well-trained and war-hardened soldiers against ruthless, intractable IRA terrorists, often resulted in the deaths of the latter. This sometimes provided IRA propagandists and supporters with opportunities to portray the SAS as a hit squad.[60] On other rare occasions, innocent civilians were caught in the crossfire, providing the IRA and its supporters fodder for their information operations and accusations that British SOF were victimizing the local population.

The facts, however, are telling and refute the IRA's propaganda. By the July 1997 ceasefire that largely ended the conflict, the SAS had killed about 38 insurgents, but its members had arrested several times more, sometimes in circumstances in which deadly force would have been unquestionably appropriate if used. As for incurring civilian casualties, five innocents died during SAS operations, some in situations in which the ambiguous circumstances justified the use of deadly force.[61] Though such deaths are tragic, surely this number is extremely small in the greater context of post-1945 COIN campaigns and underscores the fact that SOF does indeed bring precision effects that lessen civilian casualties.

As both history and current events demonstrate, counterinsurgency is a complex, difficult form of warfare that is typically protracted and may not show tangible progress for years. A determined insurgency with some degree of popular support can be extremely difficult to defeat. It is therefore useful to examine previous conflicts for lessons that may be applied now and in the future. The COIN campaign in Northern Ireland was a particularly difficult one, waged as it was by British forces on British soil against a very capable enemy with much local support and in the full glare of the media. SOF played an important role in that conflict by contributing to the development of a remarkably effective intelligence system and by acting as the action arm for that intelligence machine, particularly when circumstances called for small numbers of discreet soldiers who could bring precision, deadly force to bear instantly if required. Indeed, the successful COIN campaign in Northern Ireland, fought over a period of about 28 years, demonstrates that SOF and intelligence are mutually enabling elements that form a valuable team, one that makes concrete contributions to the long and difficult process of eroding insurgency.

NOTES

1. United States Army and Marine Corps, *Counterinsurgency,* FM 3–24/MCWP 3–33.5, 2006, 1–1 and 1–28.
2. *Ibid.,* 1–1.
3. The term intelligence is derived from the Latin verb *intellegere,* which means "to understand." Military intelligence is a military discipline that empowers a commander's decision-making process by ensuring that he has the necessary processed/analyzed data from the widest possible range of sources on the terrain, enemy and friendly forces, and environmental conditions. To furnish that informed analysis, the commander's information requirements are identified and then tasked out to organizations that are trained and equipped to gather and process the collected information. The intelligence process actually has four phases: collection, analysis, processing, and dissemination. SOF was heavily used initially for the collection of information so that the actual intelligence operators could analyze the data and provide the necessary intelligence to the requisite commanders so that they could determine the appropriate actions to take.
4. The IRA split because of political differences in 1970, shortly after the latest round of "Troubles" began. Subsequently, the "Official IRA" consisted of those who believed that they could achieve their aims using the political process. Others believed that militant action was required. They formed the Provisional IRA (PIRA) and began to use terrorist tactics. Robin Neillands, *In the Combat Zone: Special Forces Since 1945* (London: Weidenfeld and Nicholson, 1997), 225. Henceforth in this paper, the term IRA is used throughout, though it mainly refers to the Provisional IRA.
5. J. Paul de B. Taillon, *The Evolution of Special Forces in Counter-Terrorism: The British and American Experiences* (Westport, CT: Praeger Publishers, 2001), 35–36.
6. Neillands, *In the Combat Zone,* 235.
7. Tony Geraghty, *Inside the Special Air Service* (London: Methuen, 1980), 161.

8. Tony Geraghty, *Who Dares Wins* (London: Little, Brown and Company, 1992), 235. Geraghty states of the IRA, "The underdog it is not."

9. David Bonner, a lawyer who emphasizes that countering terrorist threats needs to emphasize the rule of law and use criminal legal processes, notes that the problem faced by the British in Northern Ireland was exceptional, in that the terrorist threat came from a highly organized group with significant support domestically and abroad and because of the United Kingdom's entrenched constitutional and legal traditions. David Bonner, "The United Kingdom Response to Terrorism," in *Western Responses to Terrorism,* ed. Alex P. Schmid and Ronald D. Crelinsten (London: Frank Cass, 1993), 200–01.

10. The critical role of intelligence in COIN is widely established, as is its importance to the COIN campaign in Northern Ireland. For example, Brian Jackson, a RAND Corporation scientist and researcher of homeland security and terrorism, notes that intelligence plays a central in COIN by facilitating the identification of the enemy and the determination of how to neutralize or isolate him. Brian A. Jackson, "Counterinsurgency in a Long War: The British Experience in Northern Ireland," *Military Review* January-February (2007), 74. Similarly, professor and historian John Newsinger notes that an effective intelligence architecture is a prerequisite for conducting successful COIN, as the main problem is not whether security forces can outfight the insurgents, but is simply in identifying and finding them. He adds that without good intelligence, security forces operate blindly. John Newsinger, "From Counterinsurgency to Internal Security: Northern Ireland 1969–92," *Small Wars and Insurgencies,* Vol. 6, No. 1 (1995), 96. Journalist and author Tony Geraghty states simply that "the most important weapon available to either side in this war [was] accurate intelligence." Tony Geraghty, *The Irish War: the Hidden Conflict Between the IRA and British Intelligence* (London: the John Hopkins University Press, 2000), xxix. Finally, Kiran Sarma, a professor and forensic psychologist, notes that at times during the insurgency in Northern Ireland, informers "literally crippled the IRA" by leading to the arrest or death of activists, preventing operations, and seizing arms caches. Kiran Sarma, "Informers and the Battle Against Republican Terrorism: A Review of 30 Years of Conflict," *Police Practice and Research,* Vol. 6, No. 2 (2005), 177.

11. Geraghty, *Inside the SAS,* 140.

12. Keith Jeffery, "Security Policy in Northern Ireland: Some Reflections on the Management of Violent Conflict," *Terrorism and Political Violence,* Vol. 2., No. 1 (1990), 21–34.

13. Geraghty, *Inside the SAS,* 146–47.

14. *Ibid.,* 145–47.

15. Geraghty, *The Irish War,* 123.

16. *Ibid.,* 139.

17. Anthony Kemp, *The SAS: Savage Wars of Peace* (London: Signet, 1995), 121.

18. Martin Dillon, *The Dirty War* (New York: Routledge, 1990), 363–64.

19. Dillon, 150–51. The unit was called 14 Intelligence Company since it was raised, but for years was publicly known by other names, including the Northern Ireland Training Advisory Team, HQ Company, and the Int and Sy Group. Michael Westaway McCue, "Intrigue: Britain's Shadowy 14 Company," *Military History,* Vol. 22, No. 10 (2006), 18.

20. Geraghty, *Who Dares Wins,* 222.

21. McCue, 18.

22. Neillands, 231.
23. Geraghty, *Who Dares Wins*, 221–22.
24. James Adams, Robin Morgan, and Anthony Bambridge, *Ambush: The War Between the SAS and the IRA* (London: Pan Books, 1988), 72–73. The authors note that 14 Int Company's covert deployment to Northern Ireland may have contributed to speculations, which are unfounded, that the SAS were deployed there in strength before the highly publicized deployment in January 1976.
25. Geraghty, *Who Dares Wins*, 221–22.
26. David A. Charters, "From Palestine to Northern Ireland: British Adaptation to Low-Intensity Operations," In *Armies in Low Intensity Conflict: A Comparative Analysis*, ed. David A. Charters and Maurice Tugwell (London: Brassey's Defence Publishers, 1989), 232.
27. *Ibid.*, 248 (note 224).
28. Kemp, 129.
29. Adams, Morgan, and Bambridge, 94.
30. Neillands, 230–32.
31. Jackson, 80.
32. Geraghty, *The Irish War*, 74–75 and 122–23.
33. Geraghty, *Who Dares Wins*, 244.
34. Geraghty, *The Irish War*, 119–20.
35. Gaz Hunter, *The Shooting Gallery* (London: Orion, 1998), 223–26.
36. McCue, 18.
37. Geraghty, *Who Dares Wins*, 225.
38. Geraghty, *The Irish War*, 124–25.
39. Ed Maloney, *A Secret History of the IRA* (Toronto: Penguin Canada, 2002), 306–07. Geraghty also provides details on the IRA men who conducted the Loughgall attack in *The Irish War*, 124–25.
40. Geraghty, *The Irish War*, 126–27.
41. *Ibid.*, 125.
42. It may have simply been the product of thorough intelligence analysis based on knowledge of IRA methods. The IRA had attacked police stations previously using the same plan as for the Loughgall operation. So when a digger and a van were reported stolen in Dungannon, a short distance from Loughgall, it indicated that an attack was possibly imminent. That the police station in Loughgall was one of very few lightly defended police stations in the area suggested the possible target. Key IRA members were placed under surveillance while intelligence personnel used surveillance teams to search for others indicators that an attack was imminent, such as the movement of key IRA players toward Loughgall. Adams, Morgan, and Bambridge, 110–18. These authors emphasize the role that surveillance and good analysis played in warning of the attack. However, they also state that "The decision to join forces with Lynagh's Monaghan/Armagh brigade to mount a joint and, for the IRA, mass attack had led to leaks …," indicating that these authors do not rule out than an IRA informer was involved. Adams, Morgan, and Bambridge, 117. Also, other information suggests that the intelligence was more than the product of analysis and surveillance, and that a high-level informer in the IRA, one who may have been known to intelligence services as "Steak Knife," provided the actionable intelligence. Bradley Bamford, "The Role and Effectiveness of Intelligence in Northern Ireland," *Intelligence and National*

Security, Vol. 20, No. 4 (2005), 596–97. According to Bamford, Steak Knife was a high-level agent who was a member of the IRA's internal security unit, "the Headhunters," whose job it was to identify, interrogate using torture, and execute traitors in the IRA. Steak Knife may have been directly connected to the execution of at least a dozen suspected IRA informers. Bamford makes an interesting observation, one that may be particularly relevant to the COIN campaigns being fought today, of how British intelligence ran agents. He notes that the British recruited young men who were subsequently convinced to join the IRA. He also points out that the British penetrated the IRA at various levels, which enabled them to sacrifice an informant if it was learned that the IRA suspected a traitor was at work. He states that "such methods of operating began to venture into a grey area in terms of legality and moral acceptability." Bamford, "Role and Effectiveness of Intelligence," 592. Bamford is, of course, quite correct, though given the considerable role human intelligence played in defeating the insurgency in Northern Ireland, it should perhaps be a matter of professional debate as to the extent today's intelligence services should be willing to enter the *grey area* of ethics and morality to run highly effective agents.

43. Maloney, 304–05.
44. The Tet Offensive was a plan that, like the Vietnamese original, was intended to show the world that the conflict was intensifying and that it would not be extinguished easily. The plan called for a huge wave of attacks against British forces that would force the United Kingdom into re-introducing the policy of internment, first used in 1971, that in turn would rally nationalists, inflame international opinion, and cause the British public to question its government's Northern Ireland policies. The plan was to have exploited the 95 tonnes of arms delivered to the IRA in October 1986 from Libya. The offensive never materialized because of the disaster at Loughgall, the interception of the vessel Eksund in November 1987 that was carrying arms from Libya, the disrupted IRA attack at Gibraltar in March 1988, and finally the interdicted *flying column* that attempted to attack a British checkpoint and garrison at Roslea. *Ibid.*, 327–34.
45. Maloney, 315.
46. *Ibid.*, 308.
47. Any full examination of Operation JUDY, however, should take note of the fact that the operation was not without controversy. The local population was of course unaware that a major operation was to unfold in their community, and no efforts were made to remove locals from the immediate area as a function of maintaining operations security. This attached an element of risk to the operation that unfortunately resulted in unintended casualties. Two men, the brothers Anthony and Oliver Hughes, drove close to the station just before the bomb detonated. As the men had just been repairing a truck, both were wearing blue overalls that were similar to those worn by the IRA. Upon entering the area of operations, they decided to reverse course. SAS troops assumed they were IRA and engaged their vehicle, killing Anthony and badly wounding Oliver. This tragedy was extremely unfortunate, and compensation was paid out to Anthony's spouse and to Oliver. Nevertheless, there were calls for a public inquiry, though these were rejected. There were also many remarks in the media that the IRA men should have been arrested instead of ambushed. Kemp, *Savage Wars of Peace*, 140. Such calls were common when IRA members were killed, and were typically issued either by well-meaning commentators who often did not appreciate the high risks involved in disrupting armed terrorists or by IRA supporters

who took any opportunity to portray British security forces as unnecessarily heavy handed. There was nearly even further tragedy at Loughgall. Another vehicle driving away from the scene was also engaged, this one with a female driver and her young daughter. One of the SAS troops realized that the car was not a threat and risked his life to stop the firing, an act for which he was awarded the Military Medal. Geraghty, *The Irish War*, 127. See also Jack Holland and Susan Phoenix, *Phoenix: Policing the Shadows* (London: Coronet Books, 1996), 205–18.

48. The information in this paragraph is taken from the detailed account of Operation FLAVIUS in Adams, Morgan, and Bambridge, 132–43.

49. *Ibid.*, 144–48.

50. *Ibid.*, 160. The IRA's preference for using remote-controlled bombs, and the technical development of remote detonators, was well-known to British authorities.

51. This synopsis of Op FLAVIUS is taken from the detailed account found in Adams, Morgan, and Bambridge, 144–67, and Neillands, 240–44.

52. Maloney, 329–33.

53. *Ibid.*, 336.

54. Operation FLAVIUS soon proved to be controversial for the SAS and the British government. None of the three terrorists were armed when they were shot. Furthermore, the Renault 5 car was found not to have been carrying a bomb, despite the government's first public announcements. As it turned out, the three terrorists were conducting a reconnaissance for the final mission, and the Renault 5 had been placed in Gibraltar to hold the parking spot for another car that was to contain the bomb. The actual car bomb was later found by Spanish authorities in the town of Marbela, a one-and-a-half hour drive from Gibraltar. Inside the car was 144 pounds of Semtex explosive surrounded by almost 200 rounds of AK-47 ammunition and a timer that would have initiated the bomb at 11:40 a.m., when the military parade would have been vulnerable. Bamford, "Role and Effectiveness of Intelligence," 598–99. Nevertheless, the media soon began to suspect a cover-up was underway and that the SAS had used excessive force. The central issue became whether or not the terrorists should have been arrested, and by association, if the SAS were operating on a shoot-to-kill policy. Despite the allegations of an excessive use of force, and the fact that the terrorists were unarmed, the intelligence assessment at the outset of FLAVIUS that the three were probably armed and carrying a detonator was entirely rational, given the available information. In fact, it has been argued that the personnel involved in Operation FLAVIUS could not have reasonably produced a different analytical conclusion. Adams, Morgan, and Bambridge, 159. Others correctly point out that SAS assistance was requested in the first place because the terrorists were known to be particularly dangerous and that there was a serious risk of a large bomb being detonated if the threat was not contained immediately upon confronting the terrorists. It fell to the SAS, then, to neutralize the threat in accordance with their training. It should perhaps not be surprising that lethal force was used so quickly, as the SAS troops were focused on ensuring that the terrorists would not detonate their bomb and that they would not have a chance to engage the arresting soldiers. In any event, a two-week long inquest was held in September 1988. The jury's finding, by a margin of nine jurors to two, was that the killing of the terrorists was lawful. Ultimately, the Gibraltar incident questions whether SOF are suited to conducting high-risk operations in place of the police in a COIN environment. Robin Neillands provides a valuable perspective. He indicates

that there is clearly a role for SOF in a COIN campaign, particularly to reduce the negative impact that large conventional force operations can have on the population, to conduct surveillance in high-risk scenarios, and to conduct an ambush when their expertise is called for. However, Neillands notes that there is a grey area in which the use of SOF threatens to usurp the role of police, particularly when SOF actions result in casualties that the insurgents can use for propaganda purposes. He concludes that a "winning tactical combination" exists when the collection and analysis of all-source intelligence produces targeting opportunities that police can act upon, with military participation when the police assess it is required. Neillands, 245–46. See also, Holland and Phoenix, 198–200.

55. Adams, Morgan, and Bambridge, 82–83.

56. *Ibid.*, 5–20. These authors note that an unfortunate postscript to the operation was that British authorities delayed in releasing information to the public, in part because of the mistakes made during Operation FLAVIUS when the unintentional release of inaccurate information immediately after the operation was used as fodder for criticizing security forces. This enabled IRA propagandists to fuel allegations that the SAS were murdering the IRA. By the time the true story was made public — namely, that they IRA were on a mission to conduct an assassination, the individuals were known terrorists, they were well armed, and they opened fire first — the IRA's propaganda had fed concerns that Prime Minister Thatcher's government had licensed the SAS to operate outside the bounds of law.

57. Jackson, 75.

58. As Keith Jeffery points out in a paper he prepared for a Panel on Internal Security and Political Policing at a conference at the University of Warwick, SOF is but one element that is used to counter an insurgency. Military operations alone will not end conflicts such as that experienced in Northern Ireland. Defeating insurgency is a complicated, multi-dimensional undertaking that must have an acknowledged political authority at its core that is accountable to the public. Jeffery, 32–33.

59. Geraghty, *The Irish War*, 116.

60. Some writers sympathetic to the IRA went to great lengths to portray the SAS as a British government assassination unit. At the extreme end are writers such as Raymond Murray, a Roman Catholic priest who asserts that the upper echelon of the British government, including the cabinet and prime minster, promoted a shoot-to-kill policy. He states that SAS operations progressed from intelligence gathering to destabilizing the Catholic community to "an active 'terrorist' role." Raymond Murray, *The SAS in Ireland* (Dublin: The Mercier Press, 1990), 453. Murray goes as far as assigning the SAS responsibility for some of the IRA's most spectacular terrorist acts. For example, he states that SAS activities in South Armagh led to the IRA's killing of British Ambassador Christopher Ewart-Biggs on 21 July 1979, to the murder of Earl Mountbatten on 27 August 1979, and to an attack on the Parachute Regiment in Warren Point on the same day that killed 18 soldiers. *Ibid.*, 453. Although Murray represents an extreme, if not outrageous, group of writers who accuse the SAS of dirty tricks, other writers and mainstream media have touched on his themes, leading to enormous pressure on the SAS to ensure that its operations were unquestionably consistent with the imperative to use minimum force and that the Regiment could not be perceived to be acting in ways contrary to the values of British society.

61. Geraghty, *The Irish War*, 116.

7

FIGHTING THE MUJAHIDEEN:

Lessons from the Soviet Counterinsurgency Experience in Afghanistan

Tony Balasevicius and Greg Smith

A S PART OF A North Atlantic Treaty Organization coalition, the Canadian Forces are now conducting a counterinsurgency campaign in Afghanistan against a resurgent Taliban threat. Dealing with this menace has proven to be difficult since the Taliban, realizing they cannot defeat NATO's superior military strength, have resorted to asymmetric actions that strike at the coalition's will through the cumulative effects of terror and small-scale military operations. Although NATO must contend with these tactics, concentrating solely on the military aspects of the problem will not address the real danger.

Indeed, the true nature of the Taliban's threat rests in its political strength and not in its military capability. To destroy the Taliban's influence in the region, a combination of political, social, economic, and military actions are necessary. Although the complexities of dealing with these issues in a coherent manner are significant, in the case of Afghanistan, they are not without precedent. Interestingly, the Soviets faced many of these same challenges while fighting their counterinsurgency campaign against the mujahideen throughout much of the 1980s.[1]

The Soviet experience should be of interest to coalition members as it provides a contemporary example of the challenges of conducting counterinsurgency operations in Afghanistan. Contrary to popular belief, the Soviets followed a logical and multifaceted, if somewhat brutal, counterinsurgency strategy in Afghanistan. A critical examination of their performance reveals that many of their failings can be directly attributed to a lack of resources and, in this respect, there are a surprising number of similarities between the operational environment the Soviets faced and the threat that NATO is now dealing with. As such, this chapter will explore various aspects of Soviet counterinsurgency operations during their occupation of Afghanistan. Specifically, it will examine the strengths and weaknesses of the Soviet approach and derive applicable lessons for the current situation. Before dealing with the specific aspects of the Soviet's performance, however, it is important to first comprehend the dynamics of insurgencies.[2]

In the most basic of terms, an insurgency can be viewed as an uprising against an established form of authority such as a government or an occupying military force.[3] Bard E. O'Neill, a recognized expert on the subject, defines an insurgency as a "struggle between a non-ruling group and the ruling authorities in which the non-ruling group consciously uses political resources (e.g., organizational expertise, propaganda and demonstrations) and violence to destroy, reformulate, or sustain the basis of legitimacy of one or more aspects of politics."[4] In this context, insurgencies are often used by the disaffected who recognize their inability to win against conventional military forces and therefore, resort to actions that exploit popular grievances and attack the will and motivation of the status quo authority.[5]

Conversely, counterinsurgency operations are carried out by the established authority and seek to destroy the insurgent through the use of political, social, and economic reforms that focus on satisfying the same grievances that the insurgents are attempting to exploit. The established authority must carry out reforms while simultaneously attacking the physical entities of the insurgent's military and political apparatus.[6] However, when going after the insurgent's physical capabilities, counterinsurgency forces must be cautious in their actions, because they must deprive the rebels of the basic operational and tactical conditions needed to sustain the insurgency while simultaneously limiting collateral damage on the population.

Achieving this balance is far more difficult than it may first appear. The insurgents will attempt to embed themselves within communities so that they can start to develop the tactical conditions needed for the success of the insurgency. Thus, any attempt to attack them usually also means striking the population.

Moreover, this balance underscores the fact that winning the "hearts and minds" of local populations is critical for both the insurgents and the established authority. Certainly, the co-operation of the population provides the basis for long-term operational sustainment and is a key enabler in developing the other conditions that are an essential precondition for success by both sides.

In order for the established authority to win the hearts and minds of locals, they must first be able to show that they can protect the population and defeat the insurgents.[7] As Lieutenant-Colonel John McCuen, a military officer and author on the subject of counterrevolutionary war asserts, "the most important part of a counter insurgency is having the population organized for its own self-defence ... Even in this early phase of the war, organization of local auxiliary police and militia units should be the first priority of the governing authorities."[8] Therefore, establishing a secure environment within Afghanistan was a critical first step for the success of the Soviet counterinsurgency effort. Unfortunately, developing this prerequisite for success proved to be an extremely difficult challenge for the Soviets once they entered the country.

The genesis of Soviet involvement in Afghanistan started in the late 1970s when the People's Democratic Party of Afghanistan (PDPA), a Marxist organization, seized control of the government in Kabul on 27 April 1978. Shortly after the PDPA had taken over power, the new government announced a number of broad and ill-conceived reforms that alienated large segments of the population. Moreover, they did little to implement these reforms, which alienated those who might have otherwise supported them.[9] Subsequently, rebellion broke out in the Nuristan region of eastern Afghanistan and in the following months spread throughout other parts of the country. To contend with the growing unrest the PDPA increasingly relied on Soviet military assistance. However, by October 1979 the situation had become so dire that the Afghan government was forced to formally request Soviet intervention.

Although initially hesitant, the Soviets eventually acquiesced to the request and deployed the 40th Army, which was comprised of three motorized rifle divisions, an airborne division, an assault brigade, two independent motorized rifle brigades and five separate motorized rifle regiments.[10] This force invaded Afghanistan in December 1979 rapidly taking control of large population centres and securing key lines of communication.[11]

While the occupation of the country was swift and impressive in its military efficiency, pacification of this rural, warrior society proved far more difficult. Shortly after the invasion, Afghanistan erupted into a popular revolt against the occupying forces. From the beginning of the uprising, the Soviets were confronted by a number of difficulties, including the geography of the country, a fragmented society that held no allegiance to a central authority, and a force structure that proved totally inadequate for the type of conflict they were fighting.[12] However, the most significant problem the Soviets faced during their occupation, and one that they never rectified, was a lack of resources, specifically, the necessary "boots on the ground," to establish security.[13]

The Soviets deployed and maintained a force of about 100,000 troops in Afghanistan, which was generally believed to have been totally inadequate for the task they were to undertake. According to American intelligence estimates, "An increase of perhaps 100,000 to 150,000 men might [have allowed] the Soviets to clear and hold major cities and large parts of the countryside or block infiltration from Pakistan and Iran, although it probably could not do both.... An even larger reinforcement of 200,000 to 400,000 men probably would [have allowed] Moscow to make serious inroads against the insurgency if the efforts could be sustained."[14]

There have been a number of theories put forward as to why the Soviets did not provide sufficient personnel to meet the needs of the Afghan theatre. Evidence suggests that, initially, the Soviets entered Afghanistan with the limited mandate of providing support to the established authority. According to declassified U.S. military reports, the Soviets imposed limitations on the size of their forces in Afghanistan because they believed, "that the primary purpose of [the] Soviet intervention of December 1979 was to take over security responsibilities, so that [Afghan] government forces could concentrate on putting down the ever-growing insurgency."[15]

Although the Soviets may have initially expected the Afghan Army to carry the main burden of the fighting against the insurgents, the idea quickly proved unrealistic — at least in the short term. This was because of the extremely poor quality of the average Afghan soldier, who in most cases was unwilling to fight.[16] In fact, morale in many of the units was so low and desertion to the mujahideen so common, that by August 1980 the Soviets were forced to remove all anti-armour and anti-aircraft weapons from Afghan units for fear they would fall into the hands of the resistance. The inability of the Afghans to provide any meaningful security contribution to the counterinsurgency effort forced the already overstretched Soviets to take over additional duties and in so doing they became the centre of gravity for success.[17] In essence, any hope of defeating the insurgents now lay on the shoulders of Soviets.

Unable to expand their military capabilities by increasing the Afghan Army, the Soviets focused their efforts on securing their hold of the country's cities and major towns.[18] Given the circumstances, this action was the most logical course for the Soviets to undertake as they could not regain the initiative until they had secured their own strategic bases. Unfortunately, the Soviets never had sufficient resources to move beyond the consolidation of the major cities as almost 85 percent of the approximately 100,000 troops they had available in theatre were needed to provide the basic security tasks of protecting key locations within their strategic bases and the outposts along vital supply routes from the Soviet Union.[19]

The inability to expand their control beyond their strategic bases was to prove costly for the Soviets as more than 80 percent of the country's population lived in rural areas and these people were left vulnerable to mujahideen influence.[20] In this respect, a key condition for success in the counterinsurgency effort appears to have been forfeited from the beginning of the campaign.

Interestingly, the failure of the Soviets to provide a permanent security infrastructure for the population did not deter them from attempting to persuade the people to stop supporting the insurgents. In fact, Soviet methods to win the hearts and minds of the Afghans were sophisticated, with considerable variation depending on the area they were targeting. For example, shortly after their occupation, the Soviets introduced a number of reforms that were designed to strengthen the relationship between religion and state. They gave the government in Kabul control of its own finances and this included the distribution of endowments to the country's mosques. Religious leaders were granted exemption from military service and permitted a gratuity for visits to Mecca. These concessions quickly won over the Afghan mullahs who became important sources of support for the Soviets as they preached that Islam and Marxism sought a common goal and denounced the activities of the resistance fighters.[21] Other hearts and minds initiatives included having the Afghan state media place emphasis on the government's intention to respect and observe Islam as a "sacred religion." In an attempt to showcase Afghan independence the Soviets allowed the country the use of the traditional Afghan flag. In addition, they examined land reforms, attempted a *rapprochement* with its former class enemies, and released a large number of political prisoners.[22] The Soviets also took a number of steps toward creating a more homogeneous society within Afghanistan by slowly moving the country toward a Marxist philosophy.

The Soviet-backed regime in Kabul also made extensive changes to the country's education system. The scholastic curriculum was modified to emulate the Soviet model through the use of translated Soviet textbooks heavily laden with Marxist propaganda.[23] The government also rewrote official Afghan history to reflect a more harmonious historical relationship with the Soviet Union and replaced all other foreign languages in Afghan schools with Russian, which then became a prerequisite for advancement. Such techniques were referred to simply as the "Russification" of Afghanistan and sought, over the long-term, to achieve Afghan pacification.[24] These reforms and programs were accompanied by an extensive and multifaceted propaganda campaign, which was specifically targeted at winning over the population.

In fact, propaganda and psychological warfare became a key aspect of the Soviet's hearts and minds campaign as the Russians attempted to use this advantage to legitimize the Soviet backed regime in Kabul while at the same time undermining the insurgents' belief in their cause. They did this by targeting specific groups with different massages. For example, Soviet attempts to win over the more educated urban populations focused on convincing this group of people about the benefits of their presence. To do this, the Soviets used radio, television, and literature that portrayed the Russians as heroes and defenders of Afghan freedom and as historic friends to the Afghan people. These means were also employed to convince the urban populace of the security of the Kabul regime. To illustrate the point, communist propaganda highlighted the number of refugees returning home from Pakistan because they felt it was now safe to do so.[25]

In the Hindu Kush mountain range area of northern Afghanistan, where the population is ethnically linked with the peoples of the Soviet Central Asian republics, the Soviet's propaganda took on a far different form. In these regions, ethnic ties were repeatedly emphasized and often integrated into Afghan popular culture through the conduits of documentary films and love songs. The Soviets also attempted to focus on their homogeneity with the Soviet Central Asian republics and the benefits of Communism. They continually reminded the people of their ethnic pride and their common traditions, culture, and language thereby reinforcing these messages with cultural exchanges and through various media.[26]

However, despite these efforts, the Soviets were never able to gain significant support from the population or to appreciably delegitimize the cause of the insurgents. Their lack of success was due in large part to the fact that the Soviets could not make an impact in areas where they were unable to establish a permanent security presence. Over time, the Soviets found that any efforts at convincing Afghans in rural areas, particularly in the south, of the legitimacy and benefits of their occupation proved to be useless and they eventually ended all programs aimed at winning over the people in these areas.[27] Instead, the Soviets were forced to try to gain control of the population with what is commonly referred to as the *stick technique* of winning hearts and minds.[28]

There are several ways of employing the stick technique, which can include minor punishments such as "curfews, collective fines, detention of suspects and various restrictions on individual liberties."[29] As Julian Paget explains, "One powerful 'stick' in the battle for local support is the use of reprisals and harsh punitive measures applied in the hope of making the populace more frightened of the security forces then they are of the insurgents."[30]

Over the course of the war such measures became a key part of Soviet strategy in areas where the mujahideen had established firm authority. Knowing the insurgents were receiving support from various communities throughout Afghanistan, and unable to put sufficient forces into the area to stop the support, the Soviets ruthlessly attempted to separate the mujahideen from the villages. Using Mao's comparison that guerrillas are supported by the population in the same manner that fish swimming in the sea are supported by the water, the Soviet approach in Afghanistan was to progressively empty the water out of the bowl, thereby killing the fish.[31]

The Soviets tried to "empty the bowl" through the use of reprisal attacks and terror causing what has often been referred to as migratory genocide.[32]

This strategy was based on the premise that any rebel attack against Soviet troops was quickly answered with an overwhelming military response against villages in the immediate area of the assault.[33] Moreover, in certain rural areas plagued with a strong contingent of rebel forces, the Soviets attacked using heavy mechanized forces with the simple goal of exterminating the local population.[34]

Furthermore, during these operations the Soviets destroyed the agricultural and pastoral system upon which the rural population was heavily dependent. Irrigation systems, livestock, orchards, vineyards, water wells, and crops were actively targeted with the express purpose of destroying the rural infrastructure, thus forcing civilians to choose between flight and starvation.[35] After one such attack a Swedish official reported: "Russian soldiers shot at anything alive in six villages — people, hens, donkeys — and then they plundered what remained of value."[36]

In quantitative figures, the scope of this policy was staggering. At the end of 1986, the United Nations High Commission for Refugees (UNHCR) stated there were approximately 3.2 million Afghan refugees in Pakistan with a further 50,000 scattered in Europe, India, and the United States.[37] Toward the end of the war, it was believed that there were upwards of five million refugees in Pakistan and India, with a further two million rural Afghanis seeking refuge in Kabul and other Afghan population centres. In their efforts to eliminate potential bases of support, it is believed that the Soviets killed off as much as 9 percent of Afghanistan's pre-invasion population.[38]

Although extreme, the Soviet emphasis on eliminating bases and logistic support of mujahideen through relocation is not surprising.[39] Insurgents need a secure place from which to operate, where they can rest, train, be organized, and supplied. Clearly, the importance of bases and logistic support to the insurgents make these bases an important priority for counterinsurgent forces.[40] As a result, since the Soviets were unable to secure control of many of the villages through occupation and, thus, eliminate their use by the mujahideen , they adopted a policy of utter destruction.

The main difficulty with this policy was that it backfired, causing both international indignation and increased local and international support for the mujahideen. Moreover, significant for the Soviets, this counterproductive strategy did little to address the important problem of eliminating rebel bases. This was because, besides the bases located in villages, the mujahideen had established a number of secure bases or sanctuaries along both sides of the Afghan-Pakistani border where they were able to regroup and continue to plan and execute operations.[41]

Understanding the significance of these safe havens, the Soviets made concerted efforts to close the border area in an attempt to cut off the Afghan rebels from their sanctuaries.[42] Initially, they attempted to create government posts along the Afghan-Pakistani border from which they could launch attacks against mujahideen columns. This proved unsuccessful because of the sheer length of the border, so the Soviets tried to financially co-opt tribes living in the area to harass the mujahideen bands as they attempted to move back and forth, which also proved ineffective.[43]

When these actions failed, the Soviets started to carry out direct actions on both sides of the border. Although initially hesitant to violate Pakistani air space, by 1986 the Soviets had become so desperate that they were striking all known rebel bases with air and artillery attacks. In fact, analysts estimated that 700 air and 150 artillery attacks were carried out inside Pakistan throughout the latter part of the war.[44]

In the end, all measures to separate the mujahideen from their sanctuaries proved unsuccessful. Even in 1986, which logistically speaking was the worst year for the Afghan rebels, the Soviets only intercepted one third of supplies crossing the border.[45] Their failure to destroy the sanctuaries allowed the mujahideen to continue long-term operations and this meant they maintained the ability to keep wearing down Russia's strength with the cumulative effect of long-term fighting.

In a desperate attempt to strike back at the elusive enemy, the Soviets began launching large-scale military operations with their mobile reserves on suspected rebel positions.[46] Employing techniques that the Western media often referred to as "Hammer and Anvil" operations, the Soviets established blocking positions and then conducted massive mechanized sweeps intended to crush any guerrilla forces that were caught between the two forces. Incredibly, these large-scale operations, using heavy mechanized forces, became a standard counterinsurgency tactic for the Soviets during the early part of the campaign; however, in the long term, these tactics proved futile, largely because of the poor training of the soldiers in these units and the fact that the tactics were totally inappropriate for the conditions in Afghanistan.[47]

Over time, the Soviets realized the limitations of these actions and were able to adapt their organizations and operations accordingly. Moving away from their reliance on motor rifle units they started focusing on lighter, better trained, and more professional soldiers that included airborne, air assault, and special purpose (*spetsnaz*) forces. They also introduced new types of formations including mountain motor rifle battalions, and developed training and tactics that focused specifically on in-theatre operational requirements.[48]

Despite these reforms, which did increase their operational efficiency, the Soviets were unable to achieve decisive results. This is largely because these mobile reserves were not operating in conjunction with territorial units, police forces, and local militias organized and coordinated to provide the necessary security solutions required. This lack of depth within the security apparatus, combined with a steady flow of incoming supplies, allowed the mujahideen to maintain their mobility, resulting in Soviet attacks often falling on the empty countryside, as the Russians were rarely able to achieve tactical surprise or fix the enemy.[49]

The inability of the Soviets to achieve surprise was also because the insurgents were able to obtain information about the security forces from the population, while the Soviets could not do the same. Not surprisingly, the mujahideen's control of the population allowed them to develop an extensive network of observers and messengers throughout much of the country and this network maintained an almost continuous watch over Soviet movements.[50] The Soviets, on the other hand, were forced to place their emphasis on technical intelligence through the use of aerial reconnaissance, radio intercept, and, in some cases, agents (human information sources). Unfortunately, these sources often failed to produce usable tactical intelligence in a timely manner. Moreover, since the ground forces were always short of combat elements, reconnaissance forces, that could have provided the badly needed human intelligence capability or HUMINT that the Soviets lacked, were often used in close combat duties.[51]

The Soviets also attempted to disrupt rebel actions and gain information through subversion operations, which were carried out by the Soviet intelligence services using Afghan spies and collaborators. Exploiting the fragmented nature of the country, the Soviets were able to persuade some villages to form a truce and reject rebel demands for logistic support. Such villages were often found near major population centres and would form their own militia groups that protected the village and enforced law and order within the community. In certain cases, rebel groups were bribed into switching allegiances, while tribal chiefs were bribed with land and money to renounce support for the mujahideen. These techniques of co-opting the population had the effect of creating "a stratum of people in the countryside that have a vested political and economic stake in the system and are likely to defend it."[52]

Subversion was particularly successful when used to spread conflict and division among the various resistance groups. Afghan society and the rebel groups it produced were inherently fragmented and fraught with disunity.[53] The Soviets repeatedly attempted to exploit these divisions and turn the groups against each other. Agents were infiltrated into these rebel organizations and attempted to assassinate mujahideen leaders or, at a minimum, report information on insurgent movements and tactics. Agents also spread rumours between resistance groups and employed disinformation to create conflict between bands or to discredit the mujahideen leaders in the eyes of others. The fact that the rebels acted independently and did not possess modern means of communication to resolve these artificial conflicts made this technique all the more effective. One mujahideen leader discussed the effectiveness of these techniques in some areas: "the KHAD (Democratic Republic of Afghanistan's secret police) agents have rendered mujahed groups completely useless by getting them to fight among themselves." He added, "Why should the Soviets worry about killing Afghans [insurgents] if the Mujahideen do it for them?"[54]

Despite this success, the Soviet policy of pitting the various mujahideen bands against each other proved to be of limited value. This was because the Soviets found their subversive tactics were often disrupted by the same weakness they were trying to exploit: the fragmented nature of the Afghan people. "At the root of the Soviet difficulties, military as well as political," noted one military analyst, "lies the fact that Afghanistan is less a nation than an agglomeration of some 25,000 village-states, each of which is largely self-governing and self-sufficient."[55] As one scholar put it, "Much has been written about the lack of unity within insurgent ranks, but little note has been taken of the extraordinary difficulties that such disunity poses to the counter-insurgent."[56]

Although overcoming the disunity of the country would have been a key issue for the Soviets in eventually winning the counterinsurgency campaign and pacifying Afghanistan, the reality on the ground was that they were never really able to start the process. This is because they lacked the necessary resources to do the job they were asked to carry out. As General (Retired) M.Y. Nawroz and Lieutenant-Colonel (Retired) L.W. Grau lament in their article, "The Soviet War in Afghanistan: History and Harbinger of Future War":

> The Afghanistan War forced the 40th Army to change tactics, equipment, training, and force structure. However, despite these changes, the Soviet Army never had enough forces in Afghanistan to win. Initially, the Soviets had underestimated the strength of their enemy. Logistically, they were hard-pressed to maintain a larger force and, even if they could have tripled the size of their force, they probably would still have been unable to win.[57]

The direct impact of this limitation was the Soviet's inability to establish a permanent presence in the rural areas where most of the population lived. This single factor prevented the Soviets from creating the basic security conditions necessary for winning the hearts and minds of the people and without the support of the local population, defeat was inevitable.

This lesson is the most significant for NATO forces now in theatre. In a conflict where "boots on the ground" are critical to setting the conditions for success, the coalition has only 40,000 soldiers deployed in the country.[58] This is compared to the 100,000 troops the Soviets deployed which, notably, were believed to have been totally inadequate for the task. To overcome this shortfall NATO will need to train an effective Afghan security force in sufficient numbers to adequately carry out the necessary police, militia, and territorial defence duties to establish security throughout the country as well as provide some type of mobile capability. Doing so could shift the centre of gravity for the conduct of operations from NATO to the Afghan government. However, without a significant increase in troop strength, NATO will not have the capacity to establish the necessary conditions to influence the population and, if this cannot be achieved, then the coalition is unlikely to create the operational conditions needed for success in Afghanistan.

Another failure for the Soviets was their inability to cut off the mujahideen from their supplies, especially along the country's borders. This same problem is now plaguing NATO forces. Unless the Taliban bases and sanctuaries are identified, attacked, and destroyed they will be able to continue fighting even with significantly reduced numbers. This situation, in turn, will allow them to continue striking at NATO forces, eventually wearing down the coalition's resolve as deaths, injuries, damage, and costs pile up in a struggle that appears to have no end. Consequently, NATO and Afghan national forces must eliminate Taliban bases and sanctuaries, regardless of where they are located. Moreover, destroying much of the Taliban's infrastructure in one hard punch offers the best chance of disrupting their efforts to organize and mount attacks for the time needed to get the Afghan national security forces trained, organized, and in place for territorial defence missions.

Finally, the Soviet's inability to fix the mujahideen for decisive battle was due in part to the fact that the Soviets placed far too much emphasis on technical intelligence gathering that often failed to produce intelligence in a timely manner. The important lesson that should be noted from this failure is that nothing can replace human intelligence in counterinsurgency operations. If NATO is to be successful in destroying the Taliban and other insurgents through the use of military operations, then they must first be able to find and fix the enemy, and to do this they need to have excellent intelligence. To achieve this end, a network of informers must be established throughout the country to report on insurgent movements. This must be a priority for the coalition's intelligence apparatus.

In summary, despite following a logical, multifaceted counterinsurgency strategy that clearly recognized the tenets for tactical and operational success, the Soviets were hampered throughout their campaign by a lack of resources. In the end, this prevented them from denying the insurgents any of their basic needs for success.

Key to the Soviet failure was their inability to secure the countryside thereby allowing the rebels to operate freely by maintaining bases, mobility, supplies, and information. In this respect, the Soviets were unable to influence what increasingly became a hostile population. Unable to sway the rural populations through persuasion, the Soviets turned to conventional military options in an effort to contain the growing resistance.

Unfortunately for the Soviets, when these methods did not work they started using terror tactics that eventually turned the population against them and removed any trace of legitimacy of their involvement in Afghanistan. Conversely, with the basic conditions for survival in place, the mujahideen were, despite significant causalities, able to continue with a protracted conflict that wore down the enemy's strength, eventually forcing the Soviets to withdraw. With these lessons in mind the question is: can NATO learn from Soviet mistakes?

Notes

1. Mujahideen: Those who participate in jihad (Islamic Holy War), "Soldiers of Islam," *www.rawa.org/glossary.html* (accessed 21 October 2006).

2. The concept of insurgency is not new to military operations. In fact, insurgencies have been around for almost as long as organized warfare. Examples of such struggles can be found in ancient Egypt and China, while the Roman, Ottoman, and Napoleonic empires each had to deal with various types of insurgencies throughout their histories. Gerard Chaliand, *Guerrilla Strategies: A Historical Anthology from the Long March to Afghanistan* (Berkeley: University of California Press, 1982), 1–7.

3. Canada, *Canadian Army Counter-insurgency Operations* (Draft) (Kingston: LFDTS, 2005), Chapter 1, 10–14.

4. Bard E. O'Neill, *Insurgency & Terrorism: Inside Modern Revolutionary Warfare* (Washington, DC: Brassey's Inc., 1990), 13. Over the past few years, Western nations have come to recognize the transnational nature of modern insurgencies and now refer to insurgency as, "a competition involving at least one non-state movement using means that include violence against an established authority to achieve political change." This definition was developed by a counterinsurgency study group during a focused U.S. Marine Corps Joint Urban Warrior exercise in 2005. Cited in *Canadian Army Counter-insurgency Operations*.

5. O'Neill, 11.

6. See *http://earthops.org/sovereign/low_intensity/100–20.2.html* (accessed 20 October 2006).

7. Julian Paget, *Counter-Insurgency Campaigning* (London: Faber and Faber Limited, 1967), 168.

8. John J. McCuen. *The Art of Counter-Revolutionary War: The Strategy of Counter-Insurgency* (London: Faber and Faber, 1966), 107.

9. Lester W. Grau, "The Soviet-Afghan War: A Superpower Mired in the Mountains" (Foreign Military Studies Office, Fort Leavenworth, KS). This article was previously

published in *The Journal of Slavic Military Studies*, March 2004, Vol. 17, No. 1, *http:// fmso.leavenworth.army.mil/documents/miredinmount.htm* (accessed 1 December 2007).

10. *Ibid.*

11. Stephen J. Blank. *Afghanistan and Beyond: Reflections on the Future of Warfare* (U.S. Army Strategic Studies Institute, PA, 1993, SSI Special Report), 9–10.

12. Ethnic groups in Afghanistan are broken down by percentage as follows: Pashtun, 42 percent; Tajik, 27 percent; Hazara, 9 percent; Uzbek, 9 percent; Aimak, 4 percent; Turkmen, 3 percent; Baloch, 2 percent; other, 4 percent, See *www.cbc.ca/news/background/afghanistan/canada.html* (accessed 12 October 2006).

13. Grau.

14. Defense Intelligence Agency, Directorate for Research, "The Economic Impact of Soviet Involvement in Afghanistan," May 1983 (DIA Declassification Release), 17.

15. U.S. Army, "Lessons from the War in Afghanistan," May 1989 (Army Department Declassification Release), *www.gwu.edu/~nsarchiv/NSAEBB/NSAEBB57/us.html* (accessed 1 November 2006). The initial Soviet objectives were to control the cities and towns, secure the major lines of communications and train and equip government forces.

16. General (Retired) M.Y. Nawroz and Lieutenant-Colonel (Retired) L.W. Grau. *The Soviet War in Afghanistan: History and Harbinger of Future War?* (Fort Leavenworth: Foreign Military Studies Office), 2.

17. Blank, 21.

18. Department of State Bulletin. *Afghanistan: Eight Years of Soviet Occupation* (U.S. Department of State: Vol. 88, No. 2132, March 1988), 2.

19. Nawroz and Grau, 7–9.

20. Raimo Väyrynen, "Focus on Afghanistan," *Journal of Peace Research*, Vol. 17, No. 2, (Special Issue on Imperialism and Militarization, 1980), 93–102 (JPR-1), *http:// links.jstor.org/sici?sici=0022–3433%281980%2917%3A2%3C93%3AA%3E2.0.CO %3B2–9&size=LARGE* (accessed 28 October 2006).

21. Ed R. Klass. *Afghanistan: The Great Game Revisited* (London: Freedom House, 1987), 309. See also A. Arnold, *Afghanistan: The Soviet Invasion in Perspective* (Stanford: Hoover Institution Press, 1985), 106.

22. *Ibid.*, 149.

23. J.B. Amstutz, *Afghanistan: The First Five Years of Soviet Occupation* (Washington: National Defence University, 1986), 304.

24. M. Hauner and R.L. Canfield. *Afghanistan and the Soviet Union: Collision and Transformation* (Boulder: Westview Press, 1989), 55.

25. Arnold, 106.

26. R.H. Shultz Jr., R.L. Pfaltzgraff, Jr., U. Ra'anan, W.J. Olson, and I. Lukes, *Guerrilla Warfare and Counterinsurgency: U.S.-Soviet Policy in the Third World* (Toronto: Lexington, 1989), 285.

27. *Ibid.*, 285. As a result, these people found themselves tightly targeted by the more direct and violent Soviet practices that were based on the premise: "kill one, frighten a thousand."

28. Paget, 169. Paget emphasizes that "This is not likely to be an acceptable policy to any Western power today, for it is morally unacceptable that any government should try to outdo the average insurgent force in terrorism."

29. *Ibid.*

30. *Ibid.*

31. Klass, 174.

32. T.T. Hammond, *Red Flag Over Afghanistan: The Communist Coup, the Soviet Invasion, and the Consequences* (Boulder: Westview Press, 1984), 161.

33. Klass, 341.

34. Amstutz, 145.

35. J. Laber and B.R. Rubin, *A Nation is Dying* (Evanston: Northwestern University Press, 1988), 62. The significance of these attacks was not lost on villagers: "The irrigation system was built through generations to make this landscape fitted for men to live in."

36. Amstutz, 145.

37. Klass, 91.

38. *Ibid.,* 173.

39. Klass, 343.

40. Paget, 170.

41. E.R. Girardet. "Afghanistan: Eight Years of Soviet Occupation," *Department of State Bulletin*, Vol. 88, No. 2132 (March 1988), 37. Also see "Lessons from the War in Afghanistan," 6.

42. *Ibid.,* 37. The attempt was complicated by the extremely long and rugged nature of the border between these two countries — over 2,250 kilometres with approximately 320 mountainous passes.

43. Klass, 180.

44. *Ibid.,* 181.

45. O. Roy, *The Adelphi Papers: Lessons of the Soviet/Afghan War* (London: Brassey's, 1991), 22. Also see Colonel F. Freistetter, "The Battle in Afghanistan: A View from Europe," *Strategic Review*, Vol. 9, No. 1, (Winter 1981), 41.

46. This was about 15 percent of their force or 15,000 to 20,000 troops. To use more, they would have had to take them from security duties in quiet areas.

47. Shultz, 345.

48. Nawroz and Grau, 9.

49. Arnold, 100. In fact, by 1984, Soviet casualties were as high as 30,000; with a $12 billion price tag; and the loss of 536 aircraft, 304 tanks, 436 APCs, and 2,758 other vehicles.

50. Nawroz and Grau, 10.

51. *Ibid.,* 10.

52. Alexiev, 4.

53. E.R. Girardet, *Afghanistan: The Soviet War* (New York: St. Martin's Press, 1985), 36.

54. *Ibid.,* 129.

55. Arnold, 97.

56. Shultz, 164.

57. Nawroz and Grau, 8.

58. Even with this small number, national caveats prevent many of the troops deployed to Afghanistan from being used in hot spots such as Kandahar where they are really needed.

8

UNCONVENTIONAL WARFARE OPERATIONS IN AFGHANISTAN — SEPTEMBER TO DECEMBER 2001

V.I.

MANY CLAIMS HAVE BEEN made about the role of special operations forces, SOF, in the initial stages of Operation Enduring Freedom (OEF). The facts are simple: a few hundred special operations and CIA personnel, with the assistance of air power and working with the Northern Alliance, removed the Taliban from power, and denied Al Qaeda the use of Afghanistan as a safe haven for training, organizing and staging. Few would dispute these facts. But, what exactly was the role of SOF in achieving this outcome? In the end, analysis demonstrates that SOF played a central part in ousting the Taliban as the ruling power in Afghanistan in 2001.

The early stages of OEF were undeniably an unconventional warfare, UW, campaign, though slightly different from the type anticipated by traditional U.S. Army doctrine. The campaign was successful in that it shifted the political power balance in Afghanistan, resulting in the removal of the Taliban government. This success arose from the ability to synchronize the manoeuvring capability of the Afghan resistance forces on the ground with the firepower of U.S. air assets. SOF was instrumental in this synchronization.

This chapter will examine the SOF mission in Afghanistan in 2001 and the part played by both the CIA and the U.S. Army special forces in executing the mission. The campaign demonstrates that the doctrinal conception of UW should be expanded beyond the domain of insurgency. This campaign also reveals several other practical lessons for future UW practitioners about intelligence, the degree of preparation required to conduct UW, the skills and organization that are required, as well as the necessity for interagency co-operation and training. While each of these subjects will be examined in greater detail, initially it is important to provide a summary of the campaign's key events.

SITUATION IN AFGHANISTAN — 11 SEPTEMBER 2001

Throughout its long history Afghanistan has suffered from tribal and internecine rivalries that have resulted in a continuous series of conflicts.[1] On 11 September 2001, Afghanistan was partitioned into two distinct areas. One section, in the northeastern corner of the country, was controlled by the Northern Alliance (NA). The NA was a loose coalition of Afghan warlords, primarily consisting of ethnic Uzbeks and Tajiks with a small representation of Pashtuns.[2] The remainder of the country was under the control of the Islamic fundamentalist Taliban. Both factions had been fighting since the retreat of the Soviet Union and the subsequent collapse of the Communist puppet government in 1992.[3]

Militarily the situation was stalemated. Neither side had sufficient combat power for decisive victory. An L-shaped front extended north and east from Bagram Air Base, with both sides entrenched in extensively prepared defensive positions. The NA bore much similarity to a conventional army in its organization and discipline, but was significantly lacking in its scales of equipment, both individual and collective. The Taliban were viewed as less disciplined and skilled, although the Al Qaeda units of foreign fighters that were interspersed with the Taliban were substantially better motivated and trained. Foreign fighters constituted about 25 percent of the aggregate Taliban/Al Qaeda troop strength, and were often deployed in more critical sectors of the front.[4] The best available estimates of Taliban troop strength put it in the range of 40,000 to 50,000 personnel in the fall of 2001.[5] Small arms and mortars were the most commonly employed weapons. Mobility was largely provided by car, truck, and pack animals. Both sides possessed armour and artillery in small quantities.[6] There is no indication that these assets were employed in a combined arms formation, likely because of the nature of the terrain as well as the shortage of ammunition, particularly for the artillery. Lack of training for, and experience with, large offensive operations meant that small unit actions were the dominant form of fighting.[7]

In early September 2001 the United States had limited military assets in Afghanistan and the surrounding area. Afghanistan is land-locked, and few of its neighbours would, at the time, welcome a sizable, overt U.S. military presence. Iran obviously would not host U.S. military forces and while the former Soviet satellites of Tajikistan and Uzbekistan were less vehement in their hostility toward the United States, they were hardly close allies. The Americans had worked closely with Pakistan dur-ing its sponsorship of Afghan resistance to the Soviets in the 1980s, but there was substantial internal political opposition to a U.S. military pres-ence.[8] Afghanistan's landlocked position also made it less susceptible to the projection of U.S. naval power. Ultimately, facilitating U.S. access to Afghanistan required a substantial diplomatic effort, particularly to gain the consent of Russia to a U.S. presence in its former republics.[9]

The CIA, however, had a covert presence in the area. During the Afghan war against the Soviets, the CIA provided massive support to the Afghan resistance.[10] During the early 1990s, CIA interest in the region had withered to almost nothing. But, by the late 1990s, the CIA was actively rebuilding its Afghan networks and resources to counter Osama bin Laden and Al Qaeda's growing presence. The CIA's interest in Afghanistan was initially revived by their desire to apprehend Aimal Kasi. Kasi had used an AK-47 to kill and wound several CIA employees who were waiting to enter the parking lot of CIA headquarters on 25 January 1993. The CIA believed that he was hiding in Afghanistan and began efforts to build a network of indigenous agents to locate and apprehend him. He was captured in Pakistan in 1998.[11] Rather than disband the resulting human intelligence network, the CIA reoriented its mission toward monitoring bin Laden.[12]

As the threat posed by bin Laden increased, particularly after his attacks on the U.S. embassies in Africa in August 1998[13] and the sui-cide bombing of the USS *Cole* in October 2000,[14] the importance of HUMINT and operational assets in Afghanistan increased. The possi-bility of mounting a covert operation to capture and bring bin Laden before an American court was seriously considered at the highest levels of government.[15] In the final days of the Clinton administration, the CIA developed a complete covert operations plan, costing several hundred million dollars, consisting of covert sponsorship of a NA offensive to remove the Taliban from power. In support of this planning, the CIA launched several missions into Afghanistan to revive liaison with the Northern Alliance, which was then under the leadership of Ahmed Shah Massoud.[16] By September 2001 the CIA had already established the foundation for a UW campaign plan in Afghanistan.

Mission

After 9/11 the United States had two related strategic objectives in Afghanistan. The primary mission was to remove the Taliban from power and eliminate Afghanistan as a haven for terrorist training and organization. The secondary mission was to kill or capture Osama bin Laden and his key staff.[17] SOF, as further defined below, was to be the lead U.S. government agency in executing this mission. A timely response to the 11 September attacks was essential for U.S. domestic political reasons. The geographic isolation of the country, as well as the remoteness from any appreciable U.S. military presence, ruled out a rapid response by conventional forces. The United States was left with no alternative but to call on SOF, whose agility would allow immediate deployment.

Execution — Overview

The task of removing the Taliban relied upon a UW strategy. The campaign plan largely resembled that proposed by the CIA, which was based on their earlier plans. On 17 September 2001, President Bush approved the CIA's plan, and directed that he wanted CIA personnel on the ground in Afghanistan immediately.[18] Afghan forces, with the support of U.S. SOF, were to be the primary ground element of the campaign.[19] The theory was that U.S. support would sufficiently enhance the combat power of the Afghan resistance, which, in turn, would shift the balance against the Taliban and thus break the stalemate that existed. This would then result in the replacement of the Taliban regime with one more friendly to American interests.

Reliance upon indigenous forces as the primary element of a ground campaign is known within U.S. doctrine as "unconventional warfare." The doctrinal definition of UW is:

> a broad range of military and/or paramilitary operations and activities, normally of long duration, conducted through, with, or by indigenous or other surrogate forces that are organized, trained, equipped, supported, and otherwise directed in varying degrees by an external source. UW operations can be conducted across the range of conflict against regular and irregular forces. These forces may or may not be State-sponsored.[20]

Notably, the given American UW doctrine is unnecessarily narrow and only partially describes a methodology that has broader application. Nonetheless, the key concept in the definition, and thus, the key axis upon which the United States intended to conduct OEF, is that indigenous forces would be employed as agents acting, for the most part, to advance U.S. interests.

Indeed, OEF employed a broader UW strategy than promulgated in existing U.S. military doctrine. As is evident from the above definition of UW, existing doctrine assumes that indigenous personnel can be employed to use force ("military and/or paramilitary operations") against an enemy to achieve a political result. The authors of the strategic plan for OEF had an even more ambitious goal: to not only persuade those who were already favourably disposed to U.S. interests to use force against an enemy, but to actively influence those affiliated with the Taliban and Al Qaeda to switch sides. In the words of Henry "Hank" Crumpton, the CIA officer charged with running the CIA campaign:

> the centre of gravity rested in the minds of those widespread tribal militia leaders, who were allied with the Taliban and al-Qaeda out of political convenience or necessity. The CIA understood this political dynamic and could therefore define the enemy in the narrowest terms — for example, as al-Qaeda and intransigent Taliban leaders — while viewing all of the Taliban or

> Taliban-allied militia as potential allies. In other words, the enemy was not Afghanistan, not the Afghan people, not the Afghan army, not even the Taliban per se. The enemy was al-Qaeda, foreign invaders who had hijacked the Afghan government from the Afghan people. The CIA strategy depended upon persuading militia forces allied with the Taliban of this view, and convincing potential allies that their future rested with the small CIA and U.S. military teams …[21]

Accordingly, the first step of the campaign was to persuade as many Afghans as possible to join the United States in the pursuit of its interests. Military force would only be needed to deal with those not otherwise amenable to persuasion.

Several elements had to come together to successfully execute this strategy. Initially, political relationships had to be established. There had to be agreement between the United States and the Afghan resistance with regard to basic objectives. Trust between the two parties had to be generated: trust that the Afghans would act in the interests of the United States and faith that the Americans would provide the requisite support. Once developed at the higher political level, this trust had to be replicated at the lowest tactical levels for both the United States and the resistance. Without this confidence, co-operation would be impossible.

After satisfying political needs, there were a host of military requirements. Enhancing the combat power of the NA first required a great deal of intelligence about friendly and enemy locations, equipment, and disposition. Once identified, the United States could apply air power against the Taliban. At the same time, intelligence about the resistance would allow the Americans to provide the appropriate weapons, equipment and technical advice.

It was also evident that an interagency approach would be required for the United States to conduct a UW campaign in Afghanistan in 2001. The CIA had the only relationship with NA leadership, and as such would fulfill the essential task of politically engaging them, and ensuring that they acted in accordance with American interests. The military, primarily U.S. Army Special Forces (USSF), possessed the kinetic skills required to organize and support the NA in a UW environment to achieve tactical results on the ground. Clearly, the two would have to be combined to effectively execute a UW campaign.

The interagency aspect of the campaign lent a unusual character to the concept of SOF. In America, SOF typically refers to those forces found within the U.S. Special Operations Command (USSOCOM). In OEF, the CIA made a substantial contribution to the UW campaign. By virtue of the CIA's direct involvement in tasks performed and contribution to the UW campaign, as well as the skill sets of the CIA personnel, for the purpose of this chapter, those CIA elements will also be considered as SOF.[22]

Execution — Role of CIA

In the aftermath of the 9/11 attacks, the CIA was well positioned to immediately begin operating in Afghanistan. First, there was the long history of CIA involvement during the war against the Soviet occupation of Afghanistan. Second, there existed a complete operational plan for dislodging the Taliban through the actions of the NA proxy forces. Third, five liaison missions to the NA had been completed in the late 1990s and early 2000s.[23] In fact, to facilitate insertion of officers into northern Afghanistan the CIA purchased and used a surplus Russian military helicopter (MI-17).[24] Thus, it could be said that as far as the CIA was concerned, a UW operation had commenced before 9/11, although it can only be described as embryonic at this stage.

The mission of the CIA teams after 11 September 2001 was to assess the friendly and enemy situation, convince the resistance elements to work with the United States, and make such preparations as were required to permit insertion of USSF.[25] The first CIA team (code named "Jawbreaker") was inserted on 26 September 2001 into northern Afghanistan.[26] The team was led by the equivalent of a three star general and consisted of the team leader, a deputy commander, an operations officer, two paramilitary officers, a communications technician, and a medic. Operational personnel all had extensive intelligence and paramilitary training.[27] This initial team was to be the liaison element to the commander of the NA. Since the NA was a loose coalition of local warlords, additional teams were to be placed with each local NA commander/warlord.[28] As the campaign progressed, CIA involvement extended beyond the NA to the Afghan resistance generally.

The CIA teams accomplished a great deal, particularly considering that only 110 CIA personnel were deployed to Afghanistan in 2001.[29] The teams gathered extensive intelligence about both friendly and enemy forces. Some of this intelligence was gathered from a joint intelligence cell that was established with the NA's own extensive intelligence network.[30] During the first six months of deployment, CIA teams generated almost 2,000 HUMINT reports, more than many other CIA stations combined.[31] Included within this intelligence were extensive GPS-based surveys of friendly and enemy lines that would later be used to direct precision air power and prevent fratricide.[32] Intelligence about friendly forces also permitted diagnosis of equipment and supply deficiencies that permitted a head start on provisioning from U.S. stockpiles. Finally, the CIA established drop zones and landing zones to receive both supplies and USSF forces.[33]

The teams had a limited military capability. The CIA's primary role is not to conduct military operations. Even if there had been a desire to play a larger part in military operations, capabilities were very much lacking. Throughout much of the 1990s, the CIA's covert operations and paramilitary capability had been in decline. There simply were not sufficient numbers of personnel to support extensive paramilitary operations.[34] In 2001, it was estimated that the CIA's paramilitary operations department, known as the Special Activities Division, numbered no more than 500, of which only 120 were paramilitary operators.[35] After the co-operation of resistance forces had been arranged, on a political level, it was up to the USSF to execute the military portion of the UW campaign.

Execution — Role of USSF

Traditional USSF doctrine conceived of UW as progressing through a number of stages spanning political preparation, to covert underground organization, to guerrilla warfare, to full-scale conventional fighting.[36] The situation in northern Afghanistan was different. It consisted of relatively conventional forces facing each other across fixed defensive positions. Consequently, USSF's role was closer to the support of conventional forces than to fomenting an insurgency.

It was clear to the USSF personnel from the outset that their involvement would differ from their traditional conception of UW. Although the various elements of the Afghan resistance were at different levels of combat effectiveness, it was understood that progression through the various stages could be truncated. Major-General Geoffrey Lambert, commander of USSF, believed that the slow phase by phase buildup was not required and that "the war would have a 'velocity and momentum of its own.'"[37] This belief was reflected in the guidance Major-General Lambert offered to the first Operational Detachment — Alpha (ODA) that was inserted into Afghanistan. "Be prepared," he warned, "to fight a conventional battle, including the use of armour."[38] He added, "Put unconventional warfare, a fuzzy concept in today's Army, aside."[39] Lambert continued, "Take your Special Forces and unconventional warfare training, bank it, and then combine it with what you see as necessary to fight a *conventional fight*."[40]

Accomplishing the mission of supporting the Afghan resistance entailed several tasks. First, USSF was the tactical eyes and ears on the ground. The CIA had personnel in theatre, but they were few in number and lacked the tactical appreciation that military personnel possessed. Second, USSF strengthened resistance forces by providing training and matériel support. Upon the commencement of hostilities, their third task was to attrite the enemy by guiding precision air power onto enemy targets. Finally, they also served as combat advisers to the local tactical commanders, providing intelligence, coordination, technical advice, and advocacy for U.S. foreign policy objectives.[41]

The first USSF personnel were inserted into northern Afghanistan on 20 October 2001. Two ODAs were inserted, one with General Mohammed Fahim Khan (ODA 555) and the other with General Rashid Dostum (ODA 595). Both teams were inserted by helicopter at night and were received by NA forces at the landing zone.[42]

ODA 555 was typical of the organization and mission of USSF in OEF. The 12-man team was inserted to assist General Fahim.[43] The insertion had been coordinated with the CIA Jawbreaker team whose members were on hand to receive them.[44] The team consisted of 11 USSF personnel and one U.S. Air Force (USAF) special tactics airman.[45] It was led by Chief Warrant Officer David Diaz who had spent almost a year on CIA-sponsored covert operations in Pakistan and Afghanistan in 1987.[46]

Shortly after its arrival, half of ODA 555 was taken to the front lines at Bagram Air Base, where they faced a "massive Taliban formation, with at least fifty tanks, armored personnel carriers, and trucks with ZSU anti-aircraft guns mounted on them," less than a kilometre away.[47] It took less than a day of precision-guided bombing by close air support to obliterate all Taliban opposition at Bagram, thereby allowing General Fahim's forces to begin advancing on Kabul.[48]

ODA 595 was inserted to assist General Dostum. After insertion the ODA split into two six-man elements. The first element, with the ODA commander, moved with Dostum to the front lines, while the second element remained behind to assess supply requirements and establish drop zones for resupply. The primary means of mobility with Dostum were pack animals, such as mules and horses. Initially Dostum viewed the Americans solely as a source of supply. However, upon demonstrating the effectiveness of American close air support, he quickly incorporated them into his battle plan.[49]

A battle rhythm quickly developed. USSF would target fixed Taliban positions with precision air ordnance. Nearly simultaneously NA forces would charge into the Taliban position, on foot or horseback, taking advantage of the disruption caused by the air attack. Over time, the USSF perfected their technique. To maintain continuous air support over a broad front, the ODA found it necessary to divide into four groups of three men each. This permitted broad coverage, as well as some depth.

The Taliban used reverse slope defensive positions. In particular, most of their armour was positioned on the reverse slope. Thus, it was necessary for the USSF personnel to get beside or behind the Taliban positions to be able to direct ordnance onto the reverse slope positions. By "leap-frogging" from position to position, they were able to keep up with Dostum's cavalry, while providing continuous close air support coverage.[50]

ODAs 555 and 595 are representative of the type of operations conducted by USSF throughout Afghanistan. As time progressed ODAs were inserted with more local resistance commanders and they assisted in similar fashions. Operational Detachment — Charlies, basically consisting of a ready-made, stripped-down UW battalion headquarters staff, were also inserted with key Afghan resistance leaders to enhance military liaison and coordination.[51] USSF assessed local combat power; established drop zones and organized airdrops of weapons, ammunition, equipment, and food; liaised with resistance commanders, and assisted them in developing a tactical plan; guided precision air power; and participated in the ground attack. Once a critical mass of ODAs were assembled on the ground, it did not take long for the Taliban and Al Qaeda to buckle under the pressure brought to bear by the newly invigorated resistance forces. Unrelenting U.S. air power led to the collapse of the Taliban, both physically in terms of the destruction of their fortifications and combat equipment, and morally, in terms of their realization that their loss, if not complete destruction, was certain if they continued to fight.

The annihilation of the Taliban in the north led to their withdrawal to the south. They left Kabul largely undefended, allowing the NA, which was converging from several directions, to easily occupy the capital. At this point, the United States faced a strategic dilemma. The resistance consisted almost entirely of NA forces. Very little organized resistance existed in the south of Afghanistan. Viewed along ethnic lines, the NA was a largely Tajik, Uzbek, and Hazara force. It was feared that NA domination of the country would result in post-conflict political instability. The United States wanted to see a substantial Pashtun presence in the new Afghan government.[52]

In this regard, Hamid Karzai, the future leader of Afghanistan, had infiltrated into southern Afghanistan on 8 October 2001 to organize resistance to the Taliban in that locality.[53] He had been identified by the CIA as the most promising leader in the south.[54] On 14 November 2001, ODA 574 was inserted to assist Karzai. The situation in the south was different from that in the north. There were no organized resistance forces. What personnel Karzai could gather were assembled in an ad hoc fashion. They lacked weapons, training, and organization. Although the ODA attempted to provide some rudimentary training and arranged the air drop of supplies, the combat readiness of the forces in the south (approximately 150 personnel) remained low in early November 2001.[55]

The situation in the south was especially grave because Kandahar was the base of support for the Taliban. Upon learning of Karzai's presence at Tarin Kowt, the Taliban attacked. With little in the way of local forces, the USSF had to rely almost exclusively on air support to defend against the attack. Fortunately, the ODA was able to locate a canalizing piece of ground that would serve as an excellent ambush location. Although eventually dislodged from this position, and forced to fall back, the ODA was highly successful in employing precision air ordnance against the Taliban attack, which was defeated. The remnants of the Taliban retreated to Kandahar.[56]

The victory at Tarin Kowt was important because it convinced many in the area of the effectiveness of Karzai and, consequently, helped promote the growth of his forces. By late November, Karzai's forces had grown to over 700.[57] As the resistance grew in the south, the Taliban were increasingly encircled around Kandahar, until their eventual collapse, allowing the United States and resistance forces to take Kandahar by negotiated surrender. The fall of Kandahar marked the effective victory over the Taliban and Al Qaeda whose members were thereby limited to a number of remote areas of the country. This victory was achieved by approximately 316 USSF and 110 CIA personnel who were deployed in Afghanistan at the time.[58]

Campaign Timeline

The following summary of events provides an appreciation of the chronology of the campaign:[59]

> 26 September 2001: First CIA team (Jawbreaker) inserted.
>
> 7 October 2001: Bombing begins.
>
> 20 October 2001: ODAs 555 and 595 inserted.
>
> Early November: More ODAs inserted to assist local resistance commanders.
>
> 9 November 2001: Fall of Mazar-e Sharif — Taliban crumbles in North.
>
> 11–12 November 2001: Kabul and Herat captured.
>
> 14 November 2001: ODA 574 joins Hamid Karzai and move to Tarin Kowt.
>
> 18 November 2001: Battle of Tarin Kowt — Taliban retreat to Kandahar.
>
> 1 December 2001: Karzai moves on Kandahar.
>
> 7 December 2001: Karzai and USSF take Kandahar.
>
> 3–17 December 2001: Tora Bora — Senior Al Qaeda leaders escape.

ASSESSMENT OF MISSION SUCCESS

As previously stated, the US sought two strategic objectives in Afghanistan. The first was to remove the Taliban and install a regime friendly to the United States to prevent Afghanistan from serving as a haven for terrorists. The second was to capture Osama bin Laden. The primary mission was accomplished. By 7 December 2001, Kabul was under control of the Afghan resistance and the Taliban/Al Qaeda forces were restricted to relatively isolated, strategically insignificant patches of terrain. The Taliban had clearly been dethroned and control was asserted by a U.S.-friendly coalition of Afghans. The primary mission was accomplished by employing an unconventional warfare methodology.

The secondary mission, however, remains unaccomplished. This goal, however, was not the main focus of the UW campaign. The full details of the secondary mission remain secret and thus a thorough analysis is not yet possible. Notably, since the focus of this chapter is the role played by UW in OEF, the failure to attain the secondary objective, which relied much less on UW and much more on unilateral direct action by USSO-COM, is of lesser importance to the this specific analysis.

In a broad theoretical sense, the success or failure of a UW campaign depends heavily upon a number of political, economic and social factors. The fact that victory was attained in Afghanistan is *prima facie* evidence of UW's effectiveness. However, some critics assert that the victory in Afghanistan was idiosyncratic and, without existing special circumstances, UW would have been less fruitful. A number of factors are cited in support of the claim that the situation in Afghanistan was unique and ripe for victory with the use of UW. Indeed, the following characteristics within Afghanistan have been noted:

- Poor enemy morale or motivation;
- Poor enemy military training and expertise;
- Lack of popular support for the Taliban regime;
- The ease of defection in Afghan culture;
- Surprise (i.e., speed and violence of offensive action, tactics);
- Taliban dependency on fragile sources of outside support; and
- Availability of contiguous, secure territory for resupplying and re-equipping proxy forces.[60]

Thus it is important to keep in mind that there may be a degree of uniqueness to the Afghan situation, rendering it more amenable to UW. Notwithstanding the criticism, the focus of the chapter is to determine the operational and military considerations that led to success, even given a pre-existing susceptibility to UW. In other words, given the hand that it was dealt, what did SOF do that allowed it to succeed?

REASONS FOR SUCCESS

Success in Afghanistan required altering the political balance of power: removing the Taliban from power and installing a U.S.-friendly regime. The U.S. strategy for achieving this result was two-pronged. First, the Americans had to persuade as many Afghans as possible to support American interests. Second, for those Afghans and foreign fighters who were not amenable to persuasion, the United States had to use force to destroy their ability to exert influence on Afghan affairs.

Persuading Afghans to support the United States cause took two forms: non-coercive and coercive influence. Local warlords were offered direct cash payments in exchange for their support. The co-operation of local Taliban commanders could be bought for US$50,000 to US$100,000.[61] If non-coercive persuasion failed, there were plenty of coercive resources that could be employed. In more than one instance negotiations with local Taliban leaders were expedited by dropping a precision-guided bomb close to their headquarters.[62]

Notwithstanding persuasion, there will always be a faction of intransigents who must be removed by force, which was the second part of the U.S. strategy. In the early stages of OEF, with only a few hundred SOF on the ground, it was impossible to "go it alone." UW was the means by which force was employed against those parties who could not otherwise be influenced. The indigenous Afghans were the source of combat power on the ground and they would be supported by U.S. air power. The basic tactical elements of the campaign resembled those familiar to orthodox, conventional military theorists: there was a manoeuvre element (the indigenous Afghans) supported by a fire element (U.S. air power).[63] Thus the simplest explanation for success in Afghanistan is that the United States made more effective use of the traditional elements of fire and manoeuvre than the Taliban/Al Qaeda, resulting in a military victory.

Answering the question of "how" the Americans were able to employ superior fire and manoeuvre is more difficult, but necessary to establish why UW and SOF were responsible for victory in Afghanistan. Although, tactically, the style of fighting resembled that found in many prior conventional battles, having to organize and synchronize fire and manoeuvre elements in a UW context was a highly complex task. But for the presence of SOF, the United States and resistance forces would not have been able to co-operate to the degree necessary to synchronize these two elements. The discussion that follows dissects role of SOF in achieving this outcome.

Manoeuvre Element: The Resistance

The manoeuvre elements were based entirely on the Afghan resistance forces. Although the use of the term "resistance" implies a unified entity, they were anything but. Substantial negotiation and persuasion was required to convince factions with divergent interests to participate in the campaign. Quite simply, the resistance had to be persuaded to act in line with American interests. The CIA provided persuasion and coordination at the political and strategic level where Afghan leaders had to be persuaded to co-operate with U.S. foreign policy objectives. The USSF teams had to exert influence down to the lowest tactical level, whether it meant convincing local commanders of a particular tactical course of action, or leading Afghan troops in operations. Every SOF-Afghan interaction required the exercise of influence, which occurred constantly, and was of vital importance. SOF was uniquely able to exert this influence because of their language abilities, cultural sensitivity, skill sets, and access to U.S. air power.

By employing these skills and resources, they were able to shape resistance behaviour through financial incentives, tangible matériel support, and coercion.[64] With regard to financial influence, it is estimated that the CIA disbursed US$70 million in cash in Afghanistan. Aside from the payment made to induce Taliban defections, this cash was also vital to securing co-operation and building the combat power of Afghan forces by acquiring weapons, food, and other matériel.[65]

The matériel support that was provided was key to American victory. However, the Al Qaeda opposition could not be bought off. Cash ultimately had to be converted into combat power to be of any value. Direct matériel support, such as weapons, ammunition, food, and clothing, were valuable, and often requested by the Afghans, so extensive efforts were made by SOF to supply these goods. The details of this support are included below. The important point is that the promise of physical goods helped influence resistance attitudes.

Finally, coercion was also important. The constant demonstration of the effectiveness and destructive impact of U.S. air power went a long way toward convincing those commanders who wavered in their support of American interests.

Adeptly manipulating the levers of influence assured Afghan co-operation. To translate this willingness into tactical success on the ground required much more. SOF had to ensure that the resistance forces were capable of conducting the manoeuvre task for that it was responsible. Although experienced, the NA lacked sufficient weapons, equipment, and supplies. After the CIA and USSF had assessed the state of the local Afghan forces, they requested the appropriate weapons and equipment, selected drop zones, and arranged reception parties. USAF aircraft then dropped the required cargo. The scale of these deliveries was large. From mid-October to mid-December 2001, 770,000 kilograms of matériel were dropped in 108 sorties on 41 different drop zones throughout Afghanistan.[66]

Without SOF, this effort would have been less successful and, perhaps, would have even failed. The following example is instructive. Early in the campaign it became evident that NA forces were in need of food, for both themselves and their families. CIA personnel communicated this need to higher headquarters and selected a drop zone. To deliver the food the USAF pushed the prepackaged meals, in a form very similar to the U.S. military "Meals Ready to Eat" (MRE),[67] off the aircraft without parachutes. Changes in air pressure, combined with impact with the ground caused the packages to rupture, causing much of the food to be lost or be spoiled. The lack of tangible usable food was an embarrassment and showed an inability to fulfill a promise. Moreover, the spoiled food made many people sick. In the end, this was hardly conducive to winning the confidence of the Afghan resistance. SOF on the ground quickly diagnosed the problem, the CIA requisitioned cargo parachutes through their supply channels and the problem was corrected.[68]

SOF also was intimately involved in the fighting on the ground. Some have the impression that ground forces merely walked onto the objectives after devastating air attacks had destroyed all Taliban/Al Qaeda resistance. This was not the case. Fighting on the ground was intense and necessary. As scholar and military analyst Stephen Biddle has explained:

> If SOF-directed air power had simply annihilated Taliban forces at standoff range, as some now suppose, then even a radically unsophisticated army would have been sufficient to walk in and occupy the blasted ruins. But in Afghanistan, though air power could destroy most of a hostile force, it could not annihilate well-prepared defenses outright. Nor could it defeat well-directed, skillfully concealed assaults by itself. The result was a series of close combat actions, rather than a war fought exclusively at standoff ranges. And in these actions, even a few al Qaeda survivors, properly motivated and armed with modern automatic weapons, could mow down large numbers of unsophisticated indigenous soldiers caught exposed in the open. To survive long enough to take advantage of the tremendous firepower leveled by American air support thus required the fundamental combat skills of cover, concealment, dispersed small unit maneuver and local suppressive fire.[69]

Not only was fighting on the ground essential, but SOF played a large part in this fight. Usually the first step in building the resistance force is training. The NA forces had years of experience in fighting. The traditional USSF plan of instruction for the resistance force, consisting of rudimentary training in individual and small-unit infantry tactics, was largely not required because the NA forces had already been fighting small unit battles for years.[70] However, the NA was lacking in its ability to mount large-scale offensive operations. While USSF is trained and organized to provide training and mentoring to the battalion level,[71] the time for this training was not available. The campaign unfolded too rapidly. Without the ability to train the resistance forces, SOF had to take an active role in combat operations on the ground.

The best example is the actions of ODA 574 whose members almost single-handedly conducted the battle at Tarin Kowt which was discussed earlier. In the south, the resistance was very inexperienced, leaving the task of planning and leadership almost entirely to SOF in the early stages of the fighting there. In the north, the situation was better, but SOF still performed a unique and active role, such as in the case of the capture of Mazar-e-Sharif. In essence, SOF conducted the following actions in the fight to defeat the Taliban and Al Qaeda in 2001:[72]

- Directed air strikes;
- Liaised with three separate, and previously opposed, Afghan factions, securing their agreement to be nominally subordinate to General Dostum;
- Coordinated offensive action of three separate resistance factions, none of which had operated together before, and whose commanders had little proficiency in large, coordinated offensives;
- Tracked and reported on offensive progress, as most sub-unit commanders lacked the ability to read maps;
- Provided radio communications, as NA radios were lacking or not interoperable; and
- Imposed control measures to prevent fratricide, since the NA wore no uniforms and could not be identified visually.

Clearly, SOF was instrumental in organizing the manoeuvre elements on the ground. No other entity could have done this because it required the maturity and training unique to SOF. They supplied the resistance with weapons and supplies, led them in combat, provided coordination across the theatre, and permitted synchronization with the fire element (air power).

Fire Element: Air Power

U.S. air power provided the fire element. The importance of air power in influencing resistance behaviour was a core component of American success. The promise of attriting Taliban forces with air power, and thus substantially reducing casualties for the Afghan resistance, appealed to resistance commanders and made them more willing to participate in ground operations. In fact, at the highest levels of command within the Afghan resistance, decisions to act, i.e., attack, were based on availability of American air power. As such, the initial delays in delivering air power directly to the frontlines in some Northern sectors cost SOF much credibility in the early days of the campaign.[73] At lower tactical levels, several USSF ODAs commented that it took no more than a few precision-guided sorties to win the hearts of local commanders and troops. After directly experiencing the utility of American air power, the respective ODAs were rapidly accepted and incorporated into all local tactical planning.[74]

More important, air power contributed substantial combat power to the actual conflict. Without air power, a UW victory may have been possible but it would doubtlessly have taken much longer. When conceived by military planners, the UW campaign was to take several months to equip and train Afghan resistance forces, with the ground offensive not beginning until April or May of 2002.[75] That the campaign unfolded at an accelerated rate was in part because the combat capability of the NA was underestimated in the planning. In larger part, it was because U.S. air power was effective.

The ability to precisely target and destroy Taliban and Al Qaeda positions allowed victory on the ground, at substantially reduced cost in both personnel and equipment. Without SOF, however, the application of air power would not have been as effective. It was SOF on the ground that identified and located targets, guided ordnance onto the targets, assessed bomb damage, and, most important, synchronized the ground assault. SOF had to employ many capabilities to succeed at this task, from the technical role of guiding precision ordnance, to the tactical role of determining how and when to employ such ordnance, to the diplomatic role of persuading Afghan ground commanders how to best take advantage of the destruction caused by air power. Although air power inflicted substantial damage, without SOF, those effects would not have been advantageously exploited.

LESSONS LEARNED

The success of UW in OEF offers several important lessons to UW practitioners. The following is a brief overview of some of the most obvious.

The New UW Paradigm — An Expanded Theory of UW

UW has always had a close nexus with insurgency and guerrilla warfare. The U.S. doctrinal definition of UW cited earlier does not explicitly restrict UW to an insurgent or guerrilla context but that is, quite frankly, the focus of U.S. doctrine.[76] OEF demonstrated that UW does not have to rely on guerrilla warfare. OEF involved the use of indigenous forces, in a relatively conventional conflict, with fixed lines and combined arms operations, though on a limited scale. This indicates that guerrilla-based UW is only one example of a larger concept for the use of indigenous forces under SOF sponsorship. UW can exist along a spectrum, from conventional to guerrilla warfare, and doctrine must acknowledge this broader application.[77]

OEF demonstrated that this spectrum can be very wide indeed. Attaining the ultimate end of a political result does not depend exclusively upon employing kinetic means. To quote Sun Tzu, "To fight and conquer in all your battles is not supreme excellence; supreme excellence consists in breaking the enemy's resistance without fighting."[78] In effect, this is what SOF (primarily the CIA component) accomplished in Afghanistan. Through incentives and coercion, large numbers of Taliban defections were induced, which significantly reduced the combat power of the Taliban/Al Qaeda alliance. This preparatory step made the kinetic phase of the campaign that much easier. This tactic should be incorporated into UW doctrine and employed in future as circumstances permit.

Importance of Intelligence to UW

In UW, intelligence has more dimensions than in more traditional operations because the intelligence must inform about both friendly and enemy disposition. In a conventional campaign, most intelligence concerns the enemy disposition. Understandably, if friendly forces are composed of a singular army, then there is little doubt about the friendly disposition. However, UW depends on the ability to exert influence upon indigenous agents. These indigenous agents may have varying degrees of commitment to the friendly cause. In fact, as demonstrated in the Henry Crumpton quote cited earlier, even initially hostile forces can be viewed as a potential ally, if they can be sufficiently influenced to embrace the friendly cause.

Successfully exerting the requisite influence requires information as a prerequisite. Persuasion of resistance actors requires knowledge of their preferences, political sensitivities, economic means, and military disposition. The entirety of their political, military, economic, and social disposition must be understood in order to comprehend their preferences. Based on this knowledge, the most effective form of assistance can be offered in exchange for support of U.S. objectives.

Importantly, the CIA also amassed a great deal of intelligence about friendly force disposition. HUMINT based intelligence collection accelerated in the late 1990s. On 10 September 2001, the CIA had over 100 HUMINT sources and sub-sources operating in Afghanistan. These sources spanned all social classes and ethnic groups.[79] In addition, there were five prior Jawbreaker missions into Afghanistan, as well as a number of meetings with Afghan resistance leaders outside of Afghanistan.[80] These prior contacts would have offered natural opportunities to assess attitudes of the Afghan resistance and determine the on-the-ground realities of friendly force disposition. Had the CIA not possessed this intelligence, then the UW campaign would have taken much longer, or may not have even been possible.

Intelligence about enemy forces was also important. Naturally, the CIA had extensive technical and imagery intelligence. Furthermore, HUMINT had not been overlooked. By 1999, the CIA had substantially increased intelligence collection in Afghanistan. In February 1999 the CIA began joint intelligence operations with NA forces, including information sharing, reconnaissance teams, and recruitment of human sources.[81] NA HUMINT resources extended all over Afghanistan. Native Afghans were free to circulate throughout the country relatively unimpeded. Almost unbelievably, it was customary to allow unarmed personnel to cross fortified positions so that they could proceed to other areas of the country to visit with relatives.[82] Most importantly, pre-existing relationships at all levels could be exploited. Knowing the satellite telephone number and family history of a local Taliban commander proved invaluable.

Preparation for UW

OEF showed that UW begins well before the first contact or combat. A U.S. presence in northern Afghanistan well before 2001 ensured that sufficient intelligence and interpersonal relationships existed to support a UW campaign. Furthermore, USSF were prepared for a UW campaign and well trained for its conduct. Finally, the U.S. had sufficient supporting assets available, such that they could be deployed quickly. The ability to assemble 770,000 kilograms of matériel, both humanitarian and military, and deliver this load, all within two months, demonstrates that there was a high level of preparedness for this type of campaign within the U.S. military establishment.

Undeniably, employing UW requires resources and preparation. To have the UW infrastructure ready, political and military leaders must have the foresight to predict the location of future conflicts and whether or not those theatres are susceptible to a UW campaign. Having sufficient numbers of trained and experienced UW practitioners is one of the most important preparations that also requires the longest lead time.

Personnel

The most critical asset in UW is well selected and highly trained SOF personnel who then bring the whole UW campaign together. UW in OEF offers many lessons about the type of personnel and their requisite abilities. In this campaign the UW role was split between the CIA and USSOCOM.[83]

CIA operators brought experience and diplomatic skills, and these skills were very well employed to collect and extract HUMINT and thereby achieve UW objectives. Most importantly, it was the ability to apply HUMINT to conduct UW operations that was vital to the American victory. Notably, UW and HUMINT have overlapping skill sets. For example, the ability to speak local Afghan languages was crucial to building relationships with Afghan political figures. For instance, the CIA teams included personnel who spoke Farsi/Dari, Uzbek, Russian and/or Arabic.[84] In addition, they were specialists in exerting political influence and employing strong interpersonal and relationship management skills. Performing this function required people with great experience and maturity. Indeed, the average age of CIA personnel on the Jawbreaker team was 45, with an average of 25 years of experience.[85] Jawbreaker team leader, Gary Schroen, held the CIA rank equivalent to a three-star general, and delayed his retirement to participate in the mission.[86] It is also important to note that all the CIA's functions were performed under austere conditions, in a hostile environment, requiring a baseline competence in fieldcraft, weapons, and tactics.[87]

The USSF operators in turn brought kinetic capabilities. They were the experts in weapons, tactics, and logistics. They also demonstrated the ability to employ conventional tactics in unconventional environments. There was little in U.S. doctrine to directly guide their actions, but an emphasis on flexibility and adaptability as the core of their UW training allowed them to solve the novel problems that arose.[88]

Expertise in applying force does not mean that softer, interpersonal skills were not also required. As previously noted, every level of UW, whether strategic, operational, or tactical, requires co-operation with indigenous agents and, thus, cultural sensitivity, language skills, and a certain degree of empathy. In fact, there were instances where USSF ODAs were unable to find a common language with their Afghan hosts, resulting in a delay in operations of up to weeks in some cases.[89] Accordingly, kinetic skills are necessary but not sufficient. UW operators have to possess a balance of kinetic and "softer" skills.

Interagency Co-operation

Splitting operational responsibilities between USSOCOM and the CIA created interagency co-operation issues. Political turf battles at the highest levels impaired operational effectiveness from the beginning. Additionally, military SOF entered the theatre more than one month after the CIA because the U.S. Department of Defense objected to CIA leadership during the early stages of the campaign.

Although USSOCOM routinely trains in a joint environment involving U.S. Air Force, U.S. Navy, and U.S. Army elements, there seems to be very little planning or practice of joint CIA-USSOCOM operations. This is inferred from a number of documented events. For example, USSF had difficulty gaining access to CIA intelligence about NA leaders because of a shortage of USSF personnel with a "Top Secret" security clearance. The situation was sufficiently difficult that the regulations were temporarily ignored by the commander of U.S. 5th Special Forces Group, as he viewed it as the only common sense solution to the pressing needs of the circumstance.[90]

The insertion of ODA 555 offers another example of the seeming lack of trust between the CIA and USSOCOM. ODA 555 was in full communication with the Jawbreaker team, with which it was to be colocated. Jawbreaker had reconnoitred and marked landing zones and had prepared a reception party. Regardless, ODA 555 treated the insertion as one into hostile territory. They overflew the marked landing zone, landing some distance away, in two separate teams. Additionally, they did not advise the on-site CIA team of their arrival until shortly before landing. The result was mass confusion and an elevated risk of fratricide as the ODA acted in a manner unexpected by CIA personnel.[91]

Clearly, if a UW campaign is to be conducted by different parties, those agencies have to better integrate on several levels. First, they must share a common doctrine. Second, they should participate in joint training exercises and cross-postings. These types of activities are crucial if the different agencies are to build the level of mutual trust required to conduct these types of dangerous operations. For example, USSOCOM and the CIA, if they plan to conduct similar ventures, need to share a connectedness on par with that experienced by the different service arms within USSOCOM.

CONCLUSION

SOF operations in Afghanistan during the early days of OEF provide many lessons about the use of UW. The campaign was successful for several reasons. Early involvement by the CIA provided a solid foundation of intelligence and relationships with the indigenous forces. Recognition by the CIA of the idiosyncratic nature of Afghan culture and the ability to substitute cash and persuasion for brute force greatly diminished the extent of the military task by reducing the size and resources of the opposition. The CIA was also instrumental in securing the co-operation of friendly Afghan factions to ensure their support and facilitate their employment in the use of force.

For their part, USSF did the heavy lifting of the military campaign, as the experts in weapons, tactics, and logistics. Their maturity, cultural sensitivity, and overall ability to establish rapport allowed them to effectively employ these skills in a UW context. These abilities were applied to build and strengthen the resistance forces based upon a pre-existing military infrastructure. By delivering weapons and supplies, and adding liaison, tactical advice, advanced technology, and techniques (such as radios and laser target designators), USSF was able to organize a manoeuvre element on the ground, and synchronize it with the firepower element in the air. The result was the destruction of the ability of the Taliban to maintain political control over Afghanistan. Without such control, Al Qaeda was no longer free to use the country as a safe haven. Thus, a political victory was achieved by SOF employing UW.

UW doctrine should be expanded to solidly encompass all the tactics, techniques, and procedures employed in OEF. Recognition should be given to the greater importance of intelligence, about both friend and foe, in UW and the requirement for such intelligence to be heavily sourced through HUMINT.

Preparation for UW requires skilled, experienced operators possessing both highly developed political and kinetic skills. To conduct an effective UW campaign requires that these personnel are in place well before the commencement of the actual warfighting campaign. If the skills required to prosecute a UW campaign are conducted by different government agencies, then attention must be paid to interagency friction points, and doctrine and training should be unified.

This chapter touched upon many of the most obvious lessons about UW that were learned during OEF but there remains much additional work to be done. UW campaigns are infrequent. Consequently, every effort must be made to learn what lessons we can through intensive study of what few examples are available and to then apply this new knowledge as expeditiously as possible in the form of new strategy and doctrine.

NOTES

1. See Shah M. Tarzi, "Politics of the Afghan Resistance Movement: Cleavages, Disunity, and Fragmentation," *Asian Survey*, Vol. 31, No. 6 (June 1991), 479–95, for an analysis of the politics underlying Afghan disunity. See also Stephen Tanner, *Afghanistan: A Military History from Alexander the Great to the Fall of the Taliban* (New York: Da Capo Press, 2003) for a full historical account.

2. Aside from the NA, organized resistance against the Taliban was almost non-existent. Later in the campaign it became a serious issue as to how to ensure that the Pashtun majority was fairly represented in the post-Taliban political structure. Hamid Karzai, with the help of the U.S., was ultimately able to raise a small Pashtun resistance element in the south. However, all the serious damage that was inflicted upon the Taliban arose from the combat operations of the NA. Two terms will be used throughout this paper to designate anti-Taliban elements. "Northern Alliance," or NA, refers only to the loose coalition of ethnic minorities in the north of Afghanistan. The term "Afghan resistance," or simply "resistance," will be used to denote all anti-Taliban forces, including the NA and those resistance elements that were organized during the later stage of the U.S. campaign in the south.

3. Kenneth Katzman, *Afghanistan: Post-War Governance, Security, and U.S. Policy* (Washington: Congressional Research Service, 6 November 2006), 3.

4. Stephen Biddle, *Afghanistan and the Future of Warfare: Implications for Army and Defense Policy* (Carlisle, PA: U.S. Army War College, 2002), 13–14.

5. *Ibid.,* 14, note 30.

6. The author was unable to find a concise summary of the Taliban or NA order of battle. However, several accounts of combat action support this claim. In particular see the discussions of the fighting with General Dostum in Gary Berntsen and Ralph Pezzullo, *Jawbreaker* (New York: Crown Publishers, 2005), 135; and Robin Moore, *The Hunt for Bin Laden: Task Force Dagger* (New York: Random House, 2003), 69–72.

7. "The Liberation of Mazar-e Sharif: 5th SF Group Conducts UW in Afghanistan," *Special Warfare*, Vol. 15, No. 2 (June 2002), 36.

8. Mark Anderson and Greg Barker, producers, "Campaign Against Terror," *Frontline* (Public Broadcasting Service, September 2002). Transcript online at *www.pbs.org/ wgbh/pages/frontline/shows/campaign* (accessed 15 June 2008), interview with Pervez Musharraf, 7–8.

9. *Ibid.*, cited interviews with Condoleezza Rice, Colin Powell, and Vladimir Putin, 4–11.

10. See George Crile, *Charlie Wilson's War* (New York: Grove Press, 2003) for one popular account.

11. The facts surrounding the Kasi incident are summarized in George Tenet, *At the Center of the Storm* (New York: Harper Perennial, 2007), 41–42.

12. Tenet, 112.

13. *Ibid.*, 114.

14. *Ibid.*, 127.

15. See Steve Coll, *Ghost Wars* (New York: Penguin Books, 2004), 501–06 for some of the politico-military considerations that governed the possible use of SOF to kill or capture Osama bin Laden before 11 September.

16. Steve Coll, "Ahmad Shah Massoud Links with CIA," *The Washington Post*, 23 February 2004, *www.rawa.org/massoud_cia.htm* (accessed 21 May 2008). This article is a

concise summary of the CIA-NA relationship in the late 1990s. For the exhaustive account of how the relationship evolved see Coll, *Ghost Wars.*

17. Out of necessity, this paper discusses only the primary mission. The secondary mission of killing or capturing bin Laden was also led by SOF. However, most of the details of how this mission was executed remain secret and there is little data to present or analyze.

18. Tenet, 208; and Dr. Richard L. Kiper, "'Find Those Responsible': The Beginnings of Operation Enduring Freedom," *Special Warfare,* Vol. 15, No. 3 (September 2002), 4. Note also that the CIA remained the *de facto* lead agency until late October 2001, when a memorandum of understanding was executed between the Department of Defense and the CIA granting the military greater authority over the campaign. Tenet, 216.

19. Although it appears that SOF from other countries were also present, there is little to no discussion of their activities in the literature, as a result this chapter focuses on the role of U.S. SOF.

20. *Field Manual No. 3–05 — Army Special Operations Forces* (Washington: Department of the Army, 2006), 2–1.

21. Henry A. Crumpton, "Intelligence and War: Afghanistan, 2001–2002," in *Transforming U.S. Intelligence,* ed. J. Sims and B. Gerber (Washington: Georgetown University Press, 2005), 164. Note that Henry "Hank" Crumpton was intimately involved in the UW campaign plan used to topple the Taliban, according to George Tenet, then Director of the CIA (see *Center of the Storm,* 214 and 217). Accordingly, the Crumpton paper offers an insider's version of events.

22. There are two additional factors supporting this conclusion. First, the CIA is itself an evolution of the Office of Strategic Services (OSS) of the Second World War, which is widely acknowledged to be a SOF. During the Second World War, the assets necessary to conduct UW were housed within one organization: OSS in the U.S., and the Special Operations Execution (SOE) in Britain. Almost all would agree that both the OSS and SOE are SOF. Accordingly, the separation of the intelligence capabilities and kinetic capabilities necessary to conduct UW, between USSOCOM and CIA, creates an unnecessary distinction. Both are SOF-type assets.

    Second, many of the personnel deployed by the CIA into Afghanistan were themselves former members of traditional U.S. SOF. Of the seven individuals on the first team that was inserted with the NA, two had served previously as SEALs, one with USSF, and one with the U.S. Marine Corps. That SOF training is so heavily represented speaks to the close nexus between USSOCOM and the paramilitary branch of the CIA, and their associated tasks. See Gary C. Schroen, *First In* (New York: Presidio Press, 2005), 17–24.

23. Steve Coll, "Ahmad Shah Massoud Links with CIA," *The Washington Post,* 23 February 2004, *www.rawa.org/massoud_cia.htm* (accessed 21 May 2008); and Tenet, 207.

24. Tenet, 209.

25. Schroen, 38.

26. *Ibid.,* 78.

27. *Ibid.,* 17–24.

28. Tenet, 213.

29. Bob Woodward, "CIA Led Way with Cash Handouts," *The Washington Post,* 18 November 2002, A01.

30. Schroen, 111–112.
31. Crumpton, *Intelligence and War*, 171.
32. Schroen, 121–128.
33. *Ibid.*, 165–166.
34. Douglas Waller, "The CIA's Secret Army," *Time*, Canadian ed., Vol. 161, No. 5 (3 February 2003), 18.
35. Major Vincent Paul Bramble, *Covert Action Lead — Central Intelligence Agency or Special Forces?* (Unpublished monograph prepared as part of the Advanced Military Studies Program, U.S. Army Command and General Staff College, 2007), 22. The author does not provide any citation for this information other than stating that he conducted interviews at "CIA Headquarters." This order of magnitude regarding CIA paramilitary strength agrees with anecdotal evidence about the general shortage of CIA paramilitary personnel at the time.
36. *Field Manual No. 31–20 — Doctrine for Special Forces Operations* (Washington: Department of the Army, 1990), 9–1 to 9–4.
37. Charles H. Briscoe and others, *Weapon of Choice* (Fort Leavenworth, KS: Combat Studies Institute Press, 2003), 93.
38. Robin Moore, *The Hunt for Bin Laden: Task Force Dagger* (New York: Random House, 2003), 42.
39. *Ibid.*, 40.
40. *Ibid.*, 42 [emphasis added]. Note that the expectation that the conflict would look very much like a conventional battle did not mean that everyone expected it to progress as quickly as it did. In fact, the expectation was that it would take several months to organize the resistance into a cohesive fighting force. See Dr. Kalev I. Sepp, "The Campaign in Transition: from Conventional to Unconventional War," *Special Warfare*, Vol. 13, No. 3 (September 2002), 24.
41. Moore, 40–42.
42. Briscoe and others, 96.
43. Moore, 89.
44. Schroen , 221–216.
45. Moore, 91.
46. *Ibid.*, 89.
47. *Ibid.*, 92.
48. *Ibid.*, 95.
49. *Ibid.*, 66–67.
50. *Ibid.*, 69–75.
51. Briscoe and others, 98; and Moore, 80–81.
52. Anderson and Barker, "Campaign Against Terror," 26–28.
53. Briscoe and others, 154.
54. *Ibid.*, 154.
55. *Ibid.*, 154–58.
56. *Ibid.*, 154–58.
57. Moore, 214.
58. Woodward, "CIA Led Way," A01.
59. Timeline adapted from the one found at *www.pbs.org/wgbh/pages/frontline/shows/campaign/etc/cron.html* (accessed 15 June 2008).
60. Biddle, *Afghanistan and the Future of Warfare*, 12. Biddle examines each of these

factors and argues that the evidence suggests that the Afghan situation was not idiosyncratic.

61. Woodward, "CIA Led Way," A01.

62. *Ibid.*

63. The concept of reducing the key tactical elements to fire and manoeuvre is taken from Biddle, *Afghanistan and the Future of Warfare,* 41–49, where the fighting in OEF is found to be similar, in its basic theoretical elements, to that seen in the Second World War, the Arab-Israeli Wars, and Vietnam. Biddle characterizes the victory in Afghanistan as being much more conventional than typically thought and attributes the victory to the successful employment of fire and manoeuvre, rather than to idiosyncratic circumstances.

64. This classification was implied by Henry Crumpton in *Intelligence and War,* 168–69.

65. Much is made of the value of these cash payments in securing co-operation but, in a primitive economy such as Afghanistan, increasing the supply of U.S. dollars by several orders of magnitude inevitably resulted in inflation, since there was an increasing quantity of dollars chasing a relatively fixed quantity of resources. Had the campaign lasted longer, the utility of cash payments in securing co-operation would probably have declined.

66. Crumpton, 168.

67. A plastic pouch containing retort-packed, pre-cooked food items, with each pouch containing sufficient food for a meal.

68. Schroen, 168, 180, and 188.

69. Biddle, *Afghanistan and the Future of Warfare,* 42.

70. See *Guerrilla Plan of Instruction.* Fort Bragg, NC: John F. Kennedy Special Warfare Center (undated). While USSF was surely capable of more advanced training, the rapidity with which the campaign unfolded was another major factor in preventing much utility from being derived from training of the resistance.

71. *Special Forces Basic Tasks — Soldier's Manual and Trainer's Guide, CFM 18* (STP31–18-SM-TG), (Washington: Department of the Army, 1991), 3–375.

72. This list is distilled from the lessons outlined in "The Liberation of Mazar-e Sharif," 34 to 41. This article was written by members of 5th Special Forces Group based on their experiences in OEF.

73. Schroen, 148–49 and 152–56.

74. Moore, 111, for one example.

75. Briscoe and others, 94.

76. *Field Manual No. 31–20 — Doctrine for Special Forces Operations* (Washington: Department of the Army, 1990), 9–1 to 9–16. For example, see chapter 9 where evolution through a seven phase insurgency (an extended version of Mao's famous three stages) is seen as the foundation for a UW campaign. Note that this manual has since been superseded by FM 3–05.201 — *Special Forces Unconventional Warfare Operations,* April 2003, which is not publicly available. Thus, the more dated FM 31–20 is the only publicly available source of information upon official USSF UW doctrine. If the author had access to the current field manual, some of the conclusions stated herein may have changed.

77. The implication of OEF to UW doctrine are discussed at length in Hy S. Rothstein, *Afghanistan and the Troubled Future of Unconventional Warfare* (Annapolis, MD: Naval Institute Press, 2006), which is recommended.

78. Sun Tzu, *The Art of War,* translated and edited by James Clavell (New York: Dell, 1988), 15.

79. Crumpton, 163.

80. *Ibid.,* 163 and Schroen, 89.

81. Crumpton, 163.

82. Berntsen and Pezzullo, 110–11.

83. This is not to imply that this separation was intentional. Whether it was the result of historical accident or primarily a result of bureaucratic infighting remains an open question.

84. Tenet, 213.

85. *Ibid.,* 209.

86. Schroen, 22.

87. All Jawbreaker team members were armed with carbines (AK-47), pistols (Browning Hi-Power) and night vision equipment (Schroen, 28), and presumably knew how to use them. Additional details on the paramilitary training of CIA Clandestine Service recruits can be found in Lindsay Moran, *Blowing My Cover: My Life as a CIA Spy* (New York: G.P. Putnam's Sons, 2005), 59–110. Before a six month course in intelligence tradecraft, all Clandestine Service recruits participate in a SOF-like paramilitary training course including (circa 1998) physical training and an obstacle course; general military orientation and discipline; one week of land navigation; two weeks of defensive/offensive driver training; one week of explosives and demolition; one week of small boat handling, DZ/LZ preparation, and aerial resupply operations; one week of tactical firearms/weapons training; one week of hand-to-hand combat and first aid; two weeks of static line parachute training; and a two week guerrilla warfare field training exercise (including a resistance to interrogation/survival in captivity phase).

88. "The Liberation of Mazar-e Sharif," 41.

89. ODA 585 possessed no Dari speakers and for the first two weeks after insertion was completely ineffective, not even being permitted to travel to the front lines, until a translator was later found. Moore, 108.

90. Briscoe and others, 57.

91. See Schroen, 198–201 and 212–16; and Moore, 91–93 for the CIA and USSF perspectives on this event.

9

FROM THE COLD WAR TO INSURGENCY:

Preparing Leaders for the Contemporary Operating Environment

Bernd Horn

THE CLICHÉ THAT SAYS militaries always prepare for the last conflict is ready ammunition for critics, and is normally true. With it, pundits can easily convey an air of foresight, intellect, and insightfulness that is likely as deep as their understanding of the problem. Clearly, militaries are charged with the defence of their nation and national interests. However, the task is normally daunting. Military establishments in Western industrialized democracies are rarely a government's budgetary priority. As such, most military institutions find it difficult to resource even the "must have" requirements. For its part, military leadership does tend to be conservative minded, conscious of risk and totally aware of the consequences of failure. In addition, those same leaders, at all levels, are prisoners of their experience. In the absence of a decisive, clear understanding of the future battlespace, they will default to one they know, that they are comfortable with, and that has worked in the past. Some experimentation is accepted, but to risk failure on new concepts or predictions of where conflict or warfare will go is never prudent and almost always rejected. As such, large-scale military evolution and transformation has always been a function of cataclysmic events that have forced a change in direction.

Clearly militaries should strive to anticipate, adapt, and adjust as quickly as possible to transformations in the security environment. However, this is not always possible because of organizational and political constraints such as leadership capacity/capability, professional development, resources, and government policy.

A case in point is the Canadian military evolution from the Cold War to its current emphasis on insurgency. It entered each phase of its road to Afghanistan with painful lessons learned and the accusation by its own members that they were prepared for the last rotation of the mission, not the situation on the ground they faced. For example, those who served in the early tours in Kabul in 2004, stated they were trained for a "Bosnia-like" environment and conflict (which stemmed from Canada's long-standing commitment and operations there). Similarly, when the transition was made from Kabul to the more volatile Kandahar Province in 2006, soldiers complained that they were prepared for a "Kabul-like" context instead of the reality they faced.

In the end, it is clear that it is important for militaries to prepare their leaders and soldiers to face the unknown, the ambiguous, and the complex. That, quite frankly, is the security operating environment that they face today and will face in the future. Those are also the characteristics of the insurgency they are currently fighting. As such, it is important to examine the lessons learned from the evolution the Canadian military has undergone and how it can best prepare its personnel for the operations they face, and will confront, particularly with respect to the current insurgency in Afghanistan.

Initially, it is important to understand the transformation that has occurred. The political and public debate over whether the Canadian Forces should participate in such a dangerous and often seemingly thankless task as counterinsurgency in Afghanistan is always simmering under the surface, as it is inside other Western countries. The desire to do "simple" peacekeeping operations, akin to the Cold War model, U.N. Chapter VI (traditional peacekeeping) operations, as represented, for example, by the decades long deployment by the U.N. forces in Cyprus (UNFYCYP), is understandable. Relatively speaking, they were simple operations. The peacekeeper's role was to monitor a ceasefire or peace agreement once the fighting had stopped. Their employment, agreed to by the belligerents, was always within a prescribed boundary — in the buffer zone between the two former warring parties. Their operating environment was very clear. Each side had its fortified line. Each side was clearly delineated by its front line and all participants were in clearly identifiable national uniforms. Moreover, the entire operational area was quarantined. There were rarely civilians or press to deal with. When there was, it was under carefully controlled circumstances and the outsiders were always escorted. In essence, the military was allowed to operate in almost complete isolation.

The end of the Cold War, marked by fall of the Berlin Wall in late November 1989, resulted in a dramatic shift in the international security environment. Many of the proxy states that were supported or subsidized by one or another of the superpowers were abandoned, to subsequently drift toward total collapse. The resultant chaos transformed peacekeeping operations. Where conflict in the Cold War was based on an interstate paradigm, it now took on an intrastate posture. Failed states spiralled into anarchy creating a vacuum of power that was often filled by warlords, paramilitary gangs, and criminal organizations. The civil wars and unrest that ensued were incredibly savage and frequently threatened to spill beyond their borders. In 1995, Boutros Boutros-Ghali, the secretary general of the United Nations wrote: "the end of the cold war removed constraints that had inhibited conflict in the former Soviet Union and elsewhere … [There] has been a rash of wars within newly independent States, often of a religious or ethnic character and often involving unusual violence and cruelty."[1]

The safe, templated, and well-known Cold War paradigm disappeared almost overnight. The new security environment marked by complexity, ambiguity, ever-present media, nefarious enemies, and threats, all embedded in the context of failed and failing states, changed the face of peacekeeping. Operations were no longer static, no longer conducted in isolation or with the agreement of all parties, and they were exponentially more dangerous.

A whole new lexicon was developed that now spoke of peace support operations that encompassed peacekeeping, peace enforcement, and peacemaking missions. The dynamic, fluid, and combative nature of the new security landscape spawned a whole new concept entitled the "Three Block War" that argued military forces were required to conduct humanitarian, peacekeeping, and warfighting operations, potentially all on the same day, all within three city blocks. Simply put, military forces deployed on peace support operations were required to have a wide range of skills, including combat capability.

But the evolution of peace support operations was not yet complete. The terrorist attack on the twin towers of the World Trade Centre on 11 September 2001 led to the most dramatic, if not radical, shift in Western security policy since the end of the Cold War. In fact, the influential *Economist* magazine called 9/11 "the day the world changed." It provided the rationale for two major conflicts — Afghanistan and Iraq — as well as a global anti-terror campaign that has arguably fuelled an extraordinary high level of anti-Western sentiment in much of the Muslim world. Like it or not, traditional U.N. peace support operations to bolster failing states or provide humanitarian assistance can no longer separate themselves from the larger global context of the conflict that is now raging. Globalization has allowed exponential advances in communications, as well as the transfer of information and technology. These changes have shaped the next generation of conflict.

In essence, although many threats are geographically confined, international terrorist networks (e.g., Al Qaeda) pose a global threat. Their goals, operational methodologies, and adaptability have shifted the nature of transnational insurgencies. They employ asymmetric strategies in attacks following a doctrine of propaganda by deeds. They use the tactics of terrorism and guerrilla warfare in the pursuit of their objectives and have refined other disruptive techniques including suicide bombings, improvised explosive devices, and mass casualty events. Additionally, as already mentioned, they exploit globalization (i.e., telecommunications; financing; internet interconnectivity for information operations; as well as sharing lessons learned, techniques, tactics, and procedures).[2] In addition, the proliferation of technology continues to enhance their capacity and reach. In summary, these organizations are networked, multilayered, and complex entities capable of detailed operational planning, synchronization, and execution, and are continually expanding their reach.

The "so what?" is dramatic. No region or nation is immune! The set of actors on the international scene is now much more diverse, interconnected, and ruthless. "It is a merciless enemy," explained U.S. Marine Corps Lieutenant-General James N. Mattis, "and it is up to you [military] to stop them as far from our shores as you can."[3] The enemy we face, described Major-General Robert Scales, "is dedicated to tactics, techniques, and procedures, TTPs, that are unacceptable to Western nations; they are organized and networked; passionate and fanatical; committed; relentless; and savage."[4] Additionally, respected author, scholar, and analyst Robert Kaplan warned, "[we will face] warriors — erratic primitives of shifting alliance, habituated to violence, with no stake in civil order."[5]

As such, some theorists have noted that we are now engaged in Fourth Generation Warfare (4GW), where the enemy uses largely asymmetric tactics to achieve their aim; where human (non-kinetic), not technological, solutions are paramount; and where integrated operations (i.e., co-operation and coordination between all players — joint [all four services in the military], law enforcement agencies, other government departments, coalition partners, allies, and national and international agencies) in a long war scenario provide the best hope for success.

In the current security environment, militaries need soldiers, leaders, and commanders with judgment, wisdom, and reasoning abilities — not just technical skills.

Increasingly we find that we are unwilling or unable to bring our technology superiority to bear. "You're going to have people coming at you who don't play by the rules," observed former Harvard University political scientist Michael Ignatieff, "and you're going to have people coming at you who have an infinitely greater willingness to risk anything, i.e., their lives, than you may and that's one of the challenges you have to face."[6]

Simply put, the current security operating environment is chaotic, volatile, uncertain, and ever changing. The ambiguous nature and asymmetric conditions inherent in most conflicts today require militaries to rapidly deploy forces that can apply special skill sets in a variety of environments and circumstances to achieve difficult missions in peace, conflict, or war. Although excellent equipment may provide a technological edge, deployed forces must ensure they are composed of leaders and soldiers who are adaptive and agile. In the end, it is incumbent on all militaries to prepare their personnel for the complex operations, such as insurgency, that they now face.

As such, this chapter will examine theoretical constructs to frame operations in the current security environment. Furthermore, leadership lessons that aim to prepare leaders for the contemporary operating environment will be examined, specifically within the context of the Canadian counterinsurgency engagement in Afghanistan, which, intriguingly, began as a result of the Canadian government's desire to assist U.N. efforts to rebuild a failed state.[7]

THE CONCEPT OF THE "THREE BLOCK WAR"

As noted earlier, the naïve wishes of some politicians and the public to do just "simple peacekeeping" missions is understandable. It allows forces to minimize the training and equipment requirement for their personnel and it is far less dangerous. The casualty figures were always low, and normally occurred because of an unfortunate accident or a mine strike. However, the world has changed and, arguably, the simple peacekeeping mission of yesteryear has vanished.

The transformation began in the post–Cold War period. In the early 1990s United States Marine Corps (USMC) Commandant General Charles C. Krulak coined a concept called the Three Block War (3BW). He described this as military operations other than war combined with mid-intensity conflict. Although he developed his idea based on the belief that because of urbanization, most of our future conflicts would take place in cities, the core of the issue was based on the evolution of peace support operations. He explained that in 3BW the entire spectrum of tactical challenges ranging from humanitarian assistance, to peacekeeping, to traditional warfighting, could be encountered in the span of a few hours and within the space of three contiguous city blocks.[8]

The importance of his paradigm was based on the premise, or one could argue reality, that military personnel must be capable of operating in an ambiguous, chaotic, volatile, and rapidly changing battlespace. Moreover, they must be able to think in non-traditional, non-Western ways and think in terms of the enemy's perspective. Significantly, in accordance with this concept, leaders and their followers must also be able to transition through the entire spectrum of conflict seamlessly — in essence they must be able to fight the Three Block War. Simply put, military personnel must be able to transition from humanitarian operations, peace support, or stability tasks to high intensity mid-level combat, potentially all in the same day and all in the same area of operations.[9]

Fourth Generation Warfare

The concept of 3BW dominated during the 1990s in the context of the times. Failed and failing states, such as Somalia and the former Yugoslavia, fixated U.N. and Western efforts. Nonetheless, as early as October 1989 former Lieutenant-Colonel William S. Lind had introduced the concept of Fourth Generation Warfare (4GW) in the *Marine Corps Gazette*. He attempted to forecast the future trend in warfare. Although overshadowed by other theorists at the time, his idea gained prominence after 9/11.[10]

According to Lind, First Generation Warfare was characterized by linearity and order; it reflected an environment where states held a monopoly on the use of war to obtain political ends. The next generation of war, 2GW, was ushered in by the First World War. It was a function of fire and movement captured in the mantra "artillery conquers, infantry occupies." 3GW was also introduced during the First World War by German storm troopers, but was refined and became dominant during the Second World War where it was showcased by German blitzkrieg tactics. In simplest terms, 3GW was manoeuvre warfare.

Fourth Generation Warfare refers to a nonlinear, asymmetric approach to war in that agility, decentralization, and initiative are instrumental to success. Antagonists utilizing 4GW normally favour indirect and asymmetric approaches, however, they will employ the full range of military and other capabilities to erode an adversary's power, influence, and will. In essence, 4GW "seeks to convince the enemy's political decision makers/political leaders that their strategic goals are either unachievable or too costly for perceived benefit." The struggle "is rooted in the fundamental precept that superior political will, when properly employed, can defeat greater economic and military power."[11] The conflict is fought across the entire spectrum of society and human activity — political, military, economic, and social. In short, 4GW is intended to influence and affect the non-military population of a nation. It is, as General Sir Rupert Smith asserts, "war amongst the people."[12] Its use is meant to collapse an enemy internally versus destroying them physically.

Furthermore, 4GW departs radically from the traditional model in which the conduct of war was the monopoly of states. It evolved out of the radically different conditions of the post–Cold War era. It is not a war for conquest or territory. The enemy is not a nation-state and its people. Rather, in 4GW, non-state actors such as Hamas, Al Qaeda, and the Taliban become serious opponents, capable of operations outside of their traditional areas of operation.

Moreover, in 4GW the definition of combatants diverges significantly from the traditional laws of armed conflict. 4GW is non-linear, widely dispersed, and largely undefined. It has few, if any, definable battlefields, and the difference between "civilian" and "military" is often indistinguishable.[13]

The concept of 4GW is not without criticism. Some analysts have stated that 4GW is so vague and all encompassing that it can include everything and, as a result, is of little value.[14] Nonetheless, it does provide a construct by which to examine asymmetric tactics and evolution of warfare. Moreover, placed in the context of ongoing conflicts it provides a framework to understand enemy intent, their tactics, techniques, and procedures, as well as a model to prepare one's own forces.

ASYMMETRY

As already alluded to, the asymmetric nature of current conflict has a dramatic effect on how we fight. "Asymmetry," according to American strategist Steven Metz, "is acting, organizing, and thinking differently than opponents in order to maximize one's own advantages, exploit an opponent's weaknesses, attain the initiative, or gain greater freedom of action." He adds, "It can entail different methods, technologies, values, organizations, time perspectives, or some combination of these ... [and it] can have both psychological and physical dimensions."[15] Doctrinally, an asymmetric threat is a concept "used to describe attempts to circumvent or undermine an opponent's strengths while exploiting his weaknesses, using methods that differ significantly from the opponent's usual mode of operations."[16]

At its core, asymmetry is not designed to win battlefield victory. Rather its aim is to disrupt, distract, and disconnect. In short, its goal is to wear down a normally superior opponent. "Difficult to respond to in a discriminate and proportionate manner," explained strategist Colin Gray, "it is of the nature of asymmetric threats that they are apt to pose a level-of-response dilemma to the victim. The military response readily available tends to be unduly heavy-handed, if not plainly irrelevant, while the policy hunt for the carefully measured and precisely targeted reply all too easily can be ensnared in a lengthy political process that inhibits any real action."[17]

Gray also points out that the asymmetric threat makes coercive threats less credible and even poses difficulties in going to war as was recently demonstrated in the war against terrorism and the lack of international support for the American war against Iraq in 2003. Moreover, the asymmetric threat makes the achievement of operational and tactical goals difficult. As Gray pondered, what defines success? Displacing Osama bin Laden? Ousting Saddam Hussein? Furthermore, it is not enough for responses "to asymmetric threats to be effective; in addition, they must be politically and morally tolerable."[18]

Herein lies the difficulty for the practitioner. Commanders will be required to operate in, and be comfortable with, ambiguous and uncertain surroundings. Their options for the type of force they can apply will often be restricted, and they may not be permitted to use force at all. In addition, of necessity, they will require the capability of adapting physically and theoretically to changes not only in their immediate operational area but also in the larger international security environment. The contemporary defence environment will also demand that individuals, units, and formations be agile, flexible, and capable of responding to the unforeseen and unexpected.

Complexity will also derive from the nature of the enemy that is spawned by asymmetric warfare and the evolving Western way of war. As military superiority increases, so too does the resiliency of the opponents. The enemy will work increasingly in complex networks composed of small organizations of dispersed individuals that communicate, coordinate, and conduct campaigns in an internetted manner. These associations will be diverse, robust, and redundant, thus, making it difficult to bring superior effects to bear. There will be multiple nodes, most likely with no centralized command to attack. Therefore, the question arises: how do you defeat it?[19]

LEADERSHIP LESSONS LEARNED

Having set the theoretical parameters of operating in the contemporary environment, particularly in an insurgency context, it is now timely to look at the actual execution of operations and the difficulties they entail for commanders and leaders. The lessons are many and those discussed in this chapter only scratch the surface. Many are interrelated and mutually supporting as will become evident. Indeed, Canadian operations in Afghanistan have highlighted a number of salient issues that have forced change in how military personnel are educated and trained. In most cases changes have been successfully undertaken (whether out of necessity, circumstance, or by design is a separate debate).

Preparing for Complexity

To state that the modern battlespace is complex is a huge understatement. The nature of 4GW and the enemy's asymmetric approach it entails, coupled with operations in foreign, harsh, inhospitable, and alien environments, as well as in co-operation with a multitude of players (e.g., coalition allies; host nation; other government departments; national and international agencies; and non-governmental agencies) provide challenges of Herculean proportions. Major-General Scales observes, "Victory will be defined more in terms of capturing the psycho-cultural rather than the geographical high ground." He explains:

> Understanding and empathy will be more important weapons of war. Soldier conduct will be as important as skill at arms. Cultural awareness and the ability to build ties of trust will offer protection to our troops more effectively than body armor. Leaders will seek wisdom and quick but reflective thought rather than operational and planning skills as essential intellectual tools for guaranteeing future victories.[20]

His sentiments are well supported. "The absolute truth of the complexity of the modern battle space," acknowledges Lieutenant-Colonel Shane Schreiber, a former operations officer for the NATO multinational brigade in Afghanistan, "requires mental agility and adaptability. The greatest weapon is the intellectual ability of the Canadian soldier to adapt — not new technology, surveillance, or weapons."[21]

The emphasis in the contemporary environment has shifted from a traditional focus on internal staff processes to one that must be capable of dealing with 4GW, which is inherently chaotic and fluid. Therefore, emphasis must be placed on the enemy and the situational requirements. Individual leader and soldier initiatives are more important than slavish adherence to standard operating procedures (SOPs) and obedience. Understanding and adherence to the commander's intent becomes far more important than specific detailed orders.[22] In essence, the contemporary environment has shifted:

From	To
Predictability/symmetrical threats	surprise, uncertainty and asymmetrical threats
Single focused threats	multiple complex challenges at home and abroad
Interstate threats	decentralized terrorist and criminal networks and non-state enemies
Response after a crisis	preventive action to prevent, disrupt and dislocate threats
One size fits all deterrence	tailored deterrence to rogue states, terrorists, peer competitors

The indiscriminate and asymmetric nature of 4GW necessitates agility in thinking and the rapid and flexible conduct of operations, as well as decentralization and the reliance on initiative at the lowest tactical level. It is a small unit war most of the time. As such, subordinate commanders must be allowed the freedom to conduct operations based on circumstances as they arise. A culture of adaptability and agility of thought is key. But, the operational commander must ensure that the employment of tactical forces achieves specific ends, or objectives in accordance with the operational campaign plan.

To complicate this factor is the operational context. First, the commander rarely has enough enablers (e.g., aviation, close air support, surveillance suites, artillery, psychological operations) and those that do exist in theatre are national assets and controlled as such by the respective donor nation. As a result, priority of use and national caveats are not the commander's call. Furthermore, the environment is extremely complex and the commander simply does not control the battlespace. For example, a commander may have to deal with up to 30 significant incidents a day, including a mass casualty; a catastrophic friendly-fire incident minutes before H-Hr, shorthand for the hour designated for launching a brigade offensive; and five different special operations forces, all from different countries, all operating in his active area of operations (AO), all of whom report to different chains of command. These issues are exacerbated by national caveats on force utilization; hidden international agendas; host nation limitations; as well as cultural and political factors and domestic national imperatives, just to name a few. Added to this is an extremely complex operational environment where it is hard to determine friend from foe and the terrain is some of the most difficult possible in which to conduct military operations.

In addition, the restrictions and limitations placed on the operational commander as a result of the coalition context is another huge challenge. As briefly mentioned earlier, leaders must cope with diverse, nation-centric and/or, at times, competing national interests in pursuit of the mission, all of which must be dealt with through complex chains of command. From the political/development side this also means players must seek policy directives and/or authority before engaging. Moreover, national caveats on force employment provide further restrictions. For example, as one staff officer revealed, during Operation Medusa in Kandahar Province in September 2006, the Canadian brigade commander was getting calls from the ISAF commander and his senior staff "on an hourly basis saying this is the most important thing NATO's ever done, the future of NATO rides on this, the future of Afghanistan rides on this." He added, "There was a lot of psychological pressure being put upon the commander," and that in turn was transmitted down to subordinate commanders to "get this done faster." However, at the national level, those same commanders were getting "a lot of pressure" and were clearly told "you can't have any more casualties, the political situation is precarious."[23] It became a difficult circle to square.

Adding to this complexity is the amazing reality that not all force-providing countries are prepared to let their forces fight. This coalition factor is further complicated by cultural and organizational differences and the egos of personalities, particularly commanders. The importance of building personal relations becomes paramount. Often, in this complex coalition and host nation environment, more is achieved through diplomacy, personal trust, reciprocation, and relationships than through the attempted exercise of authority, position, or rank.

Finally, perhaps one of the most difficult challenges is balancing ground truth with domestic expectations. National agendas and expectations for progress and good news stories (e.g., reconstruction for a better Afghanistan) to justify the cost in Canadian blood and treasure often run counter to the reality on the ground. Leaders face pressures "to get on with it" while still wrestling with a dangerous threat environment on the ground that does not always permit the necessary freedom of movement or collaboration required to prosecute development or reconstruction programs. In addition, coalition resource limitations and foreign national caveats on their participating forces can place an inordinate burden on select nations who are in a lead position to provide security in their assigned area of responsibility.

The actual ground also adds to the complexity of the modern battlespace, particularly with operations in urban-type centres. Small, distributed targets, primarily people, are located in a high clutter, densely populated, masked environment. The design of cities with their abundance of varied infrastructure limit and restrict current military capabilities such as stealth, mobility, C4 (command, control, communications, and computers), ISTAR (intelligence, surveillance, target acquisition, and reconnaissance), and GPS (ground positioning system) navigation and target designation. Moreover, fighting in built-up areas is not a traditional core competency of most armies. This is further exacerbated by the inability of soldiers and commanders to think in a three-dimensional manner, because they did not train in and practice the skill.

These challenges and limitations provide a levelling effect. So does the reality that cities provide physical cover for the enemy. As noted, an urban centre by its very nature tends to neutralize technology, especially long-range weapons. As a result, it relegates action to close combat — normally a slow, resource and casualty-intensive process. Moreover, the clutter and dense nature of cities allows for maximization of camouflage, concealment, deception, and surprise strikes. The most recent conflicts in Iraq and Afghanistan demonstrate that an opponent will hide combatants, equipment, and weapons in churches, mosques, community centres, hospitals, and schools. They will also shed uniforms, deploy in civilian dress, and mix in with the population in an attempt to achieve success. One unofficial after-action report revealed the enemy to be "Smart, flexible. Utilizing all means at their disposal. They have moved ammo in civilian trucks, held weapons to their own people's heads, and pretended to be doctors with asthmatic children. Pretend to surrender then open fire."[24] Not surprisingly, two Chinese strategists have warned, "There is no means which cannot be used in war [in the future] and there is no territory or method which cannot be used in combination."[25]

This movement to asymmetric and unrestricted warfare on the part of some antagonists severely increases the complexity for commanders and their soldiers. Regardless of the heinous nature of the circumstances that caused the conflict, or the moral bankruptcy of the organizations fighting it, militaries of participating democracies will be expected to uphold the principles and values that are fundamental to their societies. Pressures stemming from the political context, and constraints such as societal tolerance to friendly casualties, timelines, collateral damage, and demand for increasing precision engagements will make military operations exponentially more complex in the future.[26] When military force is authorized, the resultant action will have to be at as low a risk threshold as possible, ensuring the minimum number of casualties and collateral damage, yet, accomplished in the quickest possible timeframe.

There results an inherent paradox. Commanders are often left with the quandary of using enough force to win, but thereby risking criticism of excessive death and destruction, or using too little force and risk losing or, at a minimum, becoming the target of criticism once again for a stalled, ineffectual strategy, campaign, and/or performance (e.g., initial stages of the Kosovo, Afghanistan, and Iraq campaigns in 1999, 2001, 2003 respectively).

This realization provides opponents with another valuable reason to use urban settings — political cover. The risk of heavy casualties, specifically civilians, the danger of collateral damage, and the likelihood of a subsequent humanitarian crisis in the aftermath of a prolonged struggle in an urban area, compounded by the scrutiny of the media, provide not only a levelling of the battlefield but, in some ways, an advantage to the enemy. The resultant political constraints (i.e., restrictive rules of engagement [ROEs]) compounded by the necessity to invest heavily in humanitarian and public affairs efforts to counterbalance the negative press can potentially distract from the primary mission and sap momentum. It also will have the effect of prolonging the conflict, which, to an impatient public, is untenable.

As such, commanders and leaders at all levels must become more conversant with other methodologies and resources available. The utilization of special operations forces with their surgical kinetic precision, for example, can be leveraged to take out high-value targets in urban errors to avoid collateral damage. In addition, greater credibility, emphasis, and trust must be placed in establishing and nurturing human intelligence networks and sources. Admittedly, HUMINT is always an emotional topic as it depends on people — people who often decide to assist for a multitude of reasons. However, HUMINT provides one of the greatest keys to success since it deals with individuals who know their own communities and society, who know the cultural norms, and who fit in. Importantly, they also know the villains. Although not foolproof, it is a good means of intelligence collection. Consequently, frequent overreliance on technical means must not be allowed to blind military personnel to the vital contribution HUMINT provides to the counterinsurgency battle.

In the end, the complexity in the contemporary and future battlespace will require mental agility and adaptability. A military's greatest weapon will be the intellectual ability of the average leader and soldier to adapt, use all available resources, and do the right thing. Only internalized values, commitments, and intellectual skills will fill the bill.[27] It will not be a function of new technology, surveillance equipment, or weapons. "We must never forget that war is fought in the human dimension," General Peter Schoomaker, former chief of the U.S. Army, recalled. He explained:

> Defeating our enemies requires a shared understanding
> of the threat and a strategic consensus. It requires a con-
> certed effort, utilizing all elements of power — diplomatic,

informational, military, and economic. Finally, it requires a national commitment to recruit, train, equip, and support those in uniform and their families, something that is a matter of priorities not affordability.[28]

Dealing with the Host Nation

Yet another important leadership lesson is the importance of working with host nation forces and decision makers. T.E. Lawrence, better known as Lawrence of Arabia, the infamous practitioner of unconventional warfare in the Middle East during the First World War, wrote: "It is better to let them do it themselves imperfectly than to do it yourself perfectly. It is their country, their way and our time is short." Amazingly, his sage advice is often ignored.

Military commanders invariably approach a problem with conviction, confidence, and preconceived ideas of how they will solve it. Rarely do they have knowledge or confidence in the experience or advice of others. As a result, mistakes or delays in achieving effects are often realized. "Individuals were sent home," Lieutenant-General Andrew Leslie, a former deputy commander of the International Security Assistance Force remarked. "Immaturity and the inability to actually think outside the box made them ineffective," he continued, "What they tried to do was bring their usually limited experience from somewhere else and apply it the same way that it had been done somewhere else and that didn't work." He explained, "each mission has got its own unique drivers, cultural conditions, local nuances, relationships with your other allies or other combatants." Moreover, he emphasized that the Afghan problem needed an Afghan solution.[29]

In the final analysis, commanders must engage host nation forces and decision makers. As difficult as it may be to work with less-skilled, trained, and equipped forces and personnel — it must be understood that there is no option. To build capacity so that the host nation can eventually take over responsibilities for their own affairs, the governance and security apparatuses must be built. This can only be achieved through dedicated efforts and by building host nation capacity at all levels. Moreover, long-lasting success can only be attained if the solution is integral to the culture, society, and norms of the host nation. Transplanted ideas and structures, as well intentioned as they may be are, more often than not, ineffective.

Preparing Self and Others for the Scope of Conflict

An important leadership lesson that is not always grasped quickly enough at the beginning of a new deployment is the scope of the actual conflict. For example, the default setting, or more accurately, attitude, was often one that considered the latest deployment as "just another simple peace-keeping or peace support mission." This posture ignores the nature of contemporary operations. As said earlier, arguably, there is no longer such thing as a "simple peacekeeping mission." U.N. operations in the Balkans, Somalia, Rwanda, and Afghanistan, to name a few, have shown the tragic results of being unprepared.

As such, leaders must ensure they create, nurture, and maintain the proper combat mentality within their command by cultivating an understanding of the magnitude of the mission and the soldier's respon-sibility in making the operation a success. They must reinforce the con-cept of the Three Block War and 4GW. Importantly, this means everyone, regardless of rank, trade, or position, is a potential warfighter and, as such, must ensure they have the requisite skills and abilities.

Repeatedly, commanders on the ground lament that not everyone in theatre, or at home, has fully grasped the scope of the respective conflict they are engaged in, whether Somalia or Afghanistan, for example. The slow initial uptake of individuals in theatres of operations often trans-lates into unnecessary casualties until the hard lesson is learned. A Brit-ish SOF officer with vast experience in the new environment asserted, "The sheer velocity of the insurgent's determination to kill us had to be gripped quickly. There was no room for error." He added, "it was kill or be killed." He explained, "It is warfare where the enemy is prepared to die to achieve his objectives. That is hard to counter and the insurgent approach has forced us to think not just out of the box, but around the corner."[30] This reality is the reason an intelligence senior non-commissioned officer who provided an in-country threat brief to newly arrived personnel to Afghanistan in 2006 ended his 40 minute lecture with "Now it's important to remember, they [Taliban] ARE trying to kill you."

Ensuring that leaders and subordinates are properly prepared for the theatre of operations and the full spectrum of conflict is critical. In practical terms, it will physically save lives since individuals will ensure they adopt the correct force protection posture and mindset. Equally important, it will also steel leaders and their subordinates for the hard decisions that need to be made in crisis situations as well as prepare them to deal with the reality of violent, traumatic, and stressful events. "Mental toughness must be developed just like physical fitness," a unit regimental sergeant major counselled, "because you are going to face some hard times and hard decisions."[31]

Dealing with Casualties

Casualty-averse publics are a reality. The less a society feels they have at stake in an out of area mission, the more reluctant they are to pay in blood or national treasure to help a failed or failing state. This dynamic is well understood by the enemy and they use this knowledge as a major tool for destabilizing U.N. and NATO missions or coalitions of the willing. Asymmetric tactics assist in their ability to wreak havoc on participating nations. Opponents understand that casualties have a huge domestic impact. Deaths in far away places for reasons not always well understood by domestic populations inevitably erode support for operations.

As such, with a determined foe casualties will inevitably occur as they attempt to influence events and undermine governments and their support base. The effect in theatre is dramatic. "The biggest shock," revealed Lieutenant-Colonel Omer Lavoie, a battle group commander in Afghanistan, "is that you will lose guys and you are losing guys." He elaborated:

> It's a bit of a shock and as a leader you must put it into perspective. But, it's a huge morale issue. Soldiers see their friends, buddies and colleagues on the ground dead. They don't see the 200 enemy dead. The guys are definitely hurting. I'm just not sure how you could ever replicate that in training. I mean we certainly covered the issue in our preparatory training back in Wainwright and other places. You can get your TTPs down for doing

the casualties, but you never get that true battlefield inoculation of actually seeing 37 soldiers laying on the ground all wounded, all in pain, all in agony, all needing treatment, as well as the dead along with that. And that's just something that never gets any easier. I think your TTPs — the procedural stuff, can be ironed out and more efficient SOPs developed, but the psychological side of it never, never gets any easier that's for sure.[32]

"You can mitigate it [taking casualties] but will never be able to bring it to zero," Brigadier-General David Fraser asserted, "You need commanders who have resolve of steel to get things done."[33]

In the end, leaders themselves must come to grips, and assist their subordinates to cope, with casualties and combat death. This is the single biggest shock and most difficult psychological challenge all participants are facing in Afghanistan. Although everyone acknowledged that there would be casualties and deaths in theatre, and they all witnessed ramp ceremonies on television before deploying, almost all were unprepared for it when it occurred. Leaders at all levels struggled with making sense of the deaths themselves and then had to try to comfort and make sense of it for their subordinates. "People are choking on a richness of experience," commented Padre Robert Lauder, "they are trying to metabolize it; trying to understand the new environment, but there is too much to chew, too much to swallow but they can't spit it out."[34]

Information Operations

Another critical reality in contemporary operations is the importance of information operations. Major-General Scales, a well-known strategic analyst and author observed, "the greatest challenge in the modern battlefield is human." He continued, "it's not about technology, rather the object is to influence opinion — to win over populations." He added, "it's not about kinetic energy or kinetic solutions. Killing is not important. Cognitive dominance is the key."[35] U.S. Secretary of State Condoleezza Rice reinforced this idea when she stated, the U.S. is now engaged in a "great global struggle to determine what ideas will organize the 21st century."[36] However, prosecuting a long war or operational deployment is difficult unless the public can see a major attack or clear threat to them or their society. As such, militaries desperately need a clear moral right to be doing what they are doing. Additionally, if they step off the moral high ground they will lose support — both domestic and international. General David Petraeus, the commander of the Multinational Force in Iraq, advised, "Do not hesitate to kill or capture the enemy, but stay true to the values we hold dear." He stressed, "Living our values distinguishes us from our enemies."[37]

Within this context, one leadership lesson that seemingly remains frustratingly slow for Western militaries to acquire is the importance of information operations (IO). IO "are continuous military operations within the Military Information Environment that enable, enhance and protect the commander's decision action cycle and mission execution to achieve an information advantage across the full range of military operations."[38] In simpler terms, IO are those functions that target and affect information and information systems (human or technical) to achieve a desired effect while at the same time protecting our own people and our allies. Clearly, all operations in the contemporary environment, at all levels, are dependent on IO, which include computer network attacks, efforts to counter-propaganda, deception, electronic warfare (EW), destruction of enemy IO targets, security of friendly information and infrastructure, as well as related activities such as civil military co-operation (CIMIC) and public affairs.

One immediate requirement is the need to get information disseminated quickly to military personnel and the civilian populations of both the inhabitants in the area of operations, and the domestic and international audience. It has become apparent that the enemy is highly skilled at using tactical actions by small dispersed groups and individuals and translating the resultant kinetic action into strategic cognitive effect. This must be countered. "Be first with the truth," General Petraeus insisted, "beat the insurgents, extremists, and criminals to the headlines and pre-empt rumours."[39] This action entails the swift devolution of information, i.e., explanations of events at the scene by the tactical operators.

This action also carries a degree of risk and adds to the complexity of the task. However, a RAND study concluded, "the marginal return from leveraging an information factor — such as the media — may be greater than the marginal return of applying more firepower."[40] In the end, time becomes the critical factor — often the centre of gravity.

This has a dramatic implication for those conducting operations. First, it requires a greater concentration on IO and an understanding of the peoples/cultures of the area of operations. It also necessitates great effort in countering propaganda and informing the media, affected population, domestic audience, and the international community of the "proper and righteous" manner in which operations are being conducted. "Avoid spin and let facts speak for themselves," General Petraeus insisted. He added, "Challenge enemy disinformation [and] turn our enemies' bankrupt messages, extremist ideologies, oppressive practices and indiscriminate violence against them."[41]

A fundamental lesson is that commanders must believe and communicate that IO is an integral part of the unit or formation's mission. Their actions must mirror their words. As such, personal involvement and staff focus is critical. For instance, key personnel must be selected and dedicated to carry out IO planning and coordination. Commanders must support IO in their selection of priority intelligence requirements and they must set the tone for the vital intelligence support of IO.

In the end, it is vital to keep objectives simple. In addition, one should never take a templated, cookie-cutter approach. It is important to stay adaptive and dynamic. What worked one week will not necessarily work the next. Moreover, what worked in one area/region/country may not work in another. "Although lethal operations against insurgent fighters instill confidence in the population," as mentioned by one senior officer, "their effect can be short-lived and also open to interpretation and manipulation by the insurgent information operations campaign." He continued, "The consistent promulgation of key messages in conjunction with all other types of operations has a broader and more lasting effect on the population. IO is the best tool that can be used to have an impact on the greatest number of people."[42] General David Petraeus, the commander of the Multinational Force in Iraq, advised, "Realize that we are in a struggle for legitimacy that will be won or lost in the perception of the Iraqi people."[43] Although stated in the context of Iraq, it applies equally to Afghanistan.

Dealing with the Media

Napoleon Bonaparte shrewdly opined, "Four hostile newspapers are more to be feared than 1,000 bayonets."[44] More recently, American strategist Ralph Peters counselled, "the global media can overturn the verdict of the battlefield."[45] Not surprisingly, our opponents have clearly demonstrated they will use the mass media as a tool to defeat national resolve. In fact, their doctrinal publications underline that "Understanding the media politics of the adversaries and dealing with them is important in winning the military and political battle."[46]

As such, leaders and their subordinates will invariably operate in a politically sensitive environment where the actions of a soldier at a roadblock or in a tactical setting can have strategic ramifications. Operating in a setting that is under the constant glare of the news camera will exacerbate the complexity of the situations they face. "The Power of CNN" is no longer an idle network boast.[47] The CNN effect of instantaneous worldwide imaging will magnify tenfold the concept of the "strategic corporal" where a tactical decision/error can become a strategic issue as it is beamed across the globe in real time. In fact, it adds to the volatility of the political security environment. The media's global connectivity and instant reporting can exacerbate threats or create new ones based on viewers' reactions (and generated perceived beliefs) to news reports (e.g., collateral damage, unjust military action, disrespect of religious symbols or sites). A glaring example was the American soldier who, upon clearing a stronghold in Iraq during the 2003 invasion, raised the American flag. Although lowered almost immediately, the fleeting image of that action unleashed a barrage of controversy and debate over the act in regards to the implications of an American occupying power instead of a liberating force. "A wrong decision in the glare of the media," Colonel Paul Maillet, a former Canadian Department of National Defence director of defence ethics, warns "can have far reaching consequences that can affect peacekeeping mandates and strategic and national policies and aims."[48]

The CNN effect also feeds what has become an unrealistic impatience by both the public and the media. Military operations, arguably the most multifarious of human endeavours, even when conducted in some of the most distant and hostile environments known, is expected by a restless media and their audience to be completed within days, at best weeks. In a medium where only 90 to 100 seconds are allocated per issue on an average news story, and where the concept of "if it bleeds it leads" exists, there is a need for news to be dramatic, if not sensational. This will cause great problems for the military. News reports will be fleeting and without context. "Television as a medium has no past and no future," explained NATO spokesman Jamie Shea, "It is always the eternal present. What BBC's Nik Gowing has called the 'tyranny of real time,' with no causality, no connection to what came before or what goes next. So everything is immediately important and a few moments later completely unimportant, contrary to our experience of real life."[49]

As such, a single act can become the defining image of a battle, campaign or operation. Failure or errors of any scale carry the potential of being catastrophic. Recent examples have shown that shocking images of combat or terrorist acts can sway public opinion in an open democratic society and create intense political pressure to cease hostilities or undertake dramatic action otherwise not contemplated.[50]

Moreover, there will be no respite. In Bosnia there were 3,000 journalists on the ground throughout the NATO air campaign of 1995. "They were faster than NATO soldiers or NATO satellites," Shea conceded, "Certainly faster than our intelligence community."[51] The infamous tractor bombing incident caused NATO to lose 20 percentage points of public support in Germany alone after images were beamed all over the world.[52] In 2003, in the war against Iraq, there were approximately 810 embedded reporters with the coalition alone, more than 3,000 war correspondents in total and a multitude of others covering the conflict from strategic locations throughout the globe.[53] This has led to a universally accepted populist notion that "it isn't real unless it's on television." To conduct operations in such an environment magnifies the complexity of an already complicated profession.

As a result, integrity and credibility become paramount. As one senior commander eloquently stated: "Don't put lipstick on pigs. Acknowledge setbacks and failures and then state what we've learned and how we'll respond." He added, "Hold the press (and ourselves) accountable for accuracy, characterization and context."[54]

In the end, the reality of the strategic corporal necessitates the education and training of everyone who deploys into the theatres of operations. Since their actions become tools, if not weapons, in the ongoing information campaign waged by the enemy, individuals must be inculcated with the notion that all personnel must be conscious and accountable for their behaviour at all times.

Cultural Intelligence

"During the first year of my counterinsurgency duties," one senior officer explained, "I believe I created more insurgents than I eliminated. This was not only because of inexperience but also because I lacked fundamental knowledge of the terrain, the people and the culture. I also did not know how to sift through local intelligence effectively. A combination of my own naiveté and enthusiasm, not to mention pressure from senior commanders to deliver results, resulted in actions that alienated the locals and inadvertently, helped the insurgents."[55] Similarly, Brigadier-General Fraser conceded, "I underestimated one factor — culture. I was looking at the wrong map. I needed to look at the tribal map not the geographic map. That map was over 2,000 years old."[56]

Cultural Intelligence, or CQ, "is the ability to recognize the shared beliefs, values, attitudes, and behaviours of a group of people and to apply this knowledge toward a specific goal."[57] Dr. Emily Spencer has identified that CQ goes beyond the normal parameters of understanding the enemy. It also pertains concurrently to the national (e.g. domestic population/ society); international (e.g., allies, coalition partners, NGOs, the United Nations, and other international agencies); and host nation (e.g., governmental, military, and police agencies within the country of operations) domains, in addition to that of the enemy.

Spencer explains, "showing high CQ can be an effective force multiplier," while notably demonstrating low CQ in any of these four domains can negatively impact a mission.[58] In the final analysis, the message that is intended is less important than the message that is actually received by a target audience. As such, it is important to "understand the neighbourhood." To this end, the building of relationships is key as they are a central component of successful counterinsurgency operations. Ultimately, it is critical to see reality through the eyes of the other culture, not through the lens of your own experience and bias.

Unfortunately, the importance of seeing the reality on the ground through the eyes of the local population is most often ignored or only given token attention by most Western militaries. A few language classes that provide some common phrases, a brief history overview, and some cultural anecdotes are normally the extent of the CQ provided. However, mission success rests on in-depth CQ in all four domains so that the necessary assistance, co-operation, and support are achieved to allow for the accomplishment of the necessary objectives.

Winning "Hearts and Minds"

Current conflict that is enmeshed in 4GW inevitably centres on the violent struggle among state and non-state actors for legitimacy and influence over relevant populations. Adversaries inevitably attempt to erode each other's power, influence, and will. As such, one veteran explained, "every soldier must be made to understand to take responsibility for everything they do — from facial expressions to direct action." He stressed, "Everything you do has ramifications."[59]

An American general agreed. He proclaimed, "Every time you offend an Iraqi you are working for the insurgents."[60] A former commandant of the U.S. Marine Corps cautioned, "Do not create more enemies than you take out by some immoral act."[61] Another commander agreed. "Every action taken by the enemy and our forces has implications in the public arena," he observed. He then elaborated, "There is no tougher endeavor than the one in which we are engaged. It is often brutal, physically demanding and frustrating." He concluded, "All of us experience moments of anger, but we can neither give in to dark impulses, nor tolerate unacceptable actions by others."[62] This advice is relevant regardless of theatre of operations, or scale of belligerence within the spectrum of conflict of a respective operation.

Winning the respect and support of the host nation population is essential to the success of any mission. The local population can provide intelligence on enemy activity, location, and movements. With their co-operation, they can advance IO initiatives, governmental programs, and assist military forces operating within an AO. Without their support, they can remain at best neutral and withhold vital information required for force protection. At worst, they can assist the opponents with information, food, lodgings, caching of weapons, and, potentially, recruits.

Importantly, winning the "hearts and minds" of the people is more than just providing soccer balls and food parcels. It is the amalgam of security, governance, and development. It is about providing the population with a stake in the system and trust in the legitimacy of the government. It is not just about doing nice things; rather, it is also about how you do them. Respect for individuals and culture is critical.

However, the reality of 4GW makes winning hearts and minds difficult. For example, in the case of Afghanistan, it is often difficult to breach the cultural barrier, particularly one that is so xenophobic. Moreover, it is not unusual for soldiers who are attacked to feel angry and betrayed. They deeply believe that they are serving in Afghanistan to create a better society for its people, yet, they are continually attacked by seemingly invisible antagonists who appear to operate effortlessly in the very Afghan society that the soldiers are trying to improve and protect.[63] Although most understand the average Afghan is just trying to survive, the resentment still builds with each attack, with every casualty, and, especially, with every death.

The nature of the conflict fuels a spiral of antagonism. The enemy has learned to use our kindness against us. As coalition forces continue to be targeted by improvised explosive devices (IEDs) and suicide bombers, they have no choice but to take action to protect themselves. These decisions, however, comes with a cost. As convoys drive aggressively down the centre of the road, they force local Afghan traffic to scurry for the shoulder. As they physically bump traffic out of the way, or threaten vehicles who follow too close by pointing weapons, or create collateral damage because of attacks against them and/or defensive or offensive operations, they risk alienating Afghan nationals. With every action taken against the population at large, regardless of justification or cause, a cost is incurred. As such, coalition actions could potentially push Afghans to support the Taliban, or at least cause them to turn a blind eye to Taliban activities. Yet, to do nothing and continue to be hit without doing something about it, feeds soldier disillusionment and has the potential to lose Canadian public support for the conflict, especially, if it appears that the country's troops are being put at risk without the ability to take the necessary steps to defend themselves. Moreover, if a safe and secure environment is not created for the local population, there is almost no hope of creating support for the new Afghan national government.

As such, a careful balance must be reached between force protection and winning the hearts and minds of the population. In 4GW, combat power is not always the most effective tool or weapon. Leaders must ensure that their personnel understand that money, medicine, fuel, food, access to education, employment opportunities, public works projects, respect, and, particularly, information are all important enablers to achieving the mission. These non-kinetic, non-military tools are force multipliers that can dramatically change the threat picture and effectiveness of the insurgents. They are all weapons of counterinsurgency operations. Security and reconstruction are not mutually exclusive concepts — they are intertwined and one feeds the other.

In the end, regardless of mission or theatre of operation, winning the hearts and minds of the population is paramount. As such, cultural intelligence, a carefully targeted IO campaign, solid leadership that ensures tolerance, patience, and a sound understanding of who the enemy is, are key to a successful counterinsurgency campaign.

Integrated Approach: Whole of Government

"It's quite easy to kill people and break things," a veteran observed, "compared to putting them back together."[64] This is, in a nutshell, the dilemma. As already mentioned, successful operations in the contemporary environment necessitate joint, multinational, and multiagency co-operation, namely an integrated approach. However, this is normally a greater challenge than it sometimes appears. Within the military sphere, inter-service rivalries, differing sub-cultures, and limits on interoperability create stress and inefficiencies. Once allies or coalition partners are included, differing training standards, language barriers, and larger issues of inter-operability and national caveats muddy the water even more.

These challenges are further exacerbated when government and civilian agencies with different agendas, alien organizational cultures, and differing philosophies are included. Most often the greatest problem is one of ignorance. None of the players fully understand who the other participants are, what they do, their mandates, or how they actually operate. Other government departments (OGD) and civilian agencies are normally not accustomed to military directness or command structures. In addition, ironically, they are most often nowhere near as flexible; rather, OGDs are normally more bureaucratic and more risk-averse than the Department of National Defence. Additionally, where the military looks for quick solutions and immediate results, the developmental agencies focus on long-term sustainable development. Not surprisingly, timelines, approval mechanisms, communications, and organizational method-ologies all vary among OGDs and the military and those embarking on co-operative ventures require both patience and tolerance.[65]

Clearly, ensuring an effective integrated approach is a key chal-lenge that must be mastered. But how a leader ensures a diverse, multi-national force is welded into a coherent organization, all with a clear conception of the desired operational end state, is a real challenge. This understanding must also be extended to civilian counterparts who must be integrated into the team and into the decision-making process in an accepting way and on an equal basis. What is often lost is the fact that invisible cultural barriers (i.e., divergent attitudes, beliefs, and values, as well as methodologies and organizational practices) restrict true co-operation. Often we do not know what we do not know, and we assume our perception of the state of affairs is accurate and mutual, when in fact truth on the ground may be an entirely different reality. As such, an enormous challenge for operational commanders is to create an environment conducive to the planning, decision making, and the conduct of activities in an integrated manner that allows for the neces-sary advancement of political and economic initiatives and reforms in a safe and secure environment.

The integrated approach unquestionably creates challenges for lead-ers. Essential is the realization by all military and civilian personnel of the reality that success depends on an effective, co-operative military-civilian integrated approach to most operations in the contemporary security environment. Few conflicts, particularly insurgencies, are a function of an exclusive military problem. Rather, most are the result of political, economic, and social dysfunction that is exacerbated by, and prolonged, as a result of, insecurity. Accordingly, military presence and/ or force is but one tool to remedy the problem. Notably, it is normally ineffective without the corollary political and economic levers to fix the larger underlying problems.

ACHIEVING AN ADAPTIVE AND FLEXIBLE MINDSET

We are all prisoners of our own experience and, as such, bring personal baggage to all we do.[66] Furthermore, most military members view change as a threat. It moves us from our comfort zone — i.e., sound understanding of current TTPs, technical competence, relevance of personal experience, and proficiency, and a system that rewards those characteristics. Therefore, there is normally a resistance to change, and an undue reliance on doing things "the way we always have." Although innovation is applauded, conformance is normally rewarded.

As such, to create and nurture adaptive and flexible mindsets among all levels of leadership in a military institution requires a conducive environment that actively encourages and rewards those behaviours. It is a top-down driven function that must be supported in deed, not just in words.

In the short term, creating and nurturing an adaptive and flexible mindset requires commanders to ensure that their subordinates (as well as themselves) are continually assessing the context and situation they are facing, and adapting and adjusting TTPs accordingly. In the long term, it requires an emphasis on robust professional development (PD) programs (i.e., training, experience, education, and self-development) that emphasize innovation, creative thought, discussion, and intellectual rigour and debate.

Central to developing an adaptive and flexible mindset is training. Although training provides "a predictable response to a predictable situation," it remains a key part of the process of preparing leaders and soldiers to be adaptive and flexible. Training provides the necessary skills, technical competence, and confidence in self, group, and equipment to conduct operations. It also furnishes an understanding of capability, capacity, and function that acts as a base line for future development. Additionally, training provides a default position that can act as a safety net in crisis.

However, training must be as realistic as possible, encompassing battle and casualty simulation, realistic scenarios, unscripted enemy action, and an unrelenting tempo. Leaders and soldiers must be tested in an environment where they can make mistakes and learn without penalty or fear of career implications. They must be pushed to the limit so that they do not experience this reality for the first time on actual operations. In fact, veterans from Afghanistan insisted repeatedly, "Training can never be complex enough."[67]

The payback for good training is enormous. During a final validation exercise for a force protection platoon deploying to Afghanistan, the group underwent a scenario where a convoy they were protecting underwent 29 events in less than 24 hours. At its termination, all platoon members complained that this was totally unrealistic. On their second convoy in theatre, a supposed eight-hour convoy turned into a 36-hour ordeal that included no fewer than 19 separate incidents, including multiple suicide bombers, mortar and rocket attacks, ambushes, casualty evacuation, a vehicle accident, and mechanical breakdowns. To a person, they conceded that the only way they got through the actual convoy was the fact that they had already done it on exercise, before deploying. In essence, the rehearsal in Canada provided them with the practical experience, the mental strength and stamina, as well as context and ideas of how to react and adapt to the changing dynamics of a real world dangerous situation.

Within this context, adventure training is an important activity for leaders and soldiers to undertake. Whether mountain climbing, trekking, canoeing, or another challenging activity, the opportunities for individuals to undertake risky ventures in unfamiliar environments allows them to develop leadership skills and deal with the unforeseen events that inevitably occur. In turn, these skills force leaders to improvise, adapt, and learn to deal with adversity in real world settings versus the canned exercise scenario.

Corollary to training is experience. Experience builds confidence and individual and group competence. Experience is empirical and tangible; decisions are made, actions are taken, and results are seen, if not felt. In fact, the military culture reveres and rightfully recognizes the experience of individuals. However, this experience should be shared so that those not fortunate enough to have undergone operations or complex exercises can learn through the experiences of others and thereby gain, in essence, vicarious experience. Seminars, conferences, PD symposiums, publications such as the Canadian Defence Academy's "In Harm's Way" series (several volumes — written by individuals representing different rank levels and services — that profile operations and leadership challenges and explain how success was achieved) all provide valuable vicarious experiences to learn from.

This repertoire of experience provides individuals with a data bank of knowledge that can be accessed in a crisis or when facing a problem. It enables individuals to draw from past experience, whether their own or that of someone else, when responding to a problem. In short, experience provides the confidence and practical ideas for individuals to develop an adaptive and flexible approach to challenges they encounter. As such, a conscious program of deploying leaders of all levels on exercises, operations, and PD opportunities is very important.

Education that promotes, "the reasoned response to an unpredictable situation — critical thinking in the face of the unknown" is another vital, if not the most important, part of the process of developing adaptive and flexible mindsets.[68] Quite simply, one must be educated to deal effectively with uncertainty, which is omnipresent in the current and future security environment. In essence, "education," Major David Last, a professor in the Department of Political Science at the Royal Military College of Canada (RMC), explains "is the shaping of the mind."[69] Education assists in our reasoning ability which, in turn, is critical in responding to unanticipated circumstances.

Clearly, education rooted in critical thinking, problem solving, and analytical research better prepares individuals to think, as well as cope with problems and situations that are unexpected than mere training or rote memorization. It assists individuals to not only embrace change, but to adapt and anticipate it. More important, it instills in people the attitude and ability to constantly learn from one's environment and to prepare, as well as react, accordingly. Indeed, as the famous British military historian Sir Michael Howard wrote:

> academic studies can provide the knowledge, insight, and the analytic skills which provide the necessary basis, first for reasoned discussion, and then for action. They provide a forum, and breed the qualities, which enable the student, the teacher, the politician, the civil servant, the moral philosopher, and not least the soldier to reach a common understanding of the problems which confront them, even if inevitably there is disagreement about the solutions. This dialogue is what civilization is all about. Without it societies dissolve.[70]

Similarly, Dr. John Cowan, a former principal of RMC, reinforced the necessity of education in relation to the military. "Today, when a young officer may be called upon to be a skilled leader, a technical expert, a diplomat, a warrior, and even an interpreter and an aid expert all at once," he insisted, "there is no question that good training is not enough. Skills are not enough." He added, "The job calls for judgement, that odd distillate of education, the thing which is left when the memorized facts have either fled or been smoothed into a point of view, the thing that cannot be taught directly, but which must be learned. Without the mature judgement which flows from education, we fall back on reflexes, which are damned fine things for handling known challenges, but which are manifestly unreliable when faced with new ones."[71]

Finally, the development of an adaptable and flexible mindset also rests on self-development. Individuals, particularly leaders, must take it on themselves to continue their professional development by reading and studying the profession of arms and the evolution of conflict. They should devour material that encompasses changes to the security environment and their profession, particularly material that provides insight into the geography (human, political, and terrain) of regions to which they will deploy on operations. Reading, for example, expands their horizons and assists with their understanding of the culture, history, and practical dynamics of the environment in which they will be operating. Thus, they will be better situated to anticipate and adapt to challenges they may face.

Conclusions

The theoretical solution to any problem is always easy. It is without economic, political, or cultural restraint. It normally represents the logical, comprehensive, ideal resolution to the quandary. Generally, it is also useless as it is often unworkable within the constraints of real life. It is within this context that every government and military must balance risk with achievable solutions. In the end, whatever is decided should be based on a clear understanding of the reality of the contemporary operating environment and the risk that is acceptable. It should not be based on wishful thinking.

As such, the trends in the contemporary security environment are fairly clear. The simple peacekeeping tasks of the Cold War are unlikely to ever resurface. Militaries deploying on missions in foreign lands should be prepared to conduct operations along the entire spectrum of conflict, particularly insurgencies, such as those currently experienced in Afghanistan and Iraq.

The implication of all this for the warrior of the contemporary and future security environment is seemingly simple: to be a highly trained combat soldier is no longer enough. To operate effectively in this multifaceted environment of today and tomorrow, soldiers will have to be not only highly trained, but also highly educated. In this vein, "time dedicated to understanding the higher orders of conflict inculcates mental agility and the ability to be creative as well as technically competent," is of vital importance as Major-General Scales explains. "A well-read and educated leader," he adds, "will be better prepared to deal with the uncertainty and chaos of combat [or increasingly complex operations]."[72] Quite simply, decentralized decision making power and enlightened low-level leaders capable of making reasoned, timely decisions under pressure will determine success or failure.

As previously articulated, given globalization and its implications for the proliferation of technology, weaponry, and information, opponents seeking to undermine U.N. and coalition missions will use 4GW and all that it entails to achieve their aim. Consequently, commanders and their forces must be capable of transitioning through the spectrum of conflict on a regular, if not daily, basis to accomplish their mission. Therefore, as a minimum, leaders and troops must be trained, in simple terms, to execute the Three Block War. Units must be capable of a wide scope of operations that enable troops to perform a range of activities from humanitarian assistance, to peacekeeping, to warfighting. Moreover, leaders must be intellectually agile and adaptive so they can use innovative tactics and approaches to accomplish the higher intent of a mission, rather than being limited in the scope of their actions because of restrictive mission verbs originating from an outdated lexicon that often fails to capture the reality of the contemporary and ever-evolving security environment.

Notes

1. Boutros Boutros-Ghali, *An Agenda for Peace 1995*, 2nd ed. (New York: United Nations, 1995), 7.
2. For example, explosively formed projectiles (i.e., creates a slug) similar to anti-tank shaped charges were first used by Hezbollah in Lebanon. They then migrated to Iraq in 2004 and were later confirmed in Afghanistan in April 2007.
3. Lieutenant-General James N. Mattis, *Ethical Challenges in Contemporary Conflict: The Afghanistan and Iraq Cases* (Annapolis: United States Naval Academy, March 2001), 10.
4. Major-General Robert Scales, presentation at Cognitive Dominance Workshop, West Point, 11 July 2006. This new era of conflict has also spawned a new threat even within Western nations, namely the radicalization of elements within the society of developed nations: homegrown terrorists. Recent examples include the U.K. "shoebomber" (i.e., who attempted to destroy an aircraft with a bomb hidden in the sole of a running shoe), the terrorists who conducted the London subway bombing, and the "Toronto 17" — a group of Canadian homegrown terrorists who established a training camp in Ontario, Canada.
5. Robert Kaplan, *Warrior Politics: Why Leadership Demands a Pagan Ethos* (New York: Vintage Books, 2002), 118.
6. Michael Ignatieff, *Virtual War: Ethical Challenges* (Annapolis: United States Naval Academy, March 2001), 8.
7. See Janice Gross Stein, *The Unexpected War. Canada in Kandahar* (Toronto: Viking, 2007), for a detailed account of how Canada's politicians found themselves locked in a bitter counterinsurgency campaign in Afghanistan.
8. General Charles C. Krulak, "The Strategic Corporal: Leadership in the Three Block War," *Marine Corps Magazine,* January 1999.
9. Charles C. Krulak, "The Three Block War: Fighting in Urban Areas," National Press Club, Vital Speeches of the Day, 15 December 1997; and Charles C. Krulak, "The Urban Operations Journal. The Strategic Corporal and the Three-Block War." *www. urbanoperations.com/strategiccorporal.htm* (accessed 27 March 2003).
10. William S. Lind "The Changing Face of War: Into the Fourth Generation," *Marine Corps Gazette*, October 1989, 22–26.
11. Thomas X. Hammes, "Modern Warfare Evolves Into a Fourth Generation," *Unrestricted Warfare Symposium 2006 Proceedings,* 65.
12. General Sir Rupert Smith, *The Utility of Force: the Art of War in the Modern World* (London: Allen Lane, 2005), xiii.
13. Lind, "The Changing Face of War," 22–26.
14. For a criticism of 4GW see Vincent Curtis, "The Theory of Fourth Generation Warfare," Canadian Army Journal, Vol. 8, No. 4 (Winter 2005), 17.
15. Steven Metz and Douglas V. Johnson II, "Asymmetry and U.S. military Strategy: Definition, Background, and Strategic Concepts," U.S. Army War College, Strategic Studies Institute, January 2001, 5–6.
16. Colonel W.J. Fulton, DNBCD, "Capabilities Required of DND, Asymmetric Threats and Weapons of Mass Destruction," (Fourth Draft), 18 March 2001, 2/22.
17. Colin Gray, "Thinking Asymmetrically in Times of Terror," *Parameters*, Vol. 32, No. 1, Spring 2002, 6.

18. *Ibid.*, 9.
19. Mohammed Aideed in Somalia is one example. He used runners, burning tires, and other primitive means of communication and was able to elude capture and destruction of his power base.
20. Major-General Robert Scales, introductory remarks, Cognitive Dominance Workshop, West Point Military Academy, 11 July 2006.
21. Lieutenant-Colonel Shane Schreiber, ACOS, Multinational Brigade HQ, 1 CMBG briefing, 22 January 2007.
22. The commander's intent is the commander's personal expression of why an operation is being conducted and what he hopes to achieve. It is a clear and concise statement of the desired end-state and acceptable risk. Its strength is the fact that it allows subordinates to exercise initiative in the absence of orders, or when unexpected opportunities arise, or when the original concept of operations no longer applies.
23. Lieutenant-Colonel Shane Schreiber interview with author, 18 October 2006.
24. "3–7 CAV Lessons Learned," posted on *www.companycommand.com* (accessed 1 April 2003).
25. Qiao Liang and Wang Xiangsui, *Unrestricted Warfare* (Beijing: PLA Literature and Arts Publishing House, February 1999), 199.
26. See Jeffrey Record, "Collapsed Countries, Casualty Dread, and the New American Way of War," *Parameters,* Vol. 32, No. 2, Summer 2002, 4–23.
27. Dr. Martin Cook, "The Future Operating Environment: Ethical Implications," CCEL 7, 28 November 2006.
28. General Peter J. Schoomaker, thirty-fifth chief of staff of the army in his farewell message, 9 April 2007.
29. Interview with Major-General Andrew Leslie, 8 February 2006.
30. Michael Smith, "Secret War of the SAS," Mick Smith's Defence Blog, 18 January 2008.
31. Chief Warrant Officer Northrup, RSM TF Orion, 1 CMBG briefing, 22 January 2007.
32. Interview with author, October 2006.
33. Brigadier-General David Fraser, presentation at the Canadian Infantry Association Annual General Meeting, 25 May 2007.
34. Interview with author, 17 October 2006.
35. Major-General Robert Scales, presentation at "Cognitive Dominance Workshop," West Point, 11 July 2006. He elaborated, "His hope is to leverage our impatience to cause us to overreact with inappropriate use of physical violence. Perception control will be achieved and opinions shaped by the side that best exploits the global media."
36. Michael Tutton, "Rice Gives Nod to Military," *The Kingston-Whig Standard,* 13 September 2006, 11.
37. Memorandum, General D. H. Petraeus, "Multi-National Force — Iraq Commander's Counter-insurgency Guidance," 15 July 2008, 3. Henceforth Petraeus Memo.
38. *B-GL-300–001/FTP-000 Conduct of Land Operations — Operational Level Doctrine for the Canadian Army.*
39. Petraeus Memo, 3.
40. Sean J. A. Edwards, *Mars Unmasked* (Santa Monica: RAND Arroyo Center, 2000), xiv.
41. Petraeus Memo, 3.
42. Major Jay Adair, "A Crucible of Experience: A Company Second in Command's Perspective on Operations in Afghanistan," unpublished paper, 2007. Terrorist groups

such as Hezbollah, Hamas, Al Qaeda exploit communications — make extensive use of the media, television, and internet — in battle for hearts and minds. The computer keyboard is a weapon no less than an RPG or assault rifles.

43. Petraeus Memo, 3.
44. Quoted in McCormick Tribune Foundation, "Irregular Warfare Leadership in the 21st Century: Attaining and Retaining Positional Advantage (Wheaton, IL: McCormick Tribune Foundation, 2007), 27.
45. Ralph Peters, "Lessons So Far," *New York Post Online,* 13 August 2006, *www.nypost. com/postopinion/opedcolumnists/lessons_so_far_opedcolumnists_ralph_peters.htm* (accessed 15 August 2008).
46. Abu Bakr Naji, "The Management of Savagery: The Most Critical Stage Through Which the Umma Will Pass," Translation of document done by the John M. Olin Institute for Strategic Studies at Harvard University, 23 May 2006.
47. It is estimated that a minimum of 100 million people had access to satellite networks carrying reports on the War in Iraq during the U.S.-led invasion. International Press Institute (IPI), "Caught in the Crossfire: The Iraq War and the Media," *www.free-media.at/IraqReport2003.htm* (accessed 6 June 2003).
48. Colonel J.P.M. Maillet, "Defence Ethics, Program Ethics and Operations Project," memorandum, 20 June 2000.
49. Shea, 409.
50. See Sean J. A. Edwards, *Mars Unmasked* (Santa Monica: RAND Arroyo Center, 2000), 67.
51. Dr. Jamie Shea, "Modern Conflicts, the Media and Public Opinion. The Kosovo Example," *Militaire Spectator,* JRG 169, 8–2000, 410.
52. *Ibid.,* 411.
53. IPI, "Caught in the Crossfire," a CNN televised report, 9 April 2003.
54. Petraeus Memo, 3.
55. David Kilcullen, "'Build It and They Will Come' — Use of Parallel Hierarchies to Defeat Adversary Networks," *Unrestricted Warfare Symposium: 2006 Proceedings,* 279.
56. Brigadier-General David Fraser, presentation at the Canadian Infantry Association Annual General Meeting, 25 May 2007.
57. Dr. Emily Spencer, "Crucible of Success: Applying the Four Domain CQ Paradigm," CFLI Technical Report 2007–05, May 2007.
58. *Ibid.,* 13. The message is simply, know your audience. Terrorists stopped showing taped beheadings because they found that they had violated accepted standards, although informal, of those they relied on for support and legitimacy. It was fear of losing popular support that prompted their modified behaviour. Gary Shiffman, "Economic Analysis and Unrestricted Warfare," *Unrestricted Warfare Symposium* (Maryland: John Hopkins University, 2007), 226.
59. Interview with Master-Corporal Lars Penniston, 9 May 2007.
60. Dr. Martin Cook, "The Future Operating Environment: Ethical Implications," CCEL 7, 28 November 2006.
61. Lieutenant-General James N. Mattis, *Ethical Challenges in Contemporary Conflict: The Afghanistan and Iraq Cases* (Annapolis: United States Naval Academy, March 2001), 11.
62. Petraeus Memo, 3.
63. This reality is similar to that experienced by U.N. forces working in Somalia in 1992–93.

64. Lieutenant-Colonel Shane Schreiber, ACOS, Multinational Brigade HQ, 1 CMBG briefing, 22 January 2007.

65. The different approaches can be described as follows: Security (military operations) — effects are measured in weeks; Development (programs to provide food and build roads) — effects are measured in years; Capacity Building (training clinicians, train army, build schools) — effects measured in generations.

66. Library and Archives Canada, MG 31, G6, Vol. 9, File: Articles, Papers, Speeches — U, Major Sieberg, "Tank or Anti-Tank? Does the Spanish War Show Which is Superior?" Translation of an article appearing in the *Militar-Wochenblatt* of 11 February 1938. "We see," Major Seiberg wrote in the mid-1930s, "that the Spanish Civil War has up to now demonstrated nothing really new, and also that men only regard experience as valid when it is their own experience. Otherwise it would not be possible for the same errors that led to failure in the Great War to be repeated."

67. Lieutenant-Colonel Shane Schreiber, ACOS, Multinational Brigade HQ, 1 CMBG briefing, 22 January 2007. Schreiber repeated the sentiments of many when he said, "Casualties are a fact of life for us. Bring it into training. Practice it — test the limits of the soldiers."

68. Dr. Ron Haycock, "Clio and Mars in Canada: The Need for Military Education," presentation to the Canadian Club, Kingston, Ontario, 11 November 1999.

69. Major David Last, "Educating Officers: Post Modern Professionals to Control and Prevent Violence," in Bernd Horn, ed., *Contemporary Issues in Officership: A Canadian Perspective* (Toronto: Canadian Institute of Strategic Studies, 2000), 26.

70. Michael Howard, *The Causes of War* (New York: Harvard University Press, 1984), 83. Major-General, the Honourable W.A. Griesbach stated: "Since wars cannot be arranged in order merely to train officers, it follows that, after a long period of peace, the officers of an army must get their military education from reading and study." "Military Study: Notes of a Lecture," *Canadian Defence Quarterly*, October 1931, 19.

71. Dr. John Scott Cowan, RMC Convocation Address, 4 October 1999, Kingston, Ontario. See also Eliot Cohen and John Gooch, *Military Misfortunes. The Anatomy of Failure in War* (New York: Vintage Books, 1991), 233–37.

72. Scales, 13.

SOF FOR SALE:

The Canadian Forces and the Challenge of Privatized Security

Christopher Spearin

IN THE TWENTY-FIRST CENTURY, despite a history of ad hocery and indifference, Canada has certainly entered the elite ranks of the world's special operations forces' community.[1] The December 2001 federal budget allocated an additional C$119 million to Joint Task Force 2 (JTF-2), Canada's Tier One SOF organization, to double its capacity by increasing its ranks to as many as 600 frontline personnel. JTF-2's traditional counter-terrorism responsibilities, or *black* operations, have grown alongside *green* operations (i.e., direct action and unconventional warfare missions) in countries such as Afghanistan.[2] Additionally, in January 2006, the government announced the creation of a 750-strong special operations regiment to conduct Tier Two/Tier Three-type SOF activities. Complementing all these developments was the standing up, on 1 February 2006, of the Canadian Special Operations Force Command (CANSOFCOM) with responsibility to conduct either supported or supporting operations. As a result, SOF personnel have arguably become the fourth service of the Canadian Forces.[3]

Now that Canada, through its financial commitments, military operations and personnel increases, has identified the important contribution of SOF to the Canadian defence community, the challenge will be twofold: to maintain a robust SOF capability in a relatively small military and to massage a variety of concerns likely to be held by the army, the navy, and the air force regarding "the new kid on the block." Unfortunately, these challenges will likely be heightened by the increased attractiveness of this more prominent and larger SOF pool to international private security companies (PSCs).[4]

Currently, the United States and the United Kingdom, in spite of their larger force structures, are feeling the strain caused by the drain of SOF expertise to the private sector. In Iraq alone, there are some 20,000 PSC employees, and a significant number of them possess SOF experience. This number supports claims that Iraqi PSC service constitutes the largest reunion of American SOF personnel in history, and that there are more former British Special Air Service, SAS, personnel in Iraq than are now serving in uniform.[5] As for the CF, though official numbers have not been released, it has already lost valuable SOF personnel, thus reinforcing the CF view that, "[t]he world-renowned reputation of JTF 2 as a SOF ... unit has drawn attention from many of these security firms."[6]

This unwanted attention will continue and will likely increase because of the SOF-focus of many PSCs. Moreover, there are considerable political and military limitations in formulating a coherent Canadian response. Although the CF can use some means to overcome these limitations, those means are not likely to be entirely satisfactory. Therefore, this chapter will outline that an appropriate measure would be for the government to lobby the United States for support, given its heavy influence upon the international private security industry.

SOF AND PSCs

Although the advent of PSCs is generally linked to the end of the Cold War, precursor firms did exist, and they were largely based upon SOF credentials. The Scottish laird, Sir David Stirling, instrumental in the July 1941 creation of the SAS, later formed the company Watchguard International in 1967. This company, which was once described as the "civilian branch" of the SAS, provided security analyses, military training, and personal protection services to government clients in Africa and the Middle East.[7] Alastair Morrison, another former SAS operator, founded Defence

Systems Limited (DSL) in 1981. Morrison's SAS career was distinguished by his participation alongside German SOF in the successful storming of a hijacked Lufthansa passenger aircraft in Mogadishu, Somalia on 17 October 1977. Within the private sphere, Morrison organized DSL with a mandate to harness SOF expertise "by ensuring that an internationally recognised company would be waiting to hire former military personnel into legitimate contracts as security consultants, military trainers, or support commercial enterprises with assets in regions of conflicts."[8]

Contemporary American PSCs also highlight their SOF pedigree. For instance, former U.S. Navy SEAL personnel created and largely staff the company Blackwater USA. Similarly, the firm Triple Canopy stresses that its "[o]perators have an average of more than 20 years in the most elite military special operations units and are the highest quality personnel in the industry ... We have more former Tier One special operations professionals than any organization other than the U.S. Military."[9] Additionally, Meyer & Associates indicates that its employees are "specially trained ex-military personnel from U.S. Army Special Forces, Rangers, Intelligence Operators, Marine Recon, Navy and Coast Guard Waterborne Operators."[10]

While it is important to recognize that not all PSCs are stocked with SOF expertise, there are at least three particular reasons why former SOF personnel are attractive to PSCs. First, most PSCs are "virtual" in the sense that they possess very small permanent staffs. PSCs, therefore, rely on rosters of retired military personnel from which they draw their required personnel. Although some PSCs do openly solicit employment applications, much sourcing comes from informal networks among retirees as well between the private and public spheres. Because many PSCs are started by former SOF personnel, and because of the close bonds that exist particularly among those of the SOF community because of their common training and experiences, the preference for SOF personnel in many PSCs is understandable.

Second, because there are no consistent and rigorous qualitative standards regarding PSC personnel at the domestic level, let alone internationally, the presence of SOF expertise largely suffices as the qualitative seal of approval. It becomes a de facto industry benchmark. Though also present in conventional forces, SOF, in a generic sense, offer attributes appealing to the private sector such as language abilities, cultural appreciation, flexibility, and adaptability. Moreover, SOF serve as a "leadership nursery," because, as described by Colonel Bernd Horn, now the deputy commander of Special Operations Forces Command, SOF personnel, "have the opportunity to learn additional skills, particularly advanced leadership abilities due to their exposure to different training and operational experiences, as well as exposure to different, often more experienced, mature, highly skilled personnel."[11] While Horn suggests that SOF personnel might later return to conventional units, and thus spread the benefits of their expertise, one can contend that this expertise can equally be disseminated in the private sphere instead. This attractiveness is recognized by a senior enlisted adviser at the United States Special Operations Command (USSOCOM), Master Sergeant Robert Martens Jr. He remarked, "What makes them [SOF personnel] so valuable to us makes them highly marketable on the outside."[12]

The final reason discussed as to why SOF personnel are attractive to PSCs is related to marketability. The presence of SOF expertise serves as a valuable advertising tool for PSCs. From conducting high profile "SCUD-busting operations" in the 1990–91 Persian Gulf War, to serving successfully as force multipliers alongside anti-Taliban forces in Afghanistan, the importance of SOF has been publicly recognized by prominent government officials.[13] As Elliot Cohen attests, this sort of recognition is not startling during times of crisis because, "it is then that the public searches for heroes and politicians look for panaceas."[14] To date, SOF have largely sufficed in this role, a point reinforced by the generally positive portrayal of SOF in popular entertainment.[15] Consequently, contemporary PSCs can tap into the SOF mystique to sell their services. For example, because of the recognized elite status of forces such as the SAS, Middle Eastern and African clients saw the hiring of Watchguard International as a "mark of prestige," especially given their earlier status as British colonies or protectorates.[16]

LIMITATIONS DUE TO THE SOF DRAIN

Other factors, beyond numerical augmentation, will likely increase the attractiveness of Canadian SOF to private industry. Although Canadian SOF have been criticized in the past for their lack of experience, because of, for instance, Canada's peacekeeping traditions and its lack of colonial experiences, the present operational tempo serves to substantially reduce this learning curve.[17] In this regard, Bernd Horn makes plain SOF's current importance in comparison with conventional capabilities with respect to the terrorist and insurgent threat: "Faced with an elusive foe that relies on dispersion, complex terrain, and asymmetric tactics, political and military decision-makers recognized that only a flexible, adaptive and agile response (i.e., SOF operations) would suffice."[18] Indeed, Canada's reliance upon the CF's SOF assets serves to make Canadian SOF a known, respected, and marketable commodity. Moreover, because Canadian SOF operators often train alongside and conduct operations with foreign SOF, particularly American SOF, Canadians are further drawn into the larger SOF network. Given the Bush Administration's decision in January 2003 to assign USSOCOM the primary responsibility for prosecuting the "Global War on Terrorism," these relationships are likely to grow.

Consequently, a reduced Canadian SOF capability, (in stark contrast to the politically directed expansion), resulting from the loss of trained operators to PSCs, would pose a number of difficulties to Canada with regards to potential political and military options. As Colonel Horn observes, "properly used, small, highly trained specialized units can give even a small state a deterrent power and military and political influence far in excess of that which the simply physical size of its armed forces might suggest."[19] Limited capabilities, therefore, would constrain Canada's ability to contribute to a "SOF War" and thus minimize its influence on the international scene in this regard. It would similarly reduce the political capital Canada might accrue from other countries, particularly the United States.[20]

What is more, limited Canadian SOF capacity would restrict the particular activism of Canada's executive branch of government. The increased centralization of government in Canada has long been noted and, as identified by analysts such as Cohen and Deborah Avant, the manner by which the political control of violence is managed can further alter the distribution of power among governing institutions.[21] In the particular case of SOF, because of the secrecy that often surrounds their operations and their relationship to the achievement of strategic objectives, those in the highest echelons of government become the focus of interaction and decision making. Indeed, analysis of past operations finds that decisions to employ Canadian SOF work to deflect criticism of government policy emanating domestically or internationally because of the veiled nature of the actions; the small footprint of the SOF team(s) employed; the surgical precision and nature of their capabilities; and/or the highly skilled operators that normally ensure mission success.[22] However, this domestic or foreign policy tool, specifically the "political" elasticity of Canadian SOF, would become brittle if there was an increased brain/brawn drain to the private sector.

CHALLENGES IN HANDLING THE SOF DRAIN

There is no straightforward solution or "silver bullet" regarding how to keep Canadian SOF capability in uniform. Simply increasing SOF intake, whether for JTF-2 or the nascent special operations regiment, will not be the sole effective answer. Indeed, significant challenges exist in this regard. From one standpoint, rapidly increased intake contradicts the so-called four "enduring truths" of SOF: "Humans are more important than hardware; Quality is better than quantity; Special Operations Forces cannot be mass-produced; and competent SOF cannot be created after emergencies occur."[23] Altering the SOF selection standards, which normally results in acceptance rates of between 10 and 30 percent of those who apply depending on the particular SOF tier, threatens existing qualitative standards. Already, concerns exist about the CF's ability to maintain SOF standards if JTF-2's capabilities are doubled.[24] Even former Minister of National Defence, Gordon O'Connor, while serving as opposition defence critic, cast doubt upon whether Canada possessed the ability to maintain the requisite SOF skills and standards. He opined, "Is the Canadian military big enough to get that much talent?"[25]

From another standpoint, because existing Canadian policy is not to recruit SOF personnel directly "from the street," the navy, the air force, and, especially, the army, given that it supplies most SOF recruits, would likely be hesitant to embrace plans that would deplete their ranks, even with the incumbent Conservative government's wish to increase overall CF strength. A greater and quickly applied emphasis on SOF, if not handled delicately, serves to potentially create a substantial rift between the conventional and unconventional elements within the CF. The result would likely favour the former if Colonel J. Paul de B. Taillon's warning observation is to be taken into account: "[W]e [the CF] are a conventional force steeped in a conventional military culture, with its attendant views and opinions."[26] In essence, as history has shown — conservative, conventional forces are slow to accept or support SOF.

But more problematic from a conventional services point of view is that SOF, historically, are known to attract individuals who display great potential and ability from (and at the expense of) the conventional forces. For example, military historian Philip Warner contends that SOF volunteers "are the most enterprising, energetic, and least dispensable," and Field Marshal Viscount Slim accused SOF of "skimming the cream" from conventional forces.[27] Thus, one argument is that JTF-2, following its inception in April 1993, served to draw quality personnel away from the Canadian Airborne Regiment.[28] It is also important to recall views held by senior CF leadership as late as 1999 that Canada did not possess "special forces," in part out of the fear that such recognition would heighten the attraction of SOF, and would implicitly deem the rest of the CF as unexceptional.[29]

Heightening the "value" of uniformed service in a number of ways will also not fully remedy the situation. In 2006, financial compensation allowances for JTF-2, dictated by the level of risk, working conditions, seniority, and skill sets were increased for the first time since 1997. For instance, the annual allowance for JTF-2 assaulters, the "sharpest point of Canada's SOF spear," rose from C$21,756.00 to C$25,260.00. This development built upon a CF report issued in 2004 that examined increasing SOF remuneration to encourage retention.[30] Nevertheless, on a dollar-per-dollar basis, public expenditures are likely not to be large enough to counter salaries offered in the private sphere. Under the terms of some contracts in Iraq, for example, PSC personnel stand to receive daily payments of between US$800 and US$1,000.

Other benefits of public service are also not as robust in ensuring retention. CF officials have emphasized some benefits seemingly not available in the private sphere, such as pensions and insurance.[31] However, in the United States, where the issue of SOF retention has been more publicly studied, it is the senior SOF operators, those with earned pensions, who have been attracted to private industry. Additionally, depending on the PSC, the financial attraction has been improved by the introduction of robust insurance plans.

Finally, attention paid to the values of national service versus private employment presents limitations given the "creeping occupationalism," rather than institutionalism, that is thought to exist in the Canadian Forces.[32] For Charles Moskos, this represents the difference between value orientations and rational calculations, between "the intrinsic motivation of an institution with the extrinsic motivation of an occupation."[33] This situation is not unique to Canada. In the United Kingdom, some argue that, "[I]t's a money-driven culture now and a lot of young troopers are treating the SAS as a training school for their private careers."[34] In fact, if present patterns in the United States hold and spread to Canada, the institutional/occupational line is becoming more and more blurred because of the increased recognition the state is giving to PSC personnel, especially those that have died, through honouring them and through highlighting their patriotism.

REGULATION AND CONTROL

Suggested forms of Canadian regulation are only in their nascent stages, and they relate more to the normative and human rights impact of privately supplied security sector expertise, rather than to specifically managing the flow of Canadian personnel from the public to private spheres *per se*. As Lieutenant-Colonel David Last warns, "[I]t is not just a question of autonomy and efficiency for the state. The state must consider regulation of the private capacity for special operations, which might be misused in a global marketplace."[35] While not wishing to underplay the importance of these factors, they are understandable. This is because of the legacy of the human security agenda that still informs many activities at the Department of Foreign Affairs and International Trade. As well, it acknowledges enduring concerns about national image and respect for human rights, matters that first came to the fore in the wake of the Somalia Inquiry, and that continue today in such cases as the appropriate handling of combatants captured during anti-terrorist/insurgent operations.

The complete prohibition of CF SOF joining PSCs would not help. Ethically, it would most likely draw into question former operators' protections under the *Charter of Rights and Freedoms*. Practically, it would be difficult given the transnational personnel sourcing of the PSC industry, and the limitations of extraterritoriality. Even in earlier times, the control of personnel proved difficult for Ottawa. In 1937, Prime Minister Mackenzie King's government created the Canadian Foreign Enlistment Act (FEA) to prevent Canadian participation in the Spanish Civil War. During that conflict, no state provided more foreign fighters per capita than did Canada.[36] The act's ineffectiveness was made plain since over half the 1,200 Canadians that travelled to Spain did so *after* the FEA became law.

In the present day, U.S. experience has demonstrated that "stop loss programs" designed to prevent retirement of personnel deemed essential have been both unpopular and the subject of criticism, ranging from accusations of an unofficial draft through to servitude. As for managing PSCs, there are few Canadian PSCs, let alone those that draw regularly from Canadian SOF assets. For the most part, Canada serves as a feeder country for firms with greater presence and market share located in other countries, particularly in the United States and the United Kingdom.

Because of these limitations, one can argue that a more productive undertaking would be for the Canadian government to lobby Washington to implement controls dealing with the qualitative standards of the PSC industry. In part, this argument can be made because many Canadians are hired by U.S.-based PSCs. More important, however, is the place of the United States in the broader PSC industry. Conclusions reached by political scientist Deborah Avant point toward this issue: "Indeed, the overwhelming dominance of the US in defense spending suggests that other governments will have only limited consumer impact on the behaviour of PSCs. Regulation by other governments is likely to yield less satisfaction unless they step up their consumption of security services."[37] With respect to Canada, it is unlikely that the nation will soon become a dominant player in the international marketplace for PSC services.

To expand, it is true that, on one hand, PSCs are a part of larger international trends that feature "the erosion of Westphalian norms, the spread of neo-liberal economic tendencies, especially the privatization of services, and the globalization of production of goods and services."[38] The assumption here, however, is that the effects and implications of private security are even and the same the world over in terms of control, or the lack thereof. On the other hand, with respect to developed world states, particularly the United States, PSCs are frequently the tools of statecraft. This falls in line with arguments made by likes of Hans Morgenthau, Kenneth Waltz, and John Mearsheimer that powerful states in the international system are not only affected by global phenomena differently, they can to a certain extent shape these phenomena to their benefit.[39] Thus, Norrin Ripsman and T.V. Paul assert the question "is not whether the new challenges of globalization will overwhelm the state but in what ways will they alter the state and what mechanisms will the state use to adapt to global social forces while retaining its centrality."[40]

For the United States, because it is a major client of the international PSC industry, it possesses significant influence in terms of "the market's ecology."[41] Alongside the SOF credentials of PSC founders and managers, the substantial purchasing of PSC services by the United States has served to reinforce SOF capabilities as the gold standard for private industry. This is because the United States — the demand side — has largely ignored the role it plays with respect to determining the nature of the supply side — the qualifications and capabilities of PSCs. For example, in the case of Iraq, while some of the tasks performed by PSC personnel relate directly to SOF expertise, such as close protection, other tasks such as security advising, static protection, and convoy duties do not necessarily fall directly or solely into the SOF realm. Former SOF personnel, nevertheless, are performing them for PSCs. This is not necessarily the most beneficial use of SOF expertise, but by the United States simply purchasing what the marketplace has to offer, largely dictated by the nature of the PSCs themselves, this serves as "the mechanism through which the preferred model of professionalism is communicated."[42]

To better communicate to PSCs, and thereby alleviate and de-emphasize the importance of SOF, there are two methods, possibly advanced by Canadian prodding, that the United States might consider. One approach is to make an asserted effort to hire PSCs that either do not predominantly display their SOF credentials, or perhaps do not rely significantly upon retired SOF expertise. Similarly, a closer examination might be made of the actual abilities required for contracted tasks; SOF expertise may not be needed. The second and more expansive method would be qualitative regulations for U.S.-based PSCs, put in place by the U.S. government regarding the standards for PSC personnel. These standards would stress professionalism, capability, and respect for human rights norms, but they would not imply that the necessary qualifications are predominantly found among those with SOF experience. Because the United States forms such a great portion of the international marketplace, it is likely that PSCs in other countries would follow suit in tailoring their marketing and personnel capabilities to enhance their commercial attractiveness. The overall goal, therefore, would be to make SOF seem less "special" in the private sphere.

One can argue that such a lobbying approach, if performed by Canada, might be well received in the U.S. As indicated earlier, USSOCOM has been feeling the negative effects of the shift of expertise to PSCs. Although the Pentagon has instituted new retention measures similar to the allowances and bonuses mentioned above, the expertise drain continues. Moreover, the effects of this drain might become more acute, given the weight of value placed upon SOF in the *2006 Quadrennial Defense Review:* a 15 percent increase in SOF forces, with particular emphasis upon increasing the number of operators for the U.S. Army Special Forces and the U.S. Navy SEALs. Although U.S. measures to date have largely focused upon ensuring that SOF personnel remain in uniform, more attention can be paid to the marketplace in which they operate, should they decide to leave the U.S. military. Although not a panacea, such attention would also help the CF in managing and maintaining their SOF expertise.

CONCLUSIONS

Based upon the foregoing analysis, some issues come to the fore that policy-makers and future analysts might wish to consider. First, because of its emphasis upon developing qualitative standards that de-emphasize SOF expertise, this study implies that private personnel should be derived more consistently from state security sectors in the larger sense. Even though earlier analysis has determined that PSCs are here to stay because of supply, demand, and ideational factors, the PSC industry is still a delicate matter for political and normative reasons, and it will have to be treated accordingly.[43] As such, one future thrust of inquiry will be why, when, and under what conditions Canada officially elects to manage more closely privately controlled security sector expertise that is based in Canada and that is exported internationally. Second, and in a related fashion, it will be important to examine how the Canadian populace might respond, and what impact this would have politically, to changes regarding Canadian security sector expertise. For instance, the activities of SOF and conventional units in Afghanistan already challenge traditional views of the CF (i.e., the peacekeeping myth). It is important to recall that as late as the 1990s, senior CF officials referred to some JTF-2 operations as merely "very benign observer-type missions."[44] The fact that the government chose, in

2005, to lift slightly the veil of secrecy covering JTF-2's Afghan operations underscores government sensitivity regarding the perception of Canadians.[45] Emphasis placed not only upon SOF, but also upon Canadian PSC personnel, who, perhaps for some Canadians, constitute nothing more than mercenaries in the most pejorative sense, would pose further challenges for the government.

Overall, it is intriguing to see how the "fortunes" of both SOF and PSCs have grown since the end of the Cold War, and particularly since the terrorist events of 11 September 2001. In their own different ways, they have served the "security marketplace" characterized by terrorism and insurgency. It is not surprising that some states, particularly the United States, want to rely more upon these public and private assets. In the process, however, because of the limited and overlapping personnel pool, strains will result and challenges will be presented to feeder states such as Canada, just as the CF is attempting to increase its own SOF capabilities. Although there is no easy solution to this dilemma, the aforementioned suggestions developed in this article might hopefully reduce the possibly looming necessity of "robbing Peter to pay Paul."

NOTES

1. For a history of Canada's experience with SOF, see Sean M. Maloney, "Who has Seen the Wind? An Historical Overview of Canadian Special Operations," *Canadian Military Journal*, Vol. 5, No. 3, Autumn 2004, 39–48.
2. See Bernd Horn and Tony Balasevicius, *Casting Light on the Shadows: Canadian Perspectives on Special Operations Forces* (Toronto: Dundurn, 2007), 20–30, for explanations on definitions, roles, and tasks of SOF.
3. CANSOFCOM is often referred to as such by senior leaders in NDHQ. In fact, the former chief of the defence staff (CDS) ordered that a fourth guard made up of CANSOFCOM personnel be present at his July 2008 change of command parade alongside the army, air force, and navy guards, thus, symbolizing their status.
4. For this chapter the term private security company (PSC), rather than private military company, is employed because companies conduct a hybrid of policing and military tasks. This is in light of the environments in which these companies are frequently employed (conflict/violence-prone weak states in the developing world)

and the actual effects the companies may have in these environments. Moreover, the main goal in all cases is to make something or someone more secure. As such, the term PSC is more appropriate in the cumulative sense.

5. James Dao, "The Struggle for Iraq: Security," in *New York Times*, 2 April 2004, A1; Thomas Catan and Stephen Fidler, "The Military Can't Provide Security," in *Financial Times*, 29 September 2003, *www.nettime.org/Lists-Archives/nettime-1 -0309/msg 00169.html*.

6. Cited in David Pugliese, "Soldiers of Fortune," *Ottawa Citizen*, 12 November 2005, A17.

7. Anthony Mockler, *The New Mercenaries* (London: Sidgwick & Jackson Limited, 1985), 151; and Wilfred Burchett and Derek Roebuck, *The Whores of War* (London: Pelican Special, 1977), 166.

8. Kevin A. O'Brien, "PMCs, Myths, and Mercenaries: the debate on private military companies," in *Royal United Service Institute Journal*, Vol. 145, No. 1, February 2000, 61.

9. See *www.itd.hu/itdh/nid/IQ/pid/0/itdhArticleDisplay/oid/0/Article.4402*.

10. See *www.meyerglobalforce.com/special.html*.

11. Bernd Horn, "The Dark Side to Elites: Elitism as a Catalyst for Disobedience," in *Canadian Army Journal*, Vol. 8, No. 4, Winter 2005, 71.

12. Cited in Pauline Jelinek, "Many Elite Soldiers Leave for Better Pay," in *The Guardian*, 20 July 2004, *www.node707.com/archives/001526.shtml*.

13. For example see Donald H. Rumsfeld, "Transforming the Military," in *Foreign Affairs*, Vol. 81, No. 3, May-June 2002, 20–32.

14. Eliot A. Cohen, *Commandos and Politicians: Elite Military Units in Modern Democracies* (Cambridge: Center for International Affairs, Harvard University, 1978), 95–96.

15. Note recent productions such as *The Rock, E Ring, Tears of the Sun, and Transporter*. Older productions include *The Green Berets, The Guns of Navarone, and Where Eagles Dare*.

16. Mockler, 149.

17. For one such criticism, see David Pugliese, "JTF2 Not Ready for Afghan Duty: Expert," in *Ottawa Citizen*, 22 November 2001, A1. See also Maloney.

18. Bernd Horn, "When Cultures Collide: The Conventional Military/SOF Chasm," in *Canadian Military Journal*, Vol. 5, No. 3, Autumn 2004, 6.

19. Bernd Horn, "Special Men, Special Missions: The Utility of Special Operations Force — A Summation," in Bernd Horn, J. Paul de B. Taillon, and David Last, eds., *Force of Choice: Perspectives on Special Operations* (Kingston: McGill-Queen's University Press, 2004), 20.

20. The political and diplomatic benefits of Canadian SOF are described in Jamie Hammond, "Special Operations Forces: Relevant, Ready and Precise," *Canadian Military Journal*, Vol. 5, No. 3, Autumn 2003, 17–28; and Bernard J. Brister, "Canadian Special Operations Forces: A Blueprint for the Future," *Canadian Military Journal*, Vol. 5, No. 3, Autumn 2004, 29–37.

21. See Cohen, 70; and Deborah Avant, "The Privatization of Security and Change in the Control of Force," in *International Studies Perspectives*, Vol. 5, No. 2, May 2004, 156. Regarding the centralization of power in Canada, see Donald J. Savoie, *Governing From the Centre: The Concentration of Power in Canadian Politics* (Toronto: University of Toronto Press, 1999); and Jeffrey Simpson, *The Friendly Dictatorship* (Toronto: McClelland and Stewart Ltd., 2001).

22. An example of this analysis can be found in David Pugliese, *Canada's Secret Commandos: The Unauthorized Story of Joint Task Force Two* (Ottawa: Esprit de Corps Books, 2002), 118–21.

23. Robert D. Kaplan, *Imperial Grunts: The American Military on the Ground* (New York: Random House, Inc., 2005), 191.

24. Bruce Garvey, "Forces Struggling to Find 600 Soldiers Good Enough to Serve in Crack JTF-2 Unit," in *Ottawa Citizen*, 24 October 2003, A1.

25. Cited in David Pugliese, "Military Creates New Special Forces Unit," in *Ottawa Citizen*, 4 January 2006, A1.

26. J. Paul de B. Taillon, "Canadian Special Operations Forces: Transforming Paradigms," in *Canadian Military Journal*, Vol. 6, No. 4, Winter 2005–06, 75.

27. Horn, "When Cultures Collide," 6.

28. Pugliese, *Canada's Secret Commandos*, 121.

29. David Last, "Special Operations Forces in Conventional Armies: 'Salvation Army?' or 'Dirty Dozen'?" in *Force of Choice*, 36 and 57.

30. Stephanie Rubec, "Elite soldiers drained," 25 April 2005, *http://cnews.canoe.ca/CNEWS/Canada/2005/04/25/pf-1012118.html*; and David Pugliese, "Special Forces Get Pay Raise," *National Post*, 26 August 2006, A4.

31. Rubec, "Elite Soldiers Drained."

32. Noel Iverson, "Military Leadership and Change in the 1990's," *www.cda-cdai.ca/library/iverson.htm*.

33. Charles C. Moskos and Frank R. Wood, "Introduction," in Charles C. Moskos and Frank R. Wood, eds., *The Military: More Than Just a Job?* (Washington: Pergamon-Brassey's International Defense Publishers, 1988), 4–5.

34. "British SAS Mull Bonus to Halt Exodus," *Agence France-Presse*, 15 February 2005, *www.news.com.au/story/0,10117,12253024–1702,00.html*.

35. David Last, "Epilogue: The Next Generation of 'Special Operations'?" in Bernd Horn, J. Paul de B. Taillon, and David Last, eds., *Force of Choice: Perspectives on Special Operations* (Kingston: McGill-Queen's University Press, 2004), 208.

36. Victor Hoar, *The Mackenzie-Papineau Battalion* (Toronto: Copp Clark, 1969), 1.

37. Deborah Avant, *The Market for Force: The Consequences of Privatizing Security* (Cambridge: Cambridge University Press, 2005), 177.

38. See Dan Hellinger, "NGOs and the Privatization of the Military," in *Refugee Survey Quarterly*, Vol. 23, No. 4, December 2004, 192–220.

39. Hans J. Morgenthau, *Politics Among Nations: The Struggle for Power and Peace*, Seventh Edition (Montreal: McGraw-Hill Higher Education, 2006); Kenneth N. Waltz, *Theory of International Politics* (Reading: Addison-Wesley Publishers, 1979); John J. Mearsheimer, *The Tragedy of Great Power Politics* (New York: Norton, 2001).

40. Norrin M. Ripsman and T.V. Paul, "Globalization and the National Security State: A Framework for Analysis," in *International Studies Review*, Vol. 7, No. 2, June 2005, 224.

41. Avant, *The Market for Force*, 220.

42. *Ibid.*, 226.

43. See Peter W. Singer, *Corporate Warriors: The Rise of the Privatized Military Industry* (Ithaca, NY: Cornell University Press, 2003).

44. Pugliese, *Canada's Secret Commandos*, 11.

45. One such "trial balloon" can be found in Stephen Thorne, "Canadian commandos taking out Taliban," in *Globe and Mail*, 17 September 2005, A13.

BUILDING COALITION SPECIAL OPERATIONS FORCES FOR THE "LONG WAR"

J. Paul de B. Taillon

Now, it is an extraordinary thing that you should meet with so much opposition from allies. Allies, altogether, are really very extraordinary people. It is astonishing how obstinate they are, how parochially minded, how ridiculously sensitive to prestige and how wrapped up in obsolete political ideas. It is equally astonishing how they fail to see how broad-minded you are, how clear your picture is, how up-to-date you are and how cooperative and big-hearted you are. It is extraordinary. But let me tell you, when you feel like that about allies — and you have even worse allies than the British, believe me — when you feel like that, just remind yourself of two things. First, that you are an ally too, and all allies look just the same. If you walk to the other side of the table, you will look just like that to the fellow sitting opposite. Then the next thing to remember is that there is only one thing worse than having allies — that is not having allies.

— Field Marshal Sir William Slim[1]

TODAY, MOST MILITARY COMMANDERS, analysts, and scholars will acknowledge that special operations forces accomplish missions that are tactical but that have significant strategic impact. In this vein, over the past decade, successful operations have been conducted by coalition special operations forces (CSOF) in Bosnia, Kosovo, Afghanistan, and Iraq. This record of accomplishment underlines the necessity to support, facilitate, and expedite future CSOF operations. However, current and future coalitions face difficulties as they encompass not only so-called "traditional allies,"[2] but also non-traditional SOF partners. This raises a number of sensitive concerns, including intelligence sharing and interoperability, as well as maintaining coalitions while balancing national interests. Moreover, the deployment of coalition SOF represents the strategic interests of their respective nations. Hence, coalition operations have become the crucial enabler for success in GWOT, the Global War on Terrorism.

To appreciate the spectrum of CSOF capabilities, this chapter will explore recent operations in Afghanistan and Iraq, offering recommendations on how to enhance interoperability and integration. This includes "outreach" or coalition advocacy programs aimed at likely SOF partners and initiatives to facilitate the interoperability of partners in a fully integrated joint CSOF command structure.

THE THREAT

Although terrorism has been historically viewed as a criminal threat, since the attacks of 11 September 2001 (9/11), it has become the primary focus of the American national security efforts and those of their partners since terrorists are now viewed as a serious and persistent threat to all nations. American SOF and CSOF are leading the way, using their unusual skills, experience, language capabilities, and cultural awareness to develop personal links with the local population, thereby garnering critical intelligence, fostering all-important interpersonal relationships and forging strategically important global coalition partnerships.[3] American and coalition SOF are in regions around the world, including the Philippines, the Pacific Rim countries, the South American Tri-Border region (Brazil, Paraguay, and Argentina), the African Sahel region (Chad, Mali, Mauritania, and Niger), and work closely with local police, the military, and security authorities to counter the persistent threat from terrorism. As Major-General Gary L. Harrell, the Combined Special Operations Component commander, United States Central Command, has underlined, "CSOF are valuable contributions to GWOT, far in excess of their numbers."[4] This American acknowledgement underlines the necessity to reinforce and expand such contributions, particularly as American SOF are reportedly "so overstretched" because of their operational tempo.[5]

Today's global terrorism challenge necessitates the mobilization and maintenance of a collective will and determination, with the requisite resources and elements of national power to facilitate the efforts of coalition partners. The American strategic policy of pre-emption will result in certain U.S. government initiatives taking place beyond what has historically been understood as designated combat zones. For instance, one recent incident (or pre-emptive attack) reported by a Pakistani security official outlined how an American missile launched from an unmanned aerial drone targeted and killed an Al Qaeda trainer believed to be a chemical biological expert in Waziristan. This strike highlights the necessity for closer co-operation, as well as the development of synchronized plans that draw upon the strengths of the United States and its coalition partners to best target terrorists, while at the same time avoiding tragic collateral damage as the engagement space grows.[6]

To successfully overcome contemporary terrorism, the United States and its allies must create an environment that eschews terrorism and develop an adaptive counterterrorism strategy. This requires the support and full co-operation of the international community, the respective government agencies, as well as all U.S. departments and agencies, to effectively execute the four principles that underline an adaptive counterterrorism strategy:

- Prevent the emergence of new terrorist threats;
- Isolate terrorist threats that have emerged from their respective support bases;
- Defeat isolated terrorist threats; and
- Prevent the re-emergence of terrorist threats that have already been defeated.[7]

STRATEGIC IMPORTANCE OF PARTNERS

Politicians, military commanders, and their planners understand that the "Long War," as it is now known,[8] will not be won unilaterally by the United States. To prevail, the United States and allied coalition partners must adopt the "strategy of the indirect approach," as articulated by the renowned strategist Liddell Hart, to organize and synchronize the efforts of a global coalition. This will necessitate the development of effective coalition military forces and, in particular, the interoperability and integration of CSOF at all levels.[9]

Currently, over 80 countries support Operation Enduring Freedom and Operation Iraqi Freedom (OIF), with 64 countries providing conventional military forces and 12 countries contributing CSOF.[10] Current SOF missions undertaken by CSOF include direct action (DA), special reconnaissance (SR), unconventional warfare (UW), civil affairs (CA), and psychological operations (PsyOps).[11] Depending on the political or military situation, CSOF could expand or contract these missions as required.

STRATEGIC REQUIREMENT FOR BUILDING CSOF CAPACITY

CSOF and building partner capacity became strategically salient in early February 2006, when the Joint Staff (J-5) Planners of the Pentagon laid out a new 20-year defence strategy for the Long War. This strategy outlined the deployment of U.S. forces, often clandestinely, to fight terrorism and other non-traditional threats, as well as a 15 percent boost in the future number of SOF personnel. It also acknowledged the requirement to operate around the globe.[12]

The strategy recognized that SOF would play a major role and that U.S. "SOF will have the capacity to operate in dozens of countries simultaneously,"[13] deploying for longer periods of time with the aim of building relationships with foreign military and security forces. Moreover, the strategy emphasized that the U.S. military could not unilaterally achieve victory, thereby once again reinforcing the strategic importance of allies and coalition partners. Ryan Henry, principal deputy undersecretary of defense for policy, confirmed this belief, stating that "we cannot win this Long War by ourselves."[14]

The rationale is easy to discern. Operating in a foreign cultural environment demands those linguistic and cross-cultural skills that are inherent in SOF/CSOF. Coalition commanders have learned through operational experience that no other military force can accomplish as broad a scope of missions, conducted in as wide a spectrum of operational environments, as SOF/CSOF. In addition, historically, the operational demand for CSOF continually exceeds supply.[15] And this can be easily exacerbated should a major crisis occur requiring a "surge" in military forces. In such instance, it is only logical to predict that the United States would request higher levels of military contributions from international partners.

BUILDING PARTNER CAPACITY AND COALITION INTEROPERABILITY

In 2005, Director of Strategic Studies at the Center for Strategic and Budgetary Assessments, Michael G. Vickers, told the Committee on Armed Services Panel on Gaps — Terrorism and Radical Islam that the main tasks of SOF in the Long War are to:

- Build partner capacity and provide persistent, low visibility ground presence;
- Conduct persistent air, maritime, and ground surveillance over ungoverned areas; and
- Conduct clandestine and covert operations, counter-proliferation operations, and operations in denied areas.[16]

Depending on the level of perceived threat and political support, allied or coalition partners could plan, execute, or facilitate any one of these taskings. However, early assimilation and integration are critical to ensuring that the requisite levels of coalition SOF effectiveness are attained.

To build partner capacity, the 2006 U.S. defence budget proposed that the U.S. Special Operations Command receive $4.1 billion, with a portion designated to facilitate co-operative initiatives with allies, including training for the military forces of other nations. Major-General Harrell emphasized the importance of the contribution of coalition forces across a spectrum of operations and, the fact that given the appropriate assistance, time, and investments, future CSOF activities could be expanded, predicated on appropriate political support and coalition direction.[17]

To date, CSOF has integrated and functioned with relative ease in the Afghanistan and Iraq operational areas.[18] This is largely because of SOF from the Eastern European and Pacific regions have adopted the North Atlantic Treaty Organization standard for training and equipment.[19] In addition, Major-General Harrell acknowledged that the Central Command's (CENTCOM) SOF did much to ensure that CSOF achieved the requisite level of interoperability before deploying.[20] Nonetheless, some areas still need attention to ensure closer coalition SOF co-operation, interoperability, as well as the integration of CSOF staff in joint and combined operations. It has consistently been recognized that the earlier CSOF integration takes place, the better are the results. This can be addressed through enhancing coalition SOF training and exercises to educate, train, and sensitize participating commanders and staff to tactical, operational, and strategic issues, as well as ensuing problems. CSOF partners could also contribute other ideas on how best to address this situation. Vice-Admiral Eric Olson, then deputy commander and now Admiral Olson, commander U.S. Special Operations Command, reinforced this idea, arguing that:

> The level of coalition SOF integration, particularly early on, will determine ultimate success in joint and combined special operations. Organizational relationships and communications are always issues in such operations, but feedback from our SOF counterparts reflects fewer integration and interoperability problems at the tactical level than we experienced as recently as a couple of years ago.[21]

Admiral Olson noted, however, that the higher up the chain of command one goes, the more conceptual are the challenges. It is, therefore, important — indeed imperative — that U.S. and coalition SOF staff and their commanders meet to discuss the concept of operations before assigning and engaging CSOF at the lower level. A salient lesson acknowledged by all is that the "campaign plans, mission focus, and execution parameters must be consistent across the combined force."[22]

STRATEGIC IMPORTANCE OF U.S. SOF/CSOF INTEROPERABILITY

The momentum for embracing CSOF interoperability increased dramatically in the wake of the electrifying attacks on 9/11. Since then a spectrum of CSOF operate and fight alongside U.S. SOF on a scale never before thought possible. Moreover, the deployment and integration of CSOF lends strategically important political and military legitimacy, as well as moral weight, to the war on terrorism. In both Afghanistan and Iraq, the U.S. Army Special Forces became the core for the Combined Joint Special Operations Task Forces (CJSOTFs), the command and control umbrella for CSOF.

CENTCOM INITIATIVE IN DEVELOPING CSOF

To assist nations facing terrorism, CENTCOM has created a special operations and counterterrorist, CT, capability so that regional partners can conduct successful CT operations within their respective borders. CENTCOM is pursuing bilateral SOF operations between regional nations to develop SOF skill sets and expand their respective experience in coalition operations.[23] Recognizing that there are no simple solutions to interoperability, Major-General Harrell sewed together a patchwork of strategic, operational, and tactical initiatives to facilitate the inclusion of CSOF. These include:

- A CENTCOM Coalition Command Cell (CCC) staffed by senior national representatives and defence attachés;
- Pre-deployment and interoperability training;
- Communications security memoranda of agreements (COMSEC MOA);
- Acquisition and cross-servicing agreements (ACSA); and
- Combined training and exercises.[24]

This CENTCOM initiative has done much to address the challenge of coalition interoperability. An overview of CSOF operations in Iraq and Afghanistan underlines the challenges and successes faced in both of these theatres, and illustrates the above point.

CSOF Partners in OIF: An Overview

Over 13,000 SOF personnel were deployed during Operation Iraqi Freedom, making it the largest SOF deployment since the Vietnam War. The contingent included Australian, British, Polish, and American SOF who undertook a variety of land, air, and maritime operations throughout the Iraqi theatre. To affect those operations, the Combined Forces Special Operations Component Command (CFSOCC) was created in early 2003 and was charged with the command and control of the U.S. Army, Air Force, Navy, and SOF assets, including the CSOF provided by the respective coalition nations.[25]

To facilitate command and control during OIF, three task forces were created to conduct special operations (SO) missions within the Iraqi theatre:

- Combined Joint Special Operations Task Force — North (CJSOTF-N);
- Combined Joint Special Operations Task Force — West (CJSOTF-W); and
- Combined Joint Special Operations Task Force — South (CJSOTF-S).

These task forces were directly supported by the Combined Joint Special Operations Aviation Component (CJSOAC) which had Australian and British aviation assets under its command and control, flying over 2,181 missions, many of which were behind Iraqi lines.[26]

The CJSOTF-W was built around the U.S. Army's 5th Special Forces Group (Airborne) and reinforced by coalition special forces from the Australian and British Special Air Services, including the 4th Battalion, Royal Australian Regiment (Commando). Its area of responsibility (AOR) was the western desert — the area from Baghdad to Kuwait.[27] The primary mission of CJSOTF-W was to deny freedom of movement to the Iraqi ground forces, to plan and execute strategic reconnaissance, to conduct unconventional warfare and, most important, to restrict Iraq's ability to launch SCUD missiles at coalition and friendly forces.[28]

Australian, British, and U.S. SOF, along with USAF Special Tactics Squadron personnel, were rapidly deployed throughout CJSOTF-W AOR.

They commenced the forward reconnaissance of Iraqi defensive positions, monitored their ground movements, and conducted counter–theatre ballistic missile (CTBM) operations. Among their assigned tasks, the CSOF teams called in close air support to suppress and destroy Iraqi defensive positions, as well as providing "eyes on the sparrow" intelligence and reconnaissance to both U.S. Marine Corps and U.S. Army commanders throughout their rapid armoured advance to Baghdad.[29]

The assimilation of SOF coalition partners was facilitated by clear command relationships, a common understanding of the importance of the principle of unity of command and effort, as well as solid grounding in the doctrine employed and staff procedures. During the opening phases of the attack on Iraq, Australian, and British SOF were assigned appropriate missions and were under the tactical control of CJSOTF-W. These tasks also contributed to the counter–theatre ballistic missile operations focused in the western deserts of Iraq and were tactically and strategically sensitive.[30]

COALITION SOF INTEGRATION INTO OIF

From the outset, it was vital to ensure that CSOF were thoroughly integrated into the campaign plan for Iraq. Commanders and their staffs ensured that the integration started at the most senior levels of leadership residing at the theatre special operations command (TSOC), and then cascaded down to the CJSOTF level, to the combined Army Special Operations Task Force (ARSOF), and to the respective tactical level.[31]

In one example, the effectiveness of coalition integration in Iraq was demonstrated when an Australian SAS patrol reached a boundary of their assigned AOR. The patrol commander observed an Iraqi military convoy heading toward his position and immediately sought a close air support mission from the Airborne Warning and Control Squadron (AWACS). The British AWACS crew subsequently directed a flight of fighters onto the Iraqi convoy, all within eight minutes of the air support request.[32] It should be appreciated that such close air support procedures had been developed and fully rehearsed with USSF, coalition SOF, and with British and U.S. aircraft during three well-planned exercises that were undertaken leading up to the invasion. This instance illustrates the critical importance of consistently exercising coalition operational and support procedures before any combined deployments.

U.S. SOF AND CSOF STAFF INTEGRATION

During the initial stages of the operation in Iraq, the 5th Special Forces Group (Airborne) made up much of the staff assigned to the CJSOTF-W. Embedded and integrated coalition staff, consisting of Australian and British officers, served in many of the directorates of CJSOTF-W. Notably, the CJSOTF J3 (Operations) and the deputy commanders, as well as the J3 Western Desert and Assistant J2 (Intelligence), were all coalition allies. The British J3 and his U.S. staff were so well acquainted with the doctrine that integration "appeared to be seamless." A top-down staffing approach with coalition seniors further facilitated multinational interoperability, ensuring that CSOF integrated into each phase of operations.[33]

During the strategically important CTBM operations in Iraq, U.S. special forces became a vital asset for the combined force air component commander (CFACC). During operations, coalition SOF units rapidly adapted to new technologies by effectively employing precision-targeted air delivered ordnance. However, this coalition capability and flexibility was predicated upon years of training on well-established NATO close air support procedures that ensured interoperability with both American and coalition SOF.[34] These procedures were further exercised and honed by CSOF during follow-on air strikes against the Iraqi military targets.

While operating in Iraq's western desert, CSOF were attacked on a number of occasions by Iraqi forces. Fortunately, these contacts were short-lived as coalition SOF were rapidly supported by close air support and, therefore, could engage or disengage as required. To ensure the effective coordination of air support tasks, a combined staff of American and British officers made up the joint fires element of CJSOTF.[35]

For CSOF undertaking counter–theatre ballistic missile operations in Iraq's western desert, the most harrowing time was during the days immediately after their insertion. Initially, American, Australian, and British forces had to "deconflict" their respective operations to safely conduct a passage of lines when CSOF planned, or suddenly found it necessary, to transit each other's operating areas. This situation was further complicated by the necessity of conducting all tactical moves at night — the same period when Iraqi forces would conduct aggressive counter-SOF operations — resulting in an increased possibility of friendly fire, also known as a *blue-on-blue* incident.[36]

To mitigate potential problems, a series of rehearsals were conducted, a common radio frequency was provided and activities were tightly planned, coordinated, and controlled. It is notable that CJSOTF-W's CSOF/U.S. special forces detachments were successful and achieved their missions without loss of any CSOF personnel, while, concomitantly, inflicting substantial matériel damage and casualties upon the Iraqi formations. The success of CSOF in Iraq was predicated upon tried and true interoperable procedures, an integration of CSOF staffs, close coordination and integration of coalition partners up and down the command and control chain, as well as extensive combined training in joint operations.

CSOF Assistance to Task Force 145

The close liaison between the U.S. special forces and the Jordanian special forces witnessed a major success in the 2006 pursuit of Abu Musab al-Zarqawi, the Al Qaeda terrorist leader in Iraq. Media reports indicated that the Pentagon's Task Force 145 received intelligence from a human source working under the direction of a Jordanian SF team operating inside Iraq. While acknowledging the importance of other intelligence collection methodology and techniques, it is often a single 'informer' who can provide the critical piece of timely information to take the operation to the next level — such as the capture of a high-value target (HVT). In this case, the Iraqi informant identified Zarqawi's spiritual leader and American intelligence was then able to technically monitor their target through his mobile telephone communications. American intelligence subsequently located the spiritual leader at a safe house, where he was meeting with Zarqawi. The house was surrounded and an air strike was called in on the premises. In the wake of the air attack, Zarqawi was found alive in the rubble, but quickly succumbed to massive internal injuries. This successful mission, where Jordanian special forces played a lead role, further illustrates the critical and growing importance of CSOF in the Long War.[37]

CSOF Partners in OEF: An Overview

In 2002, the first year of Operation Enduring Freedom in Afghanistan, SOF units operated hundreds of kilometres from their headquarters, Combined Joint Special Operations Task Force–Afghanistan (CJSOTF-A). To address this situation, the CJSOTF-A commander established a special forces liaison element, better known as a coalition coordination cell, which was subsequently staffed from the 3rd SF Group and colocated with the five CSOF task groups. The coordination cell had staff representatives from J2 (intelligence), J3 (operations), J4 (logistics), and J6 (command, control, communications, and computer systems). The coordination cell provided an American C2 (command and control) umbrella, as well as the vital communications and intelligence links to coalition SOF headquarters. The coordination cell also facilitated access and the dissemination of American intelligence responding to coalition requests for information (RFIs), video feeds, surveillance and reconnaissance reports, radio frequencies, and crypto. The coordination cell ensured "deconfliction" and facilitated the incorporation of coalition SOF throughout the Afghan battlespace as they conducted special reconnaissance and direct action missions against Al Qaeda and Taliban elements.[38]

In December 2001, CSOF, drawn from seven nations, were deployed to Afghanistan to conduct operations under the auspices of OEF. In the following year, these coalition partners conducted over 200 direct action, special reconnaissance and sensitive site exploitation missions.[39] This tempo could only have been accomplished through a high degree of coordination and interoperability. American SOF and CSOF must look at all measures to facilitate the fight in the Long War, more in a "by, through, and with" attitude and means. This underscores the necessity of lead nations doing more with CSOF partners and traditional allies, as well as with non-traditional partners.[40]

While the CJSOTF-A headquarters represented interoperability at the operational level, it was truly manifested at the tactical level by an American SF battalion. When the 2nd Battalion, 3rd SF Group was assigned to, and established, its Forward Operating Base 32 (FOB 32) at Kandahar Airfield, it was colocated with five CSOF task groups embedded in the coalition coordination cell. Taking advantage of CSOF expertise in static and mobile special reconnaissance, FOB 32 commenced the operational preparations for their respective SF detachments. FOB 32 also planned and undertook combat missions with coalition SOF in the Afghan provinces of Uruzgan, Helmund, and Paktika. These initial reconnaissance missions were instrumental in subsequent successful operations against leadership cells belonging to Al Qaeda and the Taliban. Moreover, SF detachments conducted many of their missions based upon the intelligence and information provided by CSOF — a true indication of trust in their CSOF partners.[41]

During initial operations, it was quickly recognized that certain CSOF partners were particularly skilled in mobile reconnaissance missions thereby enabling the identification, seizure, and destruction of enemy arms caches. Predicated upon sound and timely intelligence, as well as close coordination, CSOF members conducted their own successful direct action missions, locating and capturing a number of members of the Taliban leadership cadre.[42]

More recently, Afghan National Army commandos and U.S. SOF freed a number of hostages incarcerated in a Taliban prison. The commandos were searching a compound where the Taliban commander Nungiala Khan had a jail. Fifteen Afghans were discovered being held for ransom and were promptly released. It is through such operations that nascent SOF forces will garner the experiences to hone their professional and operational capability and internal leadership.[43]

COALITION SOF AND 160TH SPECIAL OPERATIONS AVIATION REGIMENT

Supporting CSOF was the 3rd Battalion, 160th Special Operations Aviation Regiment, better known to those in the community as the "Night Stalkers." Both CSOF and the supporting air assets acknowledge that interoperability was vital to successful joint and combined SOF initiatives. The 160th planning staff and flight commanders understood the criticality of this and undertook to facilitate CSOF operations to the fullest extent by ensuring intimate coordination between the ground force commanders and the air planners. The Danish SOF contingent was officially commended for their exceptional planning ability as they brought with them two of their U.S.-trained pilots. Both aviators, well versed in

258 / THE DIFFICULT WAR

U.S. air planning formats and requirements were, astutely, assigned to billets on the air operations planning staff of the 160th, thus expediting CSOF air planning. On a series of occasions, the 160th inserted CSOF into their AOR, including insertions on extreme slopes at high elevations. In a number of these, 160th crews took enemy fire while conducting their approaches to drop-off points, underlining the high degree of trust and professional dedication that existed between the 160th and coalition SOF partners.[44]

Lessons Learned and Recommendations

The experiences and lessons learned from Iraq and Afghanistan underscore the critical importance of deliberate planning in coalition SOF operations. Fortuitously, the planning and decision-making processes employed by CSOF mirrored American doctrine.[45] The "commonality" of doctrine and formats for developing concept of operations, staff work, and back brief facilitated interoperability and has further cemented the professional trust between the United States and the various CSOF units engaged in operations. Moreover, under the American C2 umbrella, coalition SOF proved their ability to undertake special operations successfully at both the tactical and operational levels. Strategically, CSOF contributed directly to the legitimacy and credibility of U.S. and coalition political and military objectives and subsequent initiatives in the struggle against terrorism.

In the Long War, CSOF operations will remain a vital component of the coalition effort. Hence, it is incumbent upon military professionals to assimilate the experiences and lessons learned in Afghanistan and Iraq, and to build upon them to increase the efficiency and effectiveness of integrated CSOF operations. A key lesson from operations in Afghanistan and Iraq is the early integration of qualified CSOF personnel into senior positions in CJSOTF headquarters. This ensures a unity of effort and maximizes the skills and potential of coalition partners.[46] Multinational SOF exercises, at both the tactical and operational levels, could improve interoperability and build upon the hard-won lessons of Afghanistan and Iraq.

The following recommendations would, if incorporated, expand and enhance future CSOF interoperability and assist in our coalition efforts in the Long War. As such, they are as follows:

1. Create Coalition SOF Mobile Training Teams (CSOFMTT). Operators from Australia, Canada, New Zealand, Poland, and others under NATO (plus)[47] could develop NATO-standard SOF tactics, technologies, and procedures to enhance individual military skills, develop counterinsurgency and counterterrorist expertise, and pass on proven techniques. The January 2006 announcement of the creation of the International Special Forces Training Course (ISFTC) at Fort Bragg is an important and substantial step toward CSOF interoperability. The 15-week program takes students through a comprehensive SF program. This initiative can also be a vehicle for coalition advocacy and strategic partnering. Moreover, instructors from CSOF nations would give the course a true coalition SOF flavour. CSOF nations would benefit from sending candidates to train and develop personal connections with other students in anticipation of future coalition initiatives. Another goal is for SOF lead nations to assist nations with the skills, knowledge, and experience to secure their own borders and provide for their own internal stability.

2. Create a NATO SOF School: The international Long Range Patrol School (LRPS) at Weingarten, Germany had a cadre of instructors from various NATO nations and was a focal point in developing standardized NATO patrol techniques. A similar-style NATO SOF School would provide a base of knowledge and skills, along with standardized TTPs for a spectrum of SOF missions, enhancing future CSOF interoperability.

3. Ascertain Coalition SOF Expertise and Leverage It: Many nations have developed unique or niche

capabilities, such as the Norwegians for snow or high-altitude conditions. Coalition SOF must have an awareness and appreciation of each other's respective skills and capabilities and leverage these to the benefit of the CSOF community.[48]

4. Create a SOF "Olympics": CSOF would be tested by undertaking several operational scenarios, such as a direct-action operation, hostage rescue, strategic reconnaissance mission, and long-range patrol[49] to assess the professionalism, flexibility, and equipment of those partaking, as well as ascertain the interoperability of these CSOF partners.[50] This would provide a venue to learn from the respective experience of the participants so as to share successful TTPs in preparation for future deployment initiatives.

5. Create a SOF Staff College: The college could look at special and asymmetric operations throughout history, including the profiles and experiences of various special forces to garner insights as to their respective history, skills, and methodologies. The SOF staff college would teach new planning methodologies, emphasize the responsibilities of commanders and staff in planning sensitive, as well as normative SOF operations. The curriculum could examine the issues and experiences of CSOF partners and the development of their respective SOF.[51] Courses would be taught to enable SOF operators to understand various cultural mores, behaviours and traditions, as well as to realize that this cultural understanding is as important as the weapons they carry.[52] The SOF staff college could also conduct a series of NATO-standard exercises focusing on the spectrum of SOF missions. This would assist in talent spotting and the training and development of operational skills of U.S. SOF/CSOF personnel, as

well as staff planners, trainers/instructors and commanders. This initiative could be extended to incor-
porate the creation of a SOF planning specialty,
similar to the School of Advanced Military Studies
(SAMS) at the U.S. Command and Staff College,
Leavenworth, as well as selecting officers to become
special operations and irregular warfare strategists.
This could readily be put under the umbrella of
Joint Special Operations University (JSOU), based
in Hurlburt Field, Florida.[53]

6. Increase coalition SOF attachments and second-
   ments to various SOF/CSOF schools. The exchange
   of officers, instructors, and students would secure
   the human dimension of CSOF and put a real coalition face to, in particular, American SOF schools and
   training programs. This would ensure an increase in
   interoperability through an awareness of the various
   coalition cultures, staff, and operating methodologies, while concomitantly developing personal contacts. This has proven successful in the standing up
   of reportedly four Iraqi Special Operations battalions that are now capable of conducting operations
   and another two are at present in force generation.[54]

7. Solicit CSOF participation in US and coalition SOF
   exercises and, concomitantly, garner coalition input
   and ideas, similar to Emerald Warrior 07. CSOF
   observers/participants may have unique cultural,
   operational, or methodological insights that would
   be advantageous to the SOF/CSOF community. The
   request or invitation to participate would, in itself,
   acknowledge coalition value and importance.[55]

8. Assist coalition initiatives in the Long War. Particularly in regions where post-colonial nations are
   experiencing confrontations with terrorism and

insurgency, and where British or American presence could be problematic, coalition partners may wish to provide military assistance in the Long War through a future NATO (plus) program.[56] This multinational operational detachment Alpha team (ODA, which is a U.S. Army Special Forces "A" Team) could consist of coalition SOF members from Australia, Canada, Germany, New Zealand, Poland, et cetera. This would be an expansion of the Second World War era Jedburgh teams,[57] or "Jeds" for short. These were small units comprised of three military officers/non-commissioned officers — one British (Commonwealth), one French and one American that were parachuted into France to provide intelligence and assist the French underground in aligning underground activities to support Allied operations both before, and after, the Normandy invasion.[58] Such multinational ODAs could conduct foreign training and undertake advisory missions, essentially performing Foreign Internal Defence (FID) or Stability and Security Operations (SASO). Today, this initiative would embrace coalition SOF, taking it to a higher level through team integration — a real Rainbow 6![59]

9. Support ongoing international SOF symposiums and academic institutions that study irregular warfare and special operations. These venues could be employed to enhance coalition SOF exchanges, tap respective SOF academics, and build networks internationally within the SOF academic field. This has been demonstrated at the international SOF symposium held at the Royal Military College of Canada in Kingston, where four such events have been held to date.

10. Select, train, and return intelligence support personnel. In recent operations, a major and persistent

issue was the difficulty of intelligence sharing among coalition allies. Considering the criticality of intelligence in driving SOF initiatives, the integral SOF intelligence organizations, particularly those of the traditional or special alliance comprised of Canada, Great Britain, Australia, New Zealand, and the United States, must address how to appropriately manage SOF intelligence requirements in a coalition. While it can be appreciated that intelligence sources and sensitive technology may have to be protected, assigning coalition allies high-risk conventional or SOF missions without providing critical all source intelligence along with the assigned target package is, arguably, immoral and particularly disenfranchising. It is vital to ensure that SOF select and retain intelligence support personnel who are capable of effectively operating in a joint and coalition staff, as well as working with ambiguity, prickly intelligence issues, allied/foreign SOF operators, and allied agendas.[60]

CONCLUSION

The Long War will require great patience and a comprehensive approach to defeating the terrorism threat. More important, it must be recognized that this is not purely an American problem but an international one in which military forces alone cannot win. The war demands the concerted multidisciplinary effort of global partners and CSOF will be instrumental in conducting long-term, effective operations aimed at generating enduring effects to defeat the terrorists and their support network.[61] To ensure the strategic success in the Long War, coalition members must maintain a unity of effort. All avenues that help to seed, nurture, and renew mutual trust and coalition interoperability will do much to ensure victory on this new "battlefield." To facilitate the successful interoperability of SOF, there must be a coalition SOF standard. This will not be easy as there is no simple "silver bullet" solution to ensure interoperability.

Hence, the coalition special operations community must come together and provide the guidance, doctrine, training, and education to achieve seamless interoperability, thus ensuring that coalition special operations forces remain the "Tip of the Spear."

NOTES

1. Field Marshal Sir William Slim, "Higher Command in War," *Military Review* (May 1990), 12.

2. They are sometimes known as the "Five Eyes" community consisting of Australia, Canada, New Zealand, United Kingdom, and United States. These countries are viewed as the traditional CSOF allies. For the purposes of this paper, CSOF will encompass both traditional allies and coalition partners.

3. See also Hala Jaber and Michael Smith, "SAS Hunts Fleeing Al-Qaeda Africans," *Times* (14 January 2007). U.S. special forces and British Special Air Services assisted by Ethiopian and Kenyan forces were coordinating the destruction and trapping of AQ terrorists.

4. Major-General Gary L. Harrell, "Coalition SOF Support to the War on Terrorism," *Presentation* (29 January 2005), *www.dtic.mil/ndia/2005solic/harrell.ppt* (accessed 27 February 2006). See also Andrew Feickert, "U.S. and Coalition Military Operations in Afghanistan: Issues for Congress," *CRS Report* (9 June 2006) Order Code RL33503. For an interesting view regarding irregular warfare by a former USAF SOF officer, see Major General (Retired) Richard Cormer, "An Irregular Challenge," *Armed Forces Journal* (February 2008).

5. Alec Russell, "Overstretched American Special Forces Hit the Language Barrier," *Daily Telegraph* (4 May 2006).

6. Thom Shanker and Scott Shane, "Elite Troops Get Expanded Role on Intelligence," *New York Times* (8 March 2006); and Rowan Scarborough, "Special Operations Forces Eye Terrorists," *Washington Times* (12 August 2005).

7. Lieutenant-General Dell L. Dailey and Lieutenant-Colonel Jeffrey G. Webb, "U.S. Special Operations Command and the War on Terror," *JFQ* 40 (1st Quarter 2006), 45. See also, Andrew Feickert, "U.S. and Coalition Military Operations in Afghanistan."

8. The "Long War" was originally called the "Global War on Terrorism," or GWOT, which was also referred to simply as the "War on Terrorism" or the "War on Terror."

9. In recent times, much focus has been placed on SOF operations in the direct action mission areas. These are "attractive" operations as they are easy to see and report and have an immediate result. This reality unfortunately, overlooks or underestimates the critical importance of the indirect approach strategies that have long-term strategic effects such as foreign internal defence, national capacity building, and complementary SOF and conventional operations.

10. Harrell, "Coalition SOF Support to the War on Terrorism."

11. *Ibid.*

12. See Ann Scott Tyson, "Ability to Wage 'Long War' Is Key to Pentagon Plan," *Washington Post* (4 February 2006); and Josh White and Ann Scott Tyson, "Rumsfeld Offers Strategies for Current War: Pentagon to Release 20-Year Plan Today," *Washington Post* (3 February 2006).

13. *Ibid.*

14. Tyson, "Ability to Wage 'Long War' is Key to Pentagon Plan."

15. Admiral Eric T. Olson, Commander United States Special Operations Command, "Directing, Supporting and Maintaining the World's Best SOF," Interview, *Special Operations Technology, www.sotech-kmi.com* (accessed 28 July 2008).

16. Michael G. Vickers, "Transforming U.S. Special Operations Forces," Center for Strategic and Budgetary Assessments, Prepared for OSD Net Assessment, (August 2005), 8.

17. *Ibid.*

18. It should be underlined that in the traditional alliance context, the New Zealand Special Air Service and Canada's Joint Task Force 2 (JTF-2) worked intimately against Taliban elements in Afghanistan. As described to this writer, "Our NZSAS squadron commander would command an op [operation], then the Canadian JTF-2 squadron commander led the next op. I believe this was never done before." Interview with senior New Zealand SAS commander, Auckland, NZ (21 November 2006).

19. Harrell, "Coalition SOF Support."

20. *Ibid.*

21. Vice Admiral Eric T. Olson, "SOF Transformer," interview by Jeffrey McKaughan, *Special Operations Technology* 4, 1, 19 February 2006, *www.special-operations-technology.com/archives.cfm?CoverID=69* (accessed 10 March 2006).

22. *Ibid.*

23. Harrell, "Coalition SOF Support."

24. *Ibid.*

25. A Bid for Freedom," *Global Defence Review* (2006), *www.global-defence.com/2006/utilities/article.php?id=41* (accessed 27 February 2006).

26. *Ibid.*

27. *Ibid.*

28. *Ibid.*

29. *Ibid.*

30. Mark C. Arnold, *Special Operations Forces Interoperability with Coalition Forces,* John F. Kennedy Special Warfare Center and School (2005).

31. *Ibid.*

32. *Ibid.*

33. *Ibid.*

34. *Ibid.*

35. *Ibid.*

36. A *blue-on-blue* incident, also known as "friendly fire" is when troops from the same or an allied military accidentally fire on each other. This is also known as amicide or fratricide.

37. For an overview of this operation, see Ellen Knickmeyer and Jonathan Fines, "Insurgent Leader Al-Zarqawi Killed in Iraq," *Washington Post Foreign Service* (8 June 2006); and Claude Salhani, "Jordanian Role Larger than First Reported," *UPI* (12 June 2006).

38. Arnold, *Special Operations Forces*.

39. *Ibid*.

40. Robert Pursell, "USJFCOM Newsmaker Profile: SOCJFCOM Commander Army Colonel Wesley Rehorn," Interview (5 December 2007).

41. *Ibid*.

42. *Ibid*.

43. Specialist Anna K. Perry, "Commandos, SOF Forces Rescue Kidnap Victim," CJSOTF, *Afghanistan Public Affairs* (20 July 2008); and Anna K. Perry, "SOF Forces Train New Afghan Commandos," CJSOTF, *Afghanistan Public Affairs* (27 June 2008).

44. *Ibid*.

45. *Ibid*.

46. *Ibid*.

47. Although Australia and New Zealand are not under the NATO umbrella for the purpose of such a program, they could be invited to partake in such a NATO (plus) initiative. If not, they could be included as Commonwealth attachments.

48. During OEF operations in Afghanistan, the Norwegians were considered highly capable SOF intelligence and operational planners and their methodology was, in part, copied by Canadian SOF intelligence operators. In Afghanistan, the Canadian Special Operations Intelligence Cell (SOIC) reportedly set the standard for intelligence support for SOF operations.

49. *Ibid*.

50. Observers would note differences in equipment, intelligence requirements, communications used, risks taken, commonality of reporting formats, tactics, techniques, and procedures employed while assessing real time variations from the NATO base model.

51. For various overviews, see Roy MacLaren, *Canadian Behind Enemy Lines 1939–1945* (Vancouver: UBC, 1981); William H. Burgess, III, ed., *Inside Spetsnaz: Soviet Special Operations* (Novato, CA: Presidio, 1990); Greg Annussek, *Hitler's Raid to Save Mussolini* (Cambridge: Da Capo, 2005); Tim Saunders, *Fort Eben Emael* (Barnsley: Pen and Sword, 2005), Ian Westwell, *Brandenburgers: The Third Reich's Special Forces* (Hersham: Ian Allan, 2003); Otto Skorzeny, *My Commando Operations: The Memoirs of Hitler's Most Daring Commando* (Atglen, PA: Schiffer, 1995); Eric Lefevre, *Brandenburg Division: Commandos of the Reich* (Paris: Histoire and Collections, 2000); James E. Mrazek, *The Fall of Eben Emael* (Novato, CA: Presidio, 1970); Douglas Dodds-Parker, *Setting Europe Ablaze* (Windlesham: Springwood, 1983); T. E. Lawrence, *Revolt in the Desert* (New York: Tess Press, 1926); John Arquilla, ed., *From Troy to Entebbe: Special Operations in Ancient and Modern Times* (Lanham, MD: UP of America, 1996); and William H. McRaven, *Spec Ops: Case Studies in Special Operations Warfare* (Novato, CA: Presidio, 1995).

52. Students would also undertake a broad spectrum of initiatives in dealing with terrorists, guerrillas, and insurgents and study the notables of history, T. E. Lawrence, Vo Nguyen Giap, Mao Zedong, Sun Tzu, Chen Peng, Augusto Sandino, Ho Chi Minh, Che Guevara, and Osama bin Laden.

53. JSOU is based at Hurlburt Field, Florida, and offers a wide range of courses regarding terrorism, unconventional warfare, special operations, and staff officer training. With an academic staff comprised of in-house experts and drawing from international adjunct professors, this would be a logical expansion under JSOU and

could facilitate future U.S. SOCOM/CSOF initiatives in the Long War. For an overview as to the training for SOF staff personnel, see Commander Steven P. Schreiber (USN), Lieutenant-Colonel Greg E. Metzgar (U.S.); and Major Stephen R. Mezhir (USAF), "Behind Friendly Lines: Enforcing the Need for a Joint SOF Staff Officer," *Military Review* (May-June 2004), 2–8.

54. Statement by Ambassador Zalmay Khalilzad, U.S. permanent representative, delivered at the mid-year review of UNSCR 1790 on behalf of MNF-I, in the Security Council June 13, 2008, USUN Press Release (13 June 2008), United States Mission to the United Nations.

55. Major Scott Covode and Denise Boyd, *Air Force Print News*, (11 July 2007). "There is great value in getting SOF integrated training with joint air assets that will support them during real world operations," Navy Lieutenant-Commander Patrick Corcoran commented.

56. According to reports, SOCOM has approximately 7,000 troops overseas with a major concentration in Iraq and Afghanistan. One report noted 85 percent of these were in the Middle East, central Asia, and the Horn of Africa. Ann Scott Tyson, "New Plans Foresee Fighting Terrorism Beyond War Zones," *Washington Post* (23 April 2006).

57. Julian Thompson, *The Imperial War Museum Book of War: Behind Enemy Lines* (Washington, DC: Brassey's Inc., 2001), 299–301.

58. *Ibid.*

59. Taken from Tom Clancy's techno-thriller novel "Rainbow Six." The novel focuses upon a multinational counterterrorist unit codenamed "Rainbow." The use of the numeral six in American military jargon is for the commander.

60. Jon-Paul Hart, "Killer Spooks: Increase Human Intelligence Collection Capability by Assigning Collectors to Tactical-Level Units," *Marine Corps Gazette* (April 2005). For an overview of intelligence sharing, see Major Louis-Henri Remillard, "Intelligence Sharing in Coalition Operations: Getting it Right," Royal Military College, unpublished paper (5 May 2008).

61. Dell and Webb, 47.

Author's Note: The author would like to extend his appreciation to Brigadier Tim Brewer, New Zealand Defence Force; Dr. James D. Kiras, Assistant Professor, School of Advanced Air and Space Studies, Maxwell AFB; Colonel (Retired) Joe Celeski, U.S. Army; Lieutenant-Colonel Howard G. Coombs, Canadian Army; Lieutenant-Colonel M. J. Goodspeed, Canadian Army, for their views and advice.

CONTRIBUTORS

Major Tony Balasevicius is an infantry officer and member of The Royal Canadian Regiment (RCR). He has served in many command positions in the RCR as well as in the Canadian Airborne Regiment. He served as the deputy commanding officer of the 1st Battalion, The RCR in 2002. He has just finished a tour as staff at the Department of Applied Military Science at the Royal Military College of Canada (RMC), and is currently completing his M.A. in war studies at RMC.

Captain Andrew Brown is a serving officer in the Canadian Forces. He joined the Canadian Forces in 1988 as a non-commissioned member and has served in First and Second Battalions of The Royal Canadian Regiment; in 3 Commando, the Canadian Airborne Regiment; and as a supporting officer in the CANSOF community where he is now employed. He graduated from RMC in 2004 with a Bachelor of Military Arts and Sciences. He is currently a part-time student in the Master of Arts (War Studies) program at RMC.

Dr. Peter H. Denton is a part-time associate professor of history at RMC (where he has taught in the OPME program since 2003 and in the war studies program since 2004), as well as an instructor in technical communications and ethics at Red River College. He is also a minister in the United Church of Canada. His research applies the philosophy of technology to contemporary global issues, including environmental sustainability, social responsibility, and warfare.

Colonel Bernd Horn, Ph.D., is an experienced infantry officer who is now serving as the deputy commander of Special Operations Forces Command. He has command experience at the sub-unit and unit level and was the officer commanding 3 Commando, the Canadian Airborne Regiment, from 1993–95, and the commanding officer of the 1st Battalion, The Royal Canadian Regiment from 2001–03. Colonel Horn has an M.A. and Ph.D. in war studies from RMC where he is also an adjunct professor of history.

Lieutenant-Colonel Greg Smith is an experienced infantry officer who is now serving as the commanding officer of the Canadian Special Operations Regiment in Petawawa, Ontario.

Dr. Christopher Spearin is an associate professor in the Department of Defence Studies of the Royal Military College of Canada located at the Canadian Forces College in Toronto, Ontario. His research concerns change in militaries, global security governance, non-state actors, mercenaries, the privatization of security, and Canadian foreign and defence policy.

Dr. Emily Spencer is an assistant professor at the University of Northern British Columbia and a research associate with the Canadian Forces Leadership Institute. Her main areas of interest include the relationships of society to war and violent conflict in democracies and, in particular, the gendered elements within these relationships, as well the study of culture and war.

Colonel J. Paul de B. Taillon, Ph.D., is an adjunct professor at RMC where he specializes in courses on special operations and irregular warfare. A graduate of the U.S. Marine Corps Command and Staff College and the Amphibious Warfare School, he was a 2006 graduate of the U.S. Army War

College. As a reserve infantry officer, he has served in Oman, Bosnia, Kosovo, and Afghanistan. Additionally, he has served with both the British and American special forces. His current reserve position is the counter-insurgency adviser to the chief of land staff, Canadian Army. In his civilian job, he has worked for almost 30 years in the intelligence and security field. He is a Ph.D. graduate from the London School of Economics.

V.I. is a professional in the financial sector with previous military experience.

INDEX

Abdi House, 63, 66

Afghanistan, 11–13, 17, 19–21, 54, 57, 59, 61–62, 64, 67, 69, 72, 79–80, 82, 87–88, 93–94, 96, 98–103, 106–07, 109, 111–12, 116, 118, 147–50, 152–53, 156–58, 160–66, 168–79, 182–84, 186–89, 191, 193, 196, 198, 202, 204–06, 209–11, 213, 218, 221–22, 225–28, 231, 234, 241, 246, 250–51, 256, 258, 264–67

Al Qaeda (AQ), 19, 57, 70–71, 117–18, 163–65, 167, 173–75, 177–82, 187, 196, 200, 228, 247, 255–57, 264

All-Source Intelligence Centre (ASIC), 72

Al-Midhar, Khalid, 71

Al-Zarqawi, Abu Musab, 255

Areas of Intelligence Responsibility (AIR), 58

Asymmetry, 43, 51, 119, 200

Avant, Deborah, 235, 239

Bin Laden, Osama, 71, 118, 165–66, 175, 188–89, 201, 266

Blackwater USA, 233

British Army, 76, 125–26, 129, 131–32

Canadian Forces (CF), 7, 50–51, 56, 74, 90, 92–94, 96, 98–100, 104, 106, 108–09, 193, 231–32, 236–38, 241–42

Central Command (CENTCOM), 247, 250–51

Central Intelligence Agency (CIA), 19, 71–72, 75, 77, 163, 165–71, 173–74, 177, 177–79, 182–92

China, 24, 28–29, 38, 160

Chinese Nationalist Party (see also Kuomintang), 24

CNN, 82, 214

Coalition, 12–14, 16, 20, 42, 49, 57–58, 60, 66–69, 72, 77, 95–96, 98, 102–03, 105–06, 147, 158, 164, 169, 175, 188, 197, 202, 204–05, 215–16, 218–19, 225, 245–64

Coalition Special Operations Forces (CSOF), 20, 246–47, 249–50, 252–54, 256–63

Cohen, Elliot, 234–35

Cold War, 19, 101, 193, 195–96, 232, 242

Combined Explosives Exploitation Cell (CEXC), 62

Combined Forces Special Operations Component Command (CFSOCC), 252

Combined Joint Special Operations Task Force (CJSOTF), 251–54, 256, 258

Commander's Critical Information Requirements (CCIRs), 58

Communist, 24, 26, 152, 162, 164

Communist Party of China (CPC), 24, 27, 29–30, 35, 40

Compound Warfare, 36–37, 41

Cordesman, Anthony H., 60, 67

Counterinsurgency (COIN), 8, 12–16, 18–20, 38, 55–56, 60, 62, 64, 66–69, 71, 73–74, 80, 82, 97, 99, 105, 107–08, 113, 119–20, 123–24, 126, 130, 134, 140–42, 144–49, 151, 155, 158–60, 193, 198, 207, 216, 219, 226, 259

Counterterrorism (CT), 70–72, 77, 231, 247, 251

Counterterrorism Center, 70–72, 77

Crumpton, Henry, 167, 183, 189

Cultural Intelligence (CQ), 18, 67–69, 76, 79–80, 82–84, 88–93, 95–98, 102–08, 216–17, 219

Culture, 13, 15, 19, 46, 49–50, 56, 67, 69, 79–81, 83–84, 86–93, 95, 98–100, 107, 153, 175, 186, 203, 208, 216, 218, 222, 224, 236, 238

Defence Systems Limited (DSL), 232

Direct Action (DA), 66, 175, 217, 231, 248, 256–57, 260, 264

"Eight Remarks" (Mao's), 27–28

Europe, 112, 117, 154

Federal Bureau of Investigation (FBI), 70–72, 113

Federally Administered Tribal Areas (FATA), 118

First World War, 35, 67, 76, 199, 208

14 Intelligence Company (14 Int), 128–29, 131–32, 143

Fourth Generation Warfare (4GW), 197,

199–200, 203, 209, 217–19, 225–26

Fraser, Brigadier-General David, 15–16, 79–80, 211, 216

Gibraltar, 135–38, 144–45

Global War On Terror (GWOT), 112–13, 235, 246–47, 264

Globalization, 83, 101, 117, 196, 225, 239–40

Grau, Lieutenant-Colonel (Retired) L.W., 158

Gray, Colin, 200–01

Green Berets (see also Special Forces), 243

Guerrilla Warfare, 29, 32, 34, 45, 170, 182, 192, 196

"Hearts and Minds," 13, 26, 56, 68, 80, 93, 103–05, 149, 151–53, 158, 217–19, 228

Hezbollah, 42, 61–62, 72, 226, 228

Hope, Lieutenant-Colonel Ian, 16, 61, 75, 79–80, 83, 101–02, 106–07, 109

Horn, Colonel Bernd, 9, 11, 17–19, 82, 98–99, 234–35

Host Nation (HN), 13–14, 18, 58, 60, 68–69, 72, 75, 81, 84, 91–92, 96, 98–105, 202, 204, 205, 208, 216–17

Human Intelligence (HUMINT), 59–61, 68, 74, 77, 130, 144, 156, 159, 165, 170, 183–84, 187, 207

Huntington, Samuel P., 87–88

Ignatieff, Michael, 14, 94, 197

Improvised Explosive Device (IED), 17, 59, 61–63, 72, 102, 196, 218

Information Operations (IO), 13, 76, 99, 102–03, 118, 140, 196, 211–13, 217, 219

Insurgency, 8, 12–13, 16–20, 23–25, 29–30, 35–36, 38–39, 53–56, 58–59, 66, 68, 72, 99, 99, 111–13, 118–19, 123–26, 138, 140–42, 144, 146, 148–50, 160, 164, 170, 182, 191, 193–94, 197, 201, 242, 262

Insurgents, 13–14, 17–18, 29–30, 38, 41, 53–56, 59, 61–62, 64, 66, 68–69, 72–74, 76, 80, 88, 99–100, 102, 105, 108,

112–13, 115, 117–18, 120, 123–25, 127, 130, 134, 140, 142, 146, 148–51, 153–54, 156–57, 159, 161, 182, 209, 212, 216–17, 219, 235, 238, 266

Intelligence, 13, 17–19, 32, 36, 53–74, 76–77, 79–80, 82–83, 88–91, 106–07, 116–17, 121, 124–36, 138–39, 141–46, 150, 156, 159, 164–65, 168–71, 182–84, 186–87, 189, 192, 205, 207, 209, 213, 215–17, 219, 233, 246, 253–57, 262–63, 266

Intelligence and Security Group (Int and Sy Group), 129, 142

Intelligence Process, 141

Intergovernmental Organization (IGO), 95–97, 104

International Security Assistance Force (ISAF), 15, 53, 79, 82, 106, 204, 208

Iraq, 17, 20, 54, 60, 62, 66–68, 80–81, 85, 103, 111–12, 115, 196, 201, 206, 212–15, 225–26, 228, 232, 237, 240, 246, 250–51, 253–55, 258, 267

Irish Republican Army (IRA), 125–44, 146

Irregular Warfare, 17, 23, 54, 57, 67, 72, 261–62, 264

Jedburgh, 262

Jihad, 42, 118, 160

Joint Task Force 2 (JTF-2), 231–32, 236–37, 241–42, 244, 265

Jones, Seth, 59

Kandahar, 15, 21, 64, 79, 94, 106, 162, 173–74, 193, 204, 226, 256

Karzai, Hamid, 173–74, 188

KHAD (*see also* Secret Police), 65, 157

Khan, Nungiala, 257

Krulak, General Charles C., 198

Kuomintang (*see also* Chinese Nationalist Party), 24

Lambert, Major-General Geoffrey, 171

Laqueur, Walter, 113, 120

Lavoie, Lieutenant-Colonel Omer, 12, 14, 101, 210

Lawrence, Colonel T.E. (Lawrence of Arabia), 67, 76, 208, 266

Leadership, 9, 18–19, 21, 25, 33–34, 64, 66, 76, 104, 106, 109, 118, 166, 168, 180, 185, 193–94, 197, 201, 208–09, 212, 219, 221–22, 226, 233–34, 237, 244, 253, 257

Lessons Learned, 18, 59, 66, 90, 193, 196, 209, 258

Light Armoured Vehicle III (LAV III), 11

Lind, Lieutenant-Colonel William S., 199

"Long War," 19–20, 248–49, 256, 258–59, 261–64, 267

Loughgall, 132, 134–35, 138, 143–45

Malaya, 130

Massoud, Ahmed Shah, 166

Mattis, Lieutenant-General James N., 94, 196

Metz, Steven, 53, 119, 200

MI5, 126, 136

MI6, 126

Middle East, 67–68, 72, 76, 208, 232, 267

Military Reconnaissance Force (MRF), 127–28

Minister of National Defence (MND), 11, 236

Mobile Warfare, 32, 34–36, 41

Mountbatten, Earl, 146

Mujahideen, 56, 65, 116, 147, 151, 153–57, 159–60

Networks, 58–60, 62, 64, 66, 68, 112, 117, 165, 196, 201, 203, 207, 228, 233, 262

New York, 53, 70, 112

Non-Governmental Organizations (NGOs), 95–98, 104, 202, 216

North Atlantic Treaty Organization (NATO), 19, 67, 76, 94, 96, 110, 113, 120, 147–48, 158–60, 202, 204, 210, 215, 250, 254, 259, 262, 266

Northern Alliance (NA), 163–64, 166, 16–69, 171–73, 178–81, 183, 186, 188

Northern Ireland, 123, 125–27, 129–31, 136, 139–44, 146

Nuristan, 149

Office of Strategic Services (OSS), 189

Oil Spot Strategy, 30

Olson, Vice-Admiral Eric, 250
Operation Enduring Freedom (OEF), 163, 167, 169, 171, 175–76, 182, 184, 186–87, 191, 191, 256, 266
Operation Flavius, 135–37, 145–46
Operation Iraqi Freedom (OIF), 248, 252–54
Operation Judy, 132, 134–35, 144
Operation Medusa, 204
Operational Detachment — Alpha (ODA), 171–74, 180, 186, 192, 262
Operational Detachment — Charlies, 172

Pakistan, 88, 150, 152, 154–55, 165, 171
Palestine Liberation Organization (PLO), 63
Pashmul, 61
Pashtun, 161, 173, 188
Peacekeeping, 51, 193, 195, 198, 209, 214, 224–25, 234, 241
Peacemaking, 51, 195
Pentagon, 57, 71, 112, 241, 248
People's Democratic Party of Afghanistan (PDPA), 149
People's War, 16, 23–29, 31–32, 36–37, 39–41
Petraeus, General David, 212–13
"Principles of War" (Mao's), 31
Private Military Corporation (PMC), 19–20
Private Security Company (PSC), 232–35, 237–43
Professional Development (PD), 7, 106, 109, 193, 221–24
Propaganda, 12, 28–29, 38, 55, 111, 119–20, 140, 146, 148, 152–53, 196, 213
Provisional IRA (PIRA), 141
Psychological Operations (PSYOPS), 204, 248

RAND Corporation, 59, 142, 212
Red Army, 28, 31, 34, 36, 39–41
Red Guards, 40
Resistance, 19, 29, 31, 33–34, 65, 71, 76, 151–52, 157, 159, 163, 165–66, 168–75, 177–83, 187–88, 190–92, 221

Royal Military College of Canada (RMC), 223, 262
Royal Ulster Constabulary (RUC), 126, 128–29, 131–35, 138

Scales, Major-General Robert, 13, 69, 81, 83, 101–02, 197, 202, 211, 225
Schoomaker, General Peter, 80, 107, 207, 227
Schreiber, Lieutenant-Colonel Shane, 99, 202
Schroen, Gary, 185
Second World War, 39, 119, 189, 191, 199, 262
Secret Police, 65, 157
Security, 7, 13, 15, 17, 19–20, 23, 32, 38, 45, 49–50, 53–57, 59–60, 62–63, 66–70, 72–73, 75, 77, 79, 82, 95, 98–99, 102–03, 105–06, 109, 112, 114, 117, 119, 124, 129, 131–36, 138, 142, 144–46, 150–53, 156, 158–59, 162, 186, 188, 193, 195–97, 201, 205, 208, 208, 212, 214, 218–20, 223–25, 229, 231–33, 238–42, 246–48, 251, 262
Slim, Field Marshal Sir William, 237, 245
Social Network Analysis, 62
Somali, 63
Somalia, 108, 199, 209, 227–28, 233, 238
Soviet Union, 34, 151–52, 164, 195
Soviets, 19, 56, 60–61, 65, 147–60, 165
Special Air Service (SAS), 18, 125–40, 143–46, 232–33, 238, 244, 253, 264–65
Special Branch, 126, 131, 136
Special Forces (see also Green Berets), 19, 39, 163, 168, 171, 186, 191, 233, 237, 241, 252, 254–56, 259, 260, 262
Special Operations (SO), 252
Special Operations Executive (SOE), 189
Special Operations Forces (SOF), 12, 16, 18–20, 65–66, 121, 123–25, 127–31, 134–36, 138–41, 145–46, 163, 166, 169, 176–82, 184–89, 192, 209, 231–32, 234, 236–38, 240, 242, 246–54, 256–64, 266–67
Special Reconnaissance (SR), 248, 256–57
Spencer, Dr. Emily, 18, 67, 109, 110, 216

"Strategic Corporal," 82, 214–15
Strategic Counteroffensive, 29, 34, 36
Strategic Defensive, 29, 35
Strategic Stalemate, 29

Taliban, 16, 19–20, 57, 64–65, 80, 99, 102,
    116, 147, 159, 163–64, 166–69, 171–
    77, 179–82, 184, 187–89, 200, 209,
    218, 256–57, 265
Tasking and Coordination Group (TCG),
    131–32
Terrorism, 18, 20, 29, 54–55, 70, 111–20,
    142, 161, 196, 201, 235, 242, 246–49,
    251, 258, 261, 263–64, 266
Three Block War, 195, 198, 209, 225
"Three Rules" (Mao's), 27
Tribal, 13, 65, 68–69, 72, 74–75, 79–80,
    85–86, 102–03, 116, 118, 157, 164,
    167, 216
Theatre Special Operations Command
    (TSOC), 253

Ulster Defence Regiment (UDR), 138–39
Unconventional Warfare (UW), 19, 163–
    64, 166–72, 175–77, 181–89, 191, 208,
    231, 248, 252, 266
United Kingdom (U.K.), 111, 142, 144,
    226, 232, 238, 264
United Nations (U.N.), 50–51, 94, 96, 154,
    193, 195–96, 198–99, 209–10, 216,
    225, 228, 267
United Nations Forces in Cyprus
    (UNFYCYP), 193

United States (U.S.), 19, 25, 41, 59–60, 63,
    68, 70–71, 73, 79–81, 83, 87, 90, 96,
    100, 107–08, 111–13, 116–17, 126,
    150, 154, 160, 163, 165–71, 173–78,
    180–86, 188–91, 196, 207, 211, 217,
    228, 232–33, 235, 237–42, 247–55,
    257–58, 260–64, 267
United States Special Operations
    Command (USSOCOM), 169, 175,
    184–86, 189, 234–35, 241, 249–50
Unity of Command, 95–96, 253
Unity of Effort, 96–98, 100, 258, 263
U.S. Army Special Forces (USSF), 163,
    168–74, 177–79, 181, 184–87, 189,
    191–92, 233, 241, 251, 253, 262
U.S. Marine Corps (USMC), 38, 73, 80–81,
    87, 100, 160, 189, 196, 198–99, 217,
    253
U.S. Navy SEALs, 189, 233, 241
USS *Cole*, 71, 165

Vertefeuille, Lieutenant-Colonel François,
    98
Village-States, 157

Watchguard International, 232, 234
World Trade Center, 53, 71, 112, 196

Zedong (Tse-tung), Mao, 17, 23–37,
    39–40, 266

OF RELATED INTEREST

CASTING LIGHT ON THE SHADOWS
Canadian Perspectives on Special Operations Forces
edited by Colonel Bernd Horn and
Major Tony Balasevicius
978-1-55002-694-8
$39.95

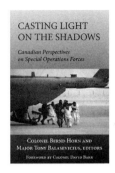

Casting Light on the Shadows features essays on issues
related to special operations forces (SOF) written by
individuals with specialized knowledge and expertise
in the field. As well as providing a solid foundation for
SOF theory, historical background, and evolution, the
book also highlights ongoing developments in SOF.

WHAT THE THUNDER SAID
Reflections of a Canadian Officer in Kandahar
by Lieutenant-Colonel John Conrad
foreword by Christie Blatchford
978-1-55488-408-7
$29.95

What the Thunder Said is an honest, raw recollection of
incidents and impressions of Canadian warfighting in
Afghanistan from the logistics perspective. It offers solid
insight into the history of military logistics in Canada
and explores in some detail the dramatic erosion of a
once-proud corner of the army from the perspective of
a battalion commander.

THE MILITARY LEADERSHIP HANDBOOK
edited by Colonel Bernd Horn and Dr. Robert W. Walker
978-1-55002-766-2
$59.95

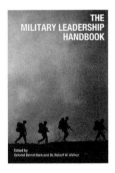

This concise and complete manual identifies, describes,
and explains the concepts, components, and ideas that
relate to military leadership. Focusing on cohesion,
command, cultural intelligence, discipline, fear, and
trust, this applied manual is invaluable to anyone who
wishes to acquire a better understanding of both the
theory and application of military leadership.

Available at your favourite bookseller.

www.dundurn.com

Tell us your story! What did you think of this book? Join the conversation at
www.definingcanada.ca/tell-your-story by telling us what you think.